Asian Pacific Americans
and Baseball

Asian Pacific Americans and Baseball

A History

Joel S. Franks

McFarland & Company, Inc., Publishers
Jefferson, North Carolina, and London

LIBRARY OF CONGRESS CATALOGUING-IN-PUBLICATION DATA

Franks, Joel S.
　　Asian Pacific Americans and baseball : a history / Joel S. Franks.
　　　　p.　　cm.
　　Includes bibliographical references and index.

　　ISBN 978-0-7864-3291-2
　　softcover : 50# alkaline paper ∞

　　1. Baseball — United States — History.　2. Baseball players —
United States — History.　3. Asian Americans — Sports — History.
4. Pacific Islander Americans — Sports — History.　I. Title.
GV863.A1F73　　2008
796.3570973 — dc22　　　　　　　　　　　　　　　　　　2008017028

British Library cataloguing data are available

©2008 Joel S. Franks. All rights reserved

*No part of this book may be reproduced or transmitted in any form
or by any means, electronic or mechanical, including photocopying
or recording, or by any information storage and retrieval system,
without permission in writing from the publisher.*

On the cover: Chinese Hawaiians representing Honolulu's Chinese
Athletic Club, ca. 1910 (courtesy Library of Congress); background
©2008 Shutterstock

Manufactured in the United States of America

*McFarland & Company, Inc., Publishers
　Box 611, Jefferson, North Carolina 28640
　　www.mcfarlandpub.com*

To Cheryl, Kaitlin, and Spencer,
the loves of my life

Acknowledgments

Several people have been helpful in putting together this book, especially in regards to tracking down photographs. These folks include Janet Marks and the special collections staff at Long Island University; Linda Wobbe and Martin Cohen of St. Mary's of Moraga's special collections department; two stalwarts of Oakland's Chinese American community, Bill Wong and Betty Wong; Jean Coffey and Tammy Lau, archivists at California State University, Fresno, and Randy Vaughn Dotta, photographer for the same institution; Marie Masumoto, senior research assistant for the Japanese American National Museum's Hirasaki National Research Center; Rob Fitts, Japanese baseball historian; Wally Yonamine, who is the worthy subject of a future biography by Rob Fitts; Kerry Howe of the Arizona State University's athletic department; and Juliana Paoli, director of corporate and public affairs for the San Jose Giants. Finally, the staff at San Jose State's interlibrary loan department has been invaluable to a scholar who does not have the time or funds to be visiting the various archives around the country.

Contents

Acknowledgments vi
Preface 1
Introduction 5

I. Baseball and Imperial America in the Philippines and Hawaii 15
II. Baseball and Asian Pacific American Communities on the Hawaiian Islands 35
III. Baseball and Asian Pacific American Communities on the American Mainland 56
IV. Asian Pacific American Amateurs and Semi-Pros 73
V. Barnstorming the Mainland with the Hawaiian Travelers, 1912–1916 101
VI. Asian Pacific American Minor Leaguers 127
VII. Asian Pacific American Big Leaguers in the United States and Japan 157

Afterword 191
Chapter Notes 193
References 209
Index 213

Preface

Asian Pacific Americans and Baseball is a legacy of personal and professional concerns. In the first place, I have long enjoyed playing and watching sports. I was too small to compete in my favorite sports such as baseball, basketball, and football well past middle school but I continued to watch sports, sometimes passionately and often admiringly. And in the last fifteen years or so I have shot hoops and played catch with my two children.

At the same time, I have long been curious about the history of sports, partly because my father inspired that interest by telling me stories about George Gipp, Red Grange, Babe Ruth, Jack Dempsey, and Joe Louis. By the time I was eight years old, I would cite to bored buddies and relatives Ty Cobb's lifetime batting average and how many home runs Joe DiMaggio hit over his career. Indeed, I think my interest in sports history helped motivate my pursuit of a career as a history teacher. Somehow digging around the past of baseball or football inspired me to dig around the past of a notable person, nation, or world.

My pursuit of an academic career in history converged with the social turmoil of the 1960s and 1970s. Like many of my contemporaries, I wondered why social divisions existed and too frequently flared into conflict in the United States. In particular, I wondered why race and ethnicity brought out both the best and the worst in Americans. My studies led me to the anti–Chinese movement which captured California and too much of the nation in the late 1800s and an eventual job teaching Asian American Studies at San Jose State University.

Meanwhile, I had married a Japanese American woman whose parents and grandparents were incarcerated in a concentration camp during World War II. Getting Asian American Studies right, therefore, combined not only professional and social priorities but also became a personal commitment. Getting Asian American Studies right involved the three dearest people in my life—not only my wife but also my two *hapa* children.

Organization

The book is organized chronologically and topically. The introduction explores the book's purpose and provides a brief history of Americans of Asian and Pacific Islander ancestry. (The term "Asian Pacific Americans," now widely accepted in both communities, refers to Americans who trace their roots to the Pacific Islands but also to Asia.) The first chapter discusses the relationship between baseball and American imperial ventures in the Asian Pacific region during the late nineteenth and early twentieth centuries. Baseball in the Philippines and Hawaii will gain the most attention since in these two areas American colonialism was controversial and remains a source of historical contention. The next two chapters cover the interaction of baseball and Asian Pacific American community development. Since this topic is so large, I have devoted the second chapter to a discussion of baseball and Asian Pacific American communities in the Hawaiian Islands. The third chapter observes the same relationship, but on the American mainland. In the fourth chapter, I analyze how, through baseball, relatively anonymous Americans of Asian Pacific Islander ancestry have journeyed over treacherous racial frontiers. Because they could have easily been discussed either in chapter one, two, or four, Hawaiian ballplayers who barnstormed the American mainland in the 1910s as members of a team variously and inaccurately described as the All Chinese, the Chinese University of Hawaii team, the Chinese Travelers, and the Hawaiian Travelers will provide the subject of the fifth chapter. The sixth chapter discusses American ballplayers of Asian Pacific Islander ancestry who have played professionally in the United States. However, this chapter stops short of taking on those who have played major league ball either in the United States or Japan. The seventh chapter covers those very talented athletes. An afterword revisits themes and advances a few ideas about the relationship between Asian Pacific Americans, baseball, and the American cultural mainstream.

Asian Pacific Americans

The field of Asian American Studies has always acknowledged the difficulty of defining the people it studies. Ronald Takaki's *Strangers from a Dif-

ferent Shore has achieved canonical status as a history of Asian Americans. Takaki's book embraces the historical experiences of people of Chinese, Japanese, Korean, East Indian, Filipino, Thai, Vietnamese, Cambodian, and Laotian descent. However, places like the Philippines and Hawaii have been historical encounter zones, where people of Asian and Pacific Islander backgrounds have, to put it somewhat politely, hooked up. Accordingly, Asian American Studies increasingly traces the experiences of Americans of Asian Pacific Islander backgrounds — that is, those people who were either born in or can trace their ancestry not only to places that we have already mentioned but also to the Pacific Islands of Hawaii, Samoa, Fiji, and Guam.

In this book, I will consider Americans of Asian Pacific Islander ancestry who have lived in the United States or in any of its territorial possessions, including the Philippines from annexation to the Tydings-McDuffie Act. I will also discuss multiracial people of Asian Pacific Islander ancestry. A son of an Italian American father and black mother, Roy Campanella is widely recognized as playing a distinguished role in African American baseball history. Today, New York Yankees star Johnny Damon is a son of a white father and a Thai mother. It makes little sense to separate Johnny Damon from Asian Pacific American baseball history, although multiracial people assuredly complicate that history.

Introduction

In March 1912, a baseball team of Hawaiians of Chinese ancestry set out for the American mainland. In order to schedule games against American college nines, promoters claimed the nine represented the fictitious Chinese University of Hawaii. At the same time, the team's purpose was to promote Hawaii and Honolulu's Chinese community on the mainland. Since Hawaii had been dragged reluctantly into the American empire as a territory more than a decade earlier, each of the Hawaiian-born players was an American citizen, regardless of how they were categorized racially.

Variously called the All Chinese, the Near Chinese, the Chinese Travelers, and The Hawaiian Travelers, these gifted athletes played well over one hundred games from one coast to another not only in 1912 but for the next four years as well. They also journeyed into Canada and Cuba. In the process, they won far more often than they lost against college, semi-professional, and even professional nines. However, by the time of their last tour of the mainland, the team no longer largely consisted of entirely Chinese Hawaiians. Rather, the roster included young men of indigenous Hawaiian, Japanese, and European ancestry as well. These Hawaiian ballplayers of Asian Pacific Islander ancestry often amazed American spectators with not only their ability to play baseball but to speak English, argue with umpires, and ridicule opposing players. Orientals were not supposed to demonstrate speed and strength, as well as a facility with American English and particularly American slang. Yet through baseball these Asian Pacific Islanders from Hawaii broke down, at least for the time they were in uniform, conventional thinking about race and nationality in early twentieth century American sport.[1]

Generally, when baseball history takes a look at Asian Pacific American baseball, it focuses on ballplayers of Japanese ancestry and neglects athletes such as the Chinese Hawaiian and multiethnic Asian Pacific Islander ballplayers who crisscrossed the Pacific from 1912 to 1916. Obviously, Japanese Americans have played baseball with enthusiasm and great skill. But all sorts of Asian Pacific Americans organized community teams, while competing as well on Little League, high school, college, and professional squads.[2]

In this book I hope to show the importance of baseball to the history of ethnically diverse Americans of Asian Pacific Islander ancestry, as well as their importance to the history of baseball. Baseball has transported Americans of Asian Pacific Islander ancestry to ballparks throughout the country—from Honolulu Stadium to Fenway Park. Historians of the Americans of Asian Pacific Islander ancestry have tended to ignore these people's experiences with sport in general and baseball in particular, as have historians of sport in general and baseball in particular.

Such neglect is understandable. We need to have the historical record of Asian Pacific Islanders in America set straight. The history of struggle against decades of exclusion, exploitation, and cultural oppression requires telling and re-telling in light of recent attempts to rationalize the confinement of over 100,000 Japanese Americans in World War II concentration camps. At the same time, historians of baseball can be excused for wishing to honor the innovative pioneers and magnificent players of the game. After all, the grand events in the history of America's venerable sport have always apparently occurred in New York City, Boston, and occasionally Chicago. And the fact that the sport spread to such places as Honolulu and Manila only seems to confirm the brilliance of entrepreneurs such as the Chicago-based A.G. Spalding and players such as the New York Yankees' "Sultan of Swat," Babe Ruth.[3]

However, a few scholars such as Samuel Regalado, Gail Nomura and Susan Zieff have demonstrated the importance of sport in the lives of Japanese and Chinese Americans. It seems that if we are to acquire a fully fleshed out history of Americans of Asian Pacific Islander ancestry that history should tell about the Chinese Hawaiians who trekked the American mainland to play baseball in small towns and big, from California to New England, as it should tell about the refuge Japanese Americans found in baseball when confined in concentration camps during World War II.[4]

However, it seems quite easy to marginalize Asian Pacific Islander experiences with baseball. After all, nearly every major racial and ethnic group has a representative in the American Baseball Hall of Fame, housed in bucolic Cooperstown, New York. But where is the Asian Pacific Islander equivalent of Hank Greenberg, Roberto Clemente, Jackie Robinson, and Joe DiMaggio?

Indeed, no person of Asian Pacific Islander ancestry is a member of the Baseball Hall of Fame, although one might expect Ichiro Suzuki to enter the hall eventually and perhaps even dynamic center fielder Johnny Damon, an American who possesses Thai ancestry.

Asian Pacific Americans and Baseball, however, takes a populist approach inspired by the Seymours' *The People's Game*. This book argues that there are myriad perspectives from which to view the value of baseball in American history. The game has been played and watched with joy by culturally diverse people from the Philippines to Maine. These people have not always played the game with the skill of a Willie Mays or a Babe Ruth, but baseball has helped give their lives a sense of community and purpose. It has allowed them to demonstrate at least a semblance of mastery of a tough to learn sport. It has encouraged them to traverse treacherous cultural borders to compete with people identified with other social and cultural groups. And in a few cases, baseball has offered them positive notoriety and healthy incomes.[5]

Neither major league ballplayers nor, for that matter, their employers own baseball. Not even the Fox Network or ESPN own it today. No country and certainly no racial group, sex, or class owns it. And baseball has not only been played in Yankee Stadium, Wrigley Field, and Fenway Park. Among those holding proprietary interest in baseball have been sugar plantation workers on the Hawaiian Islands and store clerks in San Francisco's Chinatown. Baseball's real owners have spanned the generations and now increasingly span the gender gap. They may not have played in Yankee Stadium or Fenway Park. They may have played on makeshift baseball diamonds in San Jose's Japantown or a World War II Japanese American concentration camp. In a society that has often judged success based upon fame and fortune, the Chinese and Filipino Americans who have hit and caught baseballs in crowded city streets or in the shadows of an Alaskan fish cannery may seem like losers to some of us; they are more likely objects of pity and perhaps curiosity than admiration. But there is no defeat in asserting one's humanity and one's connection to others. Through baseball Americans of Asian Pacific Islander ancestry claimed their humanity when others thought of them merely as laundry workers, maids, and busboys. Through baseball, they asserted their connections to others when America's legal-political system sought to deny them those connections.

Historical Background

This is not the place to delve deeply into the complex and often discouraging history of Asian Pacific Americans. But a brief look at America's immigration and naturalization laws will indicate how people of Asian Pacific Islander ancestry were treated by the American political-legal system. In 1790, Congress enacted a naturalization law banning non-white immigrants from citizenship. At this time, Asian Pacific Islanders were not on the minds of Congress and President Washington. But by the time Chinese immigrants started to arrive in significant numbers in California during the Gold Rush they were increasingly labeled by science and the law as racially Mongolian and, not being Caucasian, therefore ineligible for citizenship. This was confirmed in a revised naturalization law enacted in 1870—a law which somewhat redressed past wrongs by allowing immigrants of African ancestry to become citizens but as a sop to the growing anti–Chinese movement in places like California explicitly denied citizenship to so-called Mongolian immigrants.

By 1882, the anti–Chinese movement had spread eastward across the nation, making it politically expeditious for Congress to enact the Chinese Exclusion Law. The first immigration law targeting a people because of their race and nationality, the Chinese Exclusion Law restricted entry into the United States of Chinese laborers and explicitly banned all Chinese immigrants from citizenship, regardless of whether they were laborers, professionals, or business owners. The Chinese Exclusion Law would remain on the books for roughly sixty years.

Meanwhile, the issue of whether American-born children of Chinese immigrants and other Asian Pacific Islander immigrants were U.S. citizens had been adjudicated by the United States Supreme Court in the unjustly ignored case of *Wong Kim Ark vs. U.S.* (1898). Basing its decision on the 14th Amendment that stipulated anyone born in the United States was a citizen of the United States, the court decided in Wong Kim Ark's favor. That is, the United States government could not deny the San Francisco– born Wong Kim Ark's reentry into the country after a trip to China because the litigant was not an immigrant subject to the Chinese Exclusion Law but an American citizen.

However, lower courts had clearly decided that Chinese and Japanese immigrants defined as racially Mongolian were ineligible for citizenship. In addition, immigrants from other lands in East Asia and the Pacific Islands were also deemed ineligible for citizenship by the lower courts in the late 1800s and early 1900s by reason of race. The major area of legal confusion seems to have been whether Asian Indians were white since racial science at the time largely defined Asian Indians as Caucasians.[6]

By this time as well, America had added, under controversial circumstances, the Hawaiian Islands and the Philippines to its empire an, less intrusively, eastern Samoa. The status of the indigenous people on these islands varied. The Hawaiian Islands were granted territorial status by Uncle Sam. Thus, anyone born on the islands was considered a citizen, regardless of racial identification. The Philippines, on the other hand, were forced into the American empire as a protectorate. Filipinos, accordingly, were U.S. nationals, ineligible for citizenship. American Samoa, too, was provided with protectorate status and Samoans were U.S. nationals, ineligible for citizenship.

In the early 1900s, Japanese immigrants were targeted by America's anti-Asian movement. The Gentlemen's Agreement between the United States and Japan was inspired by anti–Japanese politics in San Francisco. According to this agreement, the U.S. would protect the rights of *Nikkei*, or people of Japanese ancestry, living wherever Uncle Sam claimed sovereignty and Japan would no longer issue passports to Japanese laborers wishing to migrate to America or its colonies. While it did not hinder the movement of *Nikkei* from Hawaii to the American mainland or the immigration of Japanese spouses to the United States, it did discourage Japanese immigration to the U.S. in general since most of those who had migrated to Hawaii and the American mainland were indeed laborers. Moreover, since Japan annexed Korea in the 1900s and transformed Koreans into Japanese subjects, the Gentlemen's Agreement inhibited Korean immigration as well.

World War I did not bring out the best in America when it came to immigration. The Immigration Act of 1917 was a nasty by-product of America's growing distrust of immigrants. This act eliminated immigration from British controlled India, French Indochina, as well as the Pacific Islands not held by America. The racism and nativism inspired by the war ultimately led to the even nastier National Origins Act of 1924, which pointedly denied immigration of "aliens ineligible for citizenship." Since much of Central and East Asia had been previously dealt with by Congress, this meant Japan and its colonial possessions.

A few years earlier, however, the U.S. Supreme Court handed down two troubling decisions regarding the issue of citizenship rights for Asian Pacific Island immigrants. In *Ozawa v. U.S.*, a Japanese immigrant sought American citizenship status. The Supreme Court determined, based on the available scientific evidence, that Japanese people were Mongolians and therefore ineligible for citizenship unless born in America. The court's findings inspired hope in Asian Indian and California resident Bhagat Singh Thind. Since prevailing scientific evidence considered Asian Indians as Caucasians, he expected that America's highest court would once and for all settle the matter and allow him and other Asian Indian immigrants naturalization rights. However, the court decided to throw out available scientific evidence and in a sense apply the "brown paper bag" theory to the issue of naturalization. In other words, if someone's skin was as dark or darker than a brown paper bag that person was not white and therefore ineligible for citizenship if he came from Asia. Furthermore, not only did the court decide that Thind was ineligible for citizenship but it also demanded that Asian Indians previously determined as eligible by lower courts for citizenship be stripped of that citizenship.

Intentionally adding salt to the wounds, the U.S. Congress enacted the Cable Act in 1922. The law authorized the taking away of U.S. citizenship status from anyone married to an "alien ineligible for citizenship." The Cable Act, therefore, made it harder for Asian Pacific Islander immigrants to marry citizens and raise families on American soil.

In the 1930s, the Great Depression exacerbated racial tensions in places like California, where a relatively large population of Filipino immigrants resided. At the same time, some American political leaders wanted to throw off the expense and embarrassment of America's colonial possession of the Philippines. The need to get rid of Filipino immigrants and the Philippines converged in the Tydings-McDuffie Act, which granted the Philippines eventual independence and declared Filipinos no longer U.S. nationals but "aliens ineligible for citizenship." Filipino immigration to the U.S. was essentially eliminated, although sugar plantation operators in Hawaii received a special dispensation to recruit Filipino workers if they really needed to do so.

Thus, up until World War II, Asian Pacific Islander Americans lived in a country that did not welcome them — that largely regarded them as racially unfit to become good Americans even if they were born in the U.S. More to the point, while the country regarded Hank Greenberg's parents and Joe DiMaggio's parents with often undisguised suspicion, they were still legally defined as white. Until the 1920s, Italian and Eastern European immigrants could enter the U.S. largely unrestricted and once in America they and not just their children were eligible for citizenship.

If immigration from China and Japan had not been restricted, it is very likely that someone would have emerged from a Chinatown or a Little Tokyo to claim the baseball skills mastered by elite white or black professionals. Perhaps racial discrimination would have made it hard for Chinese Americans or Japanese Americans to become major league stars. Perhaps their general lack of size would have made it hard for Chinese Americans or Japanese Americans to become home run heroes and strikeout kings. But among them would have been a few players to match the skills of standout Italian American infielders such as Frankie Crosetti or Phil Rizzuto or skilled Eastern European American pitchers such as Stan Coveleski.

World War II and the Cold War revealed some of the hypocrisy behind an American rhetoric that bragged about freedom and an American reality that denied it to millions. Accordingly, immigration and naturalization laws were liberalized. By the mid–1960s, race was no longer a legal barrier to immigration or naturalization. Since 1965, youth teams have emerged not only in Hawaii, where such organizations were long dominated by players of Asian Pacific Islander ancestry, but also in California, where Little League and Pony League squads have been composed of more than a token number of players of Asian Pacific Islander ancestry. Perhaps a future superstar of Vietnamese or East Indian descent is playing tee ball or American Legion ball at this very moment.

The Nineteenth Century

Making baseball history, therefore, has not always been easy for Asian Pacific Americans. The fact that many of them have grown up in conditions which demanded they spend more time working in sugar cane fields and their parents' restaurants and less time hitting fastballs has rendered opportunities for playing baseball impractical. Nevertheless, we can discover a very real and meaningful history of Asian Pacific American baseball.

One place to start is in the nineteenth century. By mid–nineteenth century, diasporic Chinese communities had formed in New York City, while large communities had sprouted in California as a result of the Gold Rush. By this time as well, American missionaries, business people, and sailors had come into contact with Hawaiian Islanders. Indeed, one of these folks happened to have been Alexander Cartwright, a key pioneer of the youthful sport in New York City in the 1840s. By the end of the century, a large diasporic Chinese community had developed in Hawaii as a result of the sugar plantations' insatiable hunger for labor. Japanese immigrants would join them and then make their way to the American mainland as well. While Asian Pacific American experiences with baseball on the American mainland in the nineteenth century were sporadic, they are worth exploring. However, in Hawaii, ballplayers of indigenous Hawaiian ancestry were very active by the end of the century, while Chinese and Japanese Hawaiian ballplayers pop up as well.

American colonization of the Pacific islands of Hawaii and the Philippines was steeped in contention, then and now. Neither indigenous Hawaiians nor indigenous Filipinos greeted the idea of living under the Stars and Stripes happily. Fortunately for the United States, in Hawaii resistance was largely peaceful and tamed by popular leaders such as Queen Liliuokalani. In the Philippines, resistance led to a cruel guerrilla war and atrocities committed on both sides. Moreover, in Hawaii, American annexation was preceded by years of indigenous Hawaiians interacting with American nationals — missionaries, sugar plantation owners, and teachers. Among the things that Hawaiians learned was baseball. In the Philippines, American annexation was not preceded by decades of constant interaction between Americans and Filipinos. Instead, annexation introduced Filipinos rather abruptly to America. Baseball became a small but integral part of socializing Filipinos not only to accept but also, it was hoped, to wallow happily in their status as Uncle Sam's "little brown" colonial subjects.

By the early twentieth century, thousands of people of Asian Pacific Islander ancestry lived in the United States or one of its colonial possessions. Diasporic Asian Pacific Islander communities bred durable community institutions. Among these institutions were baseball teams and leagues intended to perform the double duty of reinforcing ethnic ties while reaching out to other ethnic groups. The development of Asian Pacific Islander community teams and leagues in the twentieth century was prodigious. The Hawaiian Islands, where Asian Pacific Islanders formed a majority, nurtured talented ethnic-based teams — teams good enough to defeat many of the best amateur and semi-professional teams on the American mainland. On the American mainland, community teams and leagues also thrived, mainly, but not exclusively, on the West Coast.

Baseball helped transport individual Asian Pacific Americans across racial and ethnic barriers. This was perhaps more easily accomplished in Hawaii, where race and ethnicity were more fluid ways of identifying and marginalizing people than on the American mainland. However, even on the American mainland and even as early as the first decade of the twentieth century, ballplayers of Asian Pacific Islander ancestry competed on youth, high school, college, and semi-professional teams with people of different racial and ethnic backgrounds.

More than a handful of American ballplayers of Asian Pacific Islander background were able to reach the higher rungs of minor league baseball in addition to making the American big leagues. A few such as Ron Darling, Atlee Hammaker, Mike Lum, Tony Solaita, Benny Agbayani, Lenn Sakata, Danny Graves, and Johnny Damon have carved out solid and even outstanding major league careers in the United States. Others such as Wally Yonamine and Bozo Wakabayashi became Japanese major league stars.

While this book focuses on the players, it will also take a look at Asian Pacific Americans' relationship to baseball in other areas. Asian Pacific Americans as spectators and supporters of baseball merits attention. Moreover, Asian Pacific Americans have also contributed to baseball history as entrepreneurs, administrators, coaches and managers, as well as trainers, groundskeepers, and umpires.

Baseball and Assimilation

I am uneasy with the concept of assimilation as an effective way to explain the role of baseball in the lives of Asian Pacific Americans. While some scholars such as Milton Gordon have treated assimilation in a thoughtful and nuanced manner, many of us think of assimilation as a historical and contemporary tool to homogenize American society. Over a century of wise scholars and social critics have cast doubt upon how well assimilation has worked in America — especially for people of color. And many of the same scholars and social critics have cast doubt on whether assimilation ought to work in a healthy democratic society. After all, as John Dewey pointed out in the early decades of the twentieth century, a democratic society requires diversity of opinion to grow. It needs dialogue and not a nation of "yes men."[7]

Having made my assumptions clear, it seems that baseball did help to link Asian Pacific Americans to other Americans of varied racial and ethnic identities. Some years ago, historian Peter Levine described sport in general as a cultural middle ground in which Jewish and non–Jewish Americans could find commonality in the twentieth century. Perhaps for Asian Pacific Americans the baseball diamond has also constituted a cultural middle ground on which for a couple of hours they could share with non–Asian Pacific Americans. The positive ramifications of all this seem more durable on the Hawaiian Islands where baseball aided pidgin English in developing a Hawaiian local culture which significantly transcended ethnic and racial distinctions. Nevertheless, even on the American mainland baseball helped convince some that Kipling had it wrong — the twain could meet on the baseball diamond. Perhaps, that is, Asian Pacific Islanders and non–Asian Pacific Islanders could share other vital institutions of American life as well.[8]

At the same time, Asian Pacific American baseball has long been shadowed by what scholar Elaine Kim has called "racism's traveling eye." For years, Japanese Americans on the mainland understood that if they were going to play baseball, they would largely have to play it with one another. That is, aside from an occasional receptive high school, semi-pro, and college team, they would not be welcomed as teammates. Individual Asian Pacific Islander athletes faced overt and covert forms of discrimination. Moreover, the press frequently treated ballplayers of Asian Pacific Islander ancestry with disdain. And even when it did not intentionally try to denigrate Asian Pacific Islander people, the press fed into stereotypes of them as, to quote Ronald Takaki, "strangers from a different shore." Thus, if baseball has stood out as a melting pot dissipating the major differences between people, it has, at best, only partially succeeded with Americans of Asian Pacific Islander ancestry.[9]

CHAPTER I

Baseball and Imperial America in the Philippines and Hawaii

By 1900, the United States had claimed the Philippine Islands and the Hawaiian Islands as its own. It would spread the gospel of baseball to thousands of Filipinos not necessarily thrilled about liberation from one colonial power only to find themselves colonized by another. And while culturally diverse Hawaiians were already familiar with baseball, their reticent incorporation into the American empire perhaps helped some of Hawaii's diverse population believe that any country that invented a sport which furnished them such joy cannot be all that bad.

The Philippines

Baseball might well, according to American imperialists, ease the troubled white man's burden in the Philippines. Scholar Dean Worchester, historian Richard Drinnon notes, was a key apologist for America's disturbing expansion into the Philippines. Worchester claimed no further proof was needed that Filipinos were unfit to rule themselves than their ignorance of baseball. He boasted, therefore, that one of the benefits of the American occupation of the Philippines was that Filipinos discovered the wonders of America's national pastime. Worchester insisted, "Before the American occupation ... the Filipinos had not learned to play.... Baseball not only strengthens the muscles of the players, it sharpens the mind."[1]

Americans reported that Filipinos picked up baseball very enthusiastically, if not always adeptly. As early as 1901, an American soldier stationed in the war-torn Philippines wrote the *Sporting News*, extolling the affection in which the "natives" had lavished on baseball. He asserted, as would many after him, that the Filipino took to baseball as a "duck to water." Filipinos were "first class rooters" and while their play showed the signs of youthful ineptitude, they would eventually command baseball well enough to form their own league. Even females, he added, played catch with one another. In 1909, a letter to the *Washington Post*'s sports editor reported that Filipinos were "baseball crazy." While not always very good at the sport, Filipinos, especially the youth, had at least mastered the rules of the game.[2]

Elite Filipinos like Colonel Manuel Quezon agreed that baseball was good for the world in general and Filipinos in particular. While in Boston in 1912, Quezon asked an audience, "Did you know that the Filipino boy takes to your national game as a duck takes to water?" Then Quezon made a statement that would have warmed the heart of Dean Worchester: "Nothing less than a miracle could bring freedom to the Filipinos — lasting freedom, I mean, safe and sure — so quickly as a race of men trained early on the athlete fields with the game of base ball as the basic sport."[3]

Also in 1912, the *Sporting Life* reported on baseball's progress among Filipinos. It ran a headline that read, "Natives of the Philippines Abandoning Cockfighting for Base Ball," referring to a pastime popular in historically agrarian based societies such as the Philippines but highly unpopular among those which fancied themselves as civilized. American teachers, according to the article, expressed astonishment at how fervently Filipinos adopted baseball. This inspired the *Sporting Life* to declare that "it is not only interesting to the boys who play, but is commanding the attention of large crowds who are deserting the cockpits for the diamonds."[4]

The next year, the *Lusitania* carried a contingent of American major league baseball stars into Manila Harbor. A Filipino band struck up "The Star Spangled Banner" as the ballplayers disembarked. The advantages of American culture furnished a major theme underlying the series of games played by the major leaguers in the Philippines. Before one game, Major General J. Franklin Bell addressed the crowd and pointed out that the ballplayers' "tour [of the Philippines and Asia] would 'not only stir patriotism where Americans are encountered' but should 'impress foreign nations of the cleanness and manhood of Americans.'"[5]

Journalists commended baseball's impact on Filipino culture. John Foster, the editor of *Spalding's Official Baseball Guide 1913*, hailed baseball's influence over "Filipino boys," who were wild about the game and preferred to play it rather than bet on cockfights and other games of chance. Foster wrote:

The little fellows who wear not much more than a breechcloth play Base Ball. They have picked up many of the American terms and one of the most amusing of experiences is to stand outside the walls of old Manila and hear the little brown boys call: "Shoot it over. Line it out," and the like, returning to their native language, and jabbering excitedly in Filipino whenever they arrive at some point of play in which their command of English fails them.

A *Current Opinion* piece observed in 1913 that 482 baseball teams existed in the Philippines in order to prove "the importance of the game as a civilizing influence."[6]

In 1913, a team of Filipino ballplayers journeyed to the American mainland. In April, the *Washington Post* declared that how many games the Filipinos played in the United States was dependent upon monetary inducements. It maintained that the Filipino ballplayers mastered the game better than the average American or Japanese person, adding that the traveling team had previously and easily beaten a Japanese nine sent to the Philippines during "last carnival season." Moreover, the Filipino ballplayers had competed in the Manila League, winning well over 60 percent of the games they played. This Manila League, according to the *Post* story, equaled an American Class C or D professional league in skill. The players came from many "tribes" and the *Post* insisted that the harmony they displayed on the baseball diamond augured well for the future of the Philippines. Teams wanting to play the Filipino nine were advised to write the *San Francisco Examiner* before July 1 and the *Sporting News* after.[7]

In May, a wire story noted that "a crack all-Filipino" team was headed to the United States after playing in Japan. An American named E.F. Willets managed the tour while another American, Arthur E. McCann, served as advance agent who told the American press that the purpose of the tour was "to get the Philippines on the map, further the interest in the game, and to try to create a better feeling between the peoples of the countries visited and the Filipinos." The announced itinerary called for twelve games in Japan, one in Hawaii, and fifty on the American mainland, where the Filipinos were expected to oppose Class C and D minor leaguers, semi-professionals, and college teams. No two of the players reputedly spoke the same native language. Accordingly, "they are obliged to speak in a tongue other than their own in order to carry on a conversation among themselves." News of the team's imminent arrival stirred various comments from the American press. The *Los Angeles Times* declared, "Welcome to that Filipino baseball team. The American athletes will teach them that the bat is more powerful than the bolo," in reference to a machete-like instrument used to cut sugar cane in the Philippine Islands.[8]

During the early summer, readers of the American sporting press learned more about the team from newspapers throughout the United States. In mid-June, the *Nevada State Journal* headlined an article on the traveling squad, "Filipino Baseball Invasion." Nevadans were told, "Fifteen full-blooded Filipino youths comprise the squad, which has fair batters and pitchers and a reputation for fast fielding."[9]

In early July, Ohio's *Coshocton Tribune* announced, "America has been invaded by Chinese, Cuban, and Japanese baseball teams, but now it is the Filipino." Fourteen and not fifteen Filipino ballplayers, described as "the fastest of the Philippines," arrived in San Francisco. Baseball, according to the article proclaiming the arrival of the Filipino ballplayers, had "made wonderful strides" in the Philippines since the advent of the American occupation. Willets confidently insisted to the press, therefore, that the Filipino ballplayers could hold their own against American mainland teams.[10]

James Nealon of the *San Francisco Chronicle* bemoaned the "tardy" timing of the Filipinos' arrival in his city. Because they appeared in late June, college teams had already disbanded in the Bay Area. Thus, Bay Area college nines could not oppose the Filipino visitors. Consequently, only a semi-pro team from Santa Rosa was scheduled to take on the Filipinos in the Bay Area.[11]

Several weeks later, a photo of the "Filipino Baseball Team" was published in the *Coshocton Tribune*. According to the accompanying text, the team proved that "baseball follows the flag." "Taught by Americans" the Filipino athletes "put up a pretty good article of ball" against semi-pro and college nines. Indeed, in their first game on the American mainland, the Filipinos beat the Santa Rosa nine 8–4. Their hitting, indeed, knocked out a veteran professional pitcher, Doc Moskiman. However, according to the *San Francisco Chronicle*, "the base running of the visitors was a feature of the game." Ambrosio and San Jose formed the winning battery.[12]

The Filipinos' overall record was not all that good, however. They won but sixteen of thirty-eight games on the American mainland. They did not do all that well in their brief stay in Hawaii either. In late September, the *Honolulu Star-Bulletin* published a team photo, under which a caption read, "a grand little race war at Athletic Park" as the Filipinos were to meet the Japanese Hawaiian Asahi nine. The Honolulu daily predicted, furthermore, "Every Filipino in Honolulu who can make it will be on hand ... and it's a well-known fact that the Japanese fans turn out in force when their team is to play an international game." As it turned out, the Asahis beat the visitors. But, according to the *Star-Bulletin*, "they had to work at top speed and overdraw their account of baseball luck to turn the trick." The local Filipino and Japanese fans pulled for their favorites. Gutierrez pitched well for the

Filipinos and shortstop Platon turned in the fielding gem of the day. The *Philippines Free Press* summarized the season by claiming that that "the Filipinos were great fielders and base runners, but their hitting was poor."[13]

Despite the publicized role of E.F. Willets, Joseph Reaves claims that Filipino Alejandro Albert actually organized the tour. Called the "father of Philippine baseball," Albert served as undersecretary of public instruction for the Philippines. His son, Mariano, was the team captain, center fielder, and star. A lawyer, Mariano learned his baseball at two schools widely known for supporting the American pastime — Lico de Manila and the Philippine Normal School.[14]

In June 1915, the *Honolulu Star-Bulletin* published a photo and article on baseball in the Philippines. The headline to the photo read: "Baseball Follows the Flag." The caption asserted that the photo showed an "Igorotte" game in progress and that "[b]aseball in the Philippines has done what legislation and the Moral Progress league has failed to do in the way of pernicious gambling habits." The text quoted Worchester's take on the progress of America's national pastime in the Philippines: "We found baseball to be the keynote to Filipino morality.... The cockfighting and gambling formed the wall to advance in moral uplift and it was only by creating another sport that we were able to draw the crowds away from the cock pits." Worchester said the cockpit managers wanted legislation limiting baseball to once a week, "which shows how baseball affected the former sport."[15]

Also in 1915, the *Washington Post* ran an article claiming that American servicemen, in particular marines, were vital in spreading the gospel of baseball around the globe. It asserted that early in America's occupation of the Philippines, Filipinos had learned to love baseball by watching American marines play the game. With more than a hint of chauvinism, the *Post* insisted that "being of an imitative nature, however, the Filipinos were contented to stand by and watch. They took delight in aping the ball players, and with the aid of the marines, soon learned the rudiments of the game." The *Post* proclaimed that Filipinos had studied baseball well: "Today, the little brown men play a high brand of baseball. They are lightening like baserunners, are possessed of remarkably strong throwing arms, and are good fielders. As a general rule, they are too light to be strong hitters."[16]

Meanwhile, Manila hosted a concerted effort to organize a baseball league composed of top players of various racial and ethnic backgrounds. The appearance of a talented Chinese Hawaiian team in the spring of 1915 helped stimulate baseball fans in Manila to demand better and more baseball, as well as the introduction of an All-Chinese nine to Manila baseball. Proponents of the league wondered, however, "Are there enough native players to form at least four teams and is there a strong possibility of getting into the league an All-Chinese nine." There were, however, enough native players to help the University of Manila tie the University of Chicago nine in November 1915.[17]

In 1916, the *Baseball Monthly* published a photograph of Filipinos perched in a tree, watching a baseball game. The magazine claimed that in general baseball had become popular among "the yellow races of the Orient," but particularly so in the Philippines. Kipling was wrong, the *Monthly* asserted, the "twain" did "meet" in the Philippines thanks to baseball.[18]

In 1917, Fred O. England, the American superintendent of Manila schools, corresponded with *The Playground*, a leading voice of social and cultural reform through recreation. England assured readers that the recreational reformers had won over Filipinos, presumably just as they had been winning over working class immigrants in New York City and Chicago. Filipinos, according to England, "will turn out by the hundreds to witness a little indoor baseball [softball] game between school teams and will shout and yell their heads off."[19]

Meanwhile, Filipino teams were dispatched to the Far Eastern Games, styled as Olympic competition for Asian athletes. In 1913, a Filipino team lost the baseball championship to Meiji University of Japan. However, over the next several years Filipino baseball teams won several Far Eastern Games' baseball titles.[20]

A John Foster *Sporting News* piece in 1921 boasted of baseball's continued prosperity in the Philippine Islands. The article focused on a team of Filipino soldiers that had just taken a two out of three game series from an American military nine in Tientsin, China. In the first game, "Liboon, a little Filipino southpaw" hurled a no-hitter at the American soldiers. The Filipinos had another good pitcher in Birtulpo, "the Matty" of the Philippines. He lost the second game but pitched well. In the third game, Liboon hurled another gem to help his team to a deciding victory. To be sure, an American team went down to defeat, but the *Sporting News* urged readers not to mourn because the triumph of the Filipino team was a triumph for the American way of life. The Filipinos were inspired to embrace the American pastime even though the "perfume of incense still clings to ... [their] ... land."[21]

Earlier the same Filipino nine had defeated an American marine contingent in Bejing. One American observer noted the Filipinos' speed, adding that the Filipino nine reminded him of the "Chinese teams" that had barnstormed the mainland in the 1910s. Indeed, to this observer, the Filipinos seemed better than those teams that actually hailed from the Hawaiian Islands and consisted of American citizens of diverse Asian Pacific Islander ancestry. The American added that Birtulpo apparently had a fine future in baseball in front of him. In fact, he could even do well in American professional circles. Birtulpo possessed good size and could develop into both a "sensational pitcher" and a "sensational drawing card." The American observer expressed concerns, however, as to whether Birtulpo could adjust to the climate and society of the United States.[22]

In general, John Foster found the Filipino's mastery of the American national pastime a "marvel." Filipinos had more than simply internalized the mechanical aspects of the game. Foster was convinced that the Filipino ballplayers' alertness and "quick thinking" would stump many American mainland professionals. Foster was also impressed with the determination of Filipino teams that would travel ten days just to play one game.[23]

By the early 1920s, however, the Filipino enthusiasm for baseball had seemingly waned. A *Sporting News* article blamed a growing resentment with American rule for baseball's decline in the Philippines. Moreover, according to the "Baseball's Bible," the educators dispatched by the United States to the Philippines backed off from using baseball to "Americanize" Filipinos. It was too bad, the *Sporting News* complained, because baseball had found a home in places like Cuba, while constructing a cultural bridge between the United States and Japan.[24]

Nevertheless, in 1930, the *Sporting News* assured readers that the American pastime was far from dead in the Philippines. It reported, in fact, that "the National Game goes splendidly in the Philippine Islands." Filipinos played the game well and were convinced they surpassed the Japanese as ballplayers. Moreover, a young Filipino was interviewed on whether he would prefer the Philippines' independent without baseball or as an American colony with an active baseball program. The young man insisted he would just as soon avoid independence if exiling baseball from the Philippines was the cost. In April 1932, the St. Louis-based weekly pointed out that an all–Filipino team had just defeated a Hawaiian nine in Manila. The sport in the Philippines had produced stars such as Reginio Portucion, who surfaced as a pitching hero for National University. The Philippine Baseball League had just finished its season with teams such as the Manila Cits, McKinley, Mills, Manila, and Cavite. And fielding star Pablo Chu ranked among the league's standouts.[25]

In 1934, a major league all-star team featuring Babe Ruth, Lou Gehrig, and several other baseball immortals performed in Manila. The city accorded the major leaguers a "royal welcome." However, the Filipino Olympic team did not give the American ballplayers much of a battle, losing 9-1, thanks largely to Gehrig's heavy hitting. A few years later, the U.S. granted the Philippines semi-autonomy as a commonwealth member of the American empire. According to the Tydings-McDuffie Act the Philippines would gain independence in 1945. However, World War II stalled Filipino independence until 1946.[26]

Hawaii

Culturally diverse Hawaiians had been playing baseball for several years before the United States officially took over the islands in 1898. An inaccurate 1915 *Washington Post* article told readers that U.S. marines were largely responsible for transporting the American national pastime to the Hawaiian Islands. It traced the origins of baseball in Hawaii to the early 1890s. At the time, American marines, presumably stationed at Pearl Harbor, were ordered to "quell a revolution," presumably Queen Liliuokalani's attempt to weaken the power of the *haole* elite during the waning days of the Hawaiian monarchy. Learning baseball from the marines, the "childlike and enthusiastic" Hawaiians "played the game for all it was worth." The *Post* added, "The Hawaiians, it might be mentioned, are possessed of unusual speed and although they play barefooted, run and slide bases in a way that would do credit to our own players."[27]

Yet baseball's history in the Hawaiian Islands goes back to at least the 1860s if not earlier. One of the founders of the sport, Alexander Cartwright, trekked to Hawaii in the late 1840s and apparently proved crucial in transplanting baseball to Hawaiian soil. Meanwhile, Americans traveling to the islands as missionaries, educators, business people, as well as military personnel, brought their love of baseball to Hawaii before 1890. Moreover, by 1900 many Japanese immigrants to Hawaii carried their developing knowledge of the sport to the islands, although baseball was relatively inaccessible to the Japanese peasants and workers most likely to head to the islands to perform plantation labor.

Hawaiians of Asian Pacific Islander ancestry were playing baseball soon after the sport was introduced to the islands. Albert G. Spalding, who took a team of major leaguers to the islands in the late 1880s, noted that by then "the natives were also developing skill at the pastime." Speaking at a banquet celebrating the return of Spalding's all-star team from its world tour, Mark Twain found it odd that baseball had grown roots in Hawaiian soil. Baseball, to Twain and other Americans, represented a powerful and irrepressible alternative to the exotic primitiveness that they believed permeated the Pacific Islands. Twain called baseball in his oft-quoted declaration: "The very symbol, the outward and visible expression of the drive and push and struggle of the ranging, tearing, booming nineteenth century."[28]

Pacific Islanders were clearly important participants in Hawaiian baseball by the end of the twentieth century. In 1890, Kamehameha had won the Hawaii Baseball League championship over teams called the All-Stars, Honolulu, and Punahou. In the mid–1890s, the *Honolulu Gazette* noted the play of the "Kamehameha boys"— athletes who represented a Hawaiian private school established to educate youth of indigenous Hawaiian ancestry. However, for some reason the Hawaii Baseball League reportedly was torn by friction over whether to allow the Kamehameha team into the league in 1895. In addition, the Kamehameha baseball team did not draw well in the spring of 1895. Ballgames in Honolulu were usually played on Saturday but a recent switch in Kamehameha's schedule called for classes on Saturday. Thus, many Kamehameha students who would have wanted to personally support their team lingered in classrooms instead.[29]

The Kamehameha nine more than held its own against other Honolulu teams, although the *Gazette* insisted that the "Kams" could not play from behind but blew their advantage because they became "extremely cocky" when they got off to an early lead. In 1895, Kamehameha defeated a team called the Unknowns. The box score listed young men surnamed Pahau, Crowell, Bridges, Lemon, Aea, Ahia, Davis, and Lawelawe in the Kamehameha lineup. In 1896, the Kam team included players such as Ako Aki, James Kauka, James Cockett, Kauhaneo, Oana, Kaloi, Ainana, Nawahane, and Paulo. In 1899, F. Cockett, Burgess, Kalua, Reuter, Kekeuewa, Mahoe, Venetta, Paehaole, and Harbottle represented Kamehameha. That year the *Gazette* noted that the Native Hawaiian ballplayers had beaten the Battery K nine 22-13. The daily insisted that the Kamehameha team could hit but as defenders were unfortunately puzzled by anything hit in their direction.[30]

The *Gazette* also reported on teams comprising players of diverse Asian Pacific Islander backgrounds. In 1895, it declared that a Kalani and other Native Hawaiians played for the Unknowns. In a game pitting the Unknowns against the Stars, an umpire named Kaia made some decisions that offended the Stars. Consisting primarily of *haoles*, the Stars contended that Kaia acted on the Hawaiian language instructions imparted by an Unknown player. The next year, the daily reported on a game between news carriers of the *Hawaii Star* and their counterparts employed by the *Pacific Commercial Advertiser*. Kipi, Kikila, Kealo, and Kolio played for the Stars, while Makaohe, Kealoha, and Keahinui competed for the *Advertiser* nine. In 1897, Mahuka, Pahau, and Koki played for the Stars, while Luahiwa and Kaanohi represented a nine called the Regiments. Guarding third base for the St. Louis College nine was a player with the Chinese surname of Wong, while Kaaua roamed right field for the educational institution, which was actually a Catholic run secondary school. In 1899, Punahou, a private school for elite *haoles* that at the time occasionally admitted non-*haoles*, fielded a team with a player surnamed Ah Fook. The same year, Joy, perhaps the Native Hawaiian Barney Joy who pitched in Organized Baseball in the early 1900s, took the box for a team called Palama Chapel against the Battery K team.[31]

Asian Pacific Islanders competed in baseball in the late 1800s on other

Hawaiian islands than Oahu. On Maui, the *Hawaiian Gazette* reported, a game took place in the spring of 1895 between Wailuku and Makawao. Apparently, two Kamehameha graduates competed for Makawao. In 1896, the Maui team had players such as Willie Kia, as well as Kaluakaini, Kanewani, and Kaawakao, while the Wailuku team fielded athletes surnamed Akina, Kauka, and Palia.[32]

In the 1890s, Chinese and Japanese Hawaiians appeared decidedly interested and skilled in baseball. By the 1890s, Chinese Hawaiians had become proficient enough in the American national pastime that two of them helped pioneer the sport in China by coaching students at Shanghai's St. John's College. Meanwhile, Dr. Khai Fai Li had organized and managed the first Chinese Hawaiian baseball team, called Aala. In the late 1890s, Reverend Takie Okumura established the first Japanese American nine on the islands. Okumura operated a settlement house in the Honolulu working class district of Palama for *Nikkei* boys, and his wards generally comprised the new baseball team. Okumura shared the concerns of social reformers throughout the industrializing, modernizing world — that working class people and particularly working class youth needed healthy and wholesome pastimes to divert them from crime, alcohol abuse, and political radicalism. Whether in Chicago or Honolulu, reformers saw baseball as a useful tool to keep working class males out of trouble. Called the Excelsiors, Okumura's nine competed against teams representing other ethnic groups.[33]

In 1903, the *Hawaiian Gazette* appeared stunned that the Wailuku nine fielded a "full-blooded Chinese," who played "satisfactorily." The daily asked, as a result, "Who says Western Civilization is too difficult for the Oriental?" Indeed, the Wailukus not only had one Chinese Hawaiian on the roster but two.[34]

Haole Lorrin Andrews, who served as the new territory's attorney general, corresponded with the *Cincinnati Enquirer* in 1904 and told the Ohio daily that baseball had become clearly a multicultural affair on the islands. A Hawaiian "championship team" consisted of "three full-blooded natives," three "half-castes," as well as two "mixtures of American Negro and Hawaiian." Moreover, Andrews declared, "the star first baseman of the league is a full-blooded Chinaman."[35]

In 1906, the *Washington Post* quoted L.W. Wolff, who represented the Spalding sports equipment company in Honolulu. Wolff maintained that Honolulu was a "sports crazy" town and the city's residents of Chinese, Japanese, Hawaiian, and European American backgrounds all engaged in athletic competition. Describing the Honolulu Baseball League, Wolff claimed that "games take on more of a factional fight." One team had Japanese and Hawaiians, another Chinese and Japanese, and still another had "whites and

Hawaiians." He asserted that all of the nationalities retained enthusiastic supporters and the games were accordingly fiercely contested.³⁶

In 1909, another *Washington Post* article noted the popularity and civilizing mission of baseball on the Hawaiian Islands. The article asked, "Who says the Orient isn't being civilized?" It answered the question by pointing out a narration of a game between the Fifth Cavalry and the Waialae nines in an unspecified Honolulu newspaper. The soldiers, the *Post* stressed, lost to the Hawaiian team which had players such as Thomas Kahiwahiwa, J. Kuoha, Mon Sing, Pohina, A. Kana, and Kuhea. The correspondent predicted that eventually the major leagues would recruit Kanakas, forgetting, as will be discussed later, a Hawaiian named Barney Joy had already been signed by a major league team and quite well discussed in the *Washington Post*.³⁷

Two articles published in the *Decatur Review* in September 1910 referred to the cultural diversity of Hawaiian baseball. The first called attention to a piece spotted in Honolulu's *Pacific Commercial Advertiser* which reported on a tempestuous game between the "Chinese" and the Japanese "Asahis." A fan angered an Asahi hitter and the "dusky batsman" flung his bat into a crowd of spectators and then jumped into the stands to search out the source of his rage. Moreover, the Chinese Athletic Club (CAC) nine almost got into a fight with the Asahis when the CAC shortstop allegedly threw at an Asahi base runner heading for first. Sam Hop, who would subsequently pilot the barnstorming Chinese Hawaiian nine, served as the umpire. He wanted to call the game, but was persuaded to let it go on until the CAC nine could claim a 14–0 victory. A *Review* writer expressed curiosity about the batting orders of the two teams. The writer understood that one team was composed of Chinese but suspected that the Asahis were both Japanese and "Kanakas." Nevertheless, the writer did "learn that there is some word in the Japanese language which will cause a batter to hurl bats into the bleachers and then to hurl himself after the bats. " The *Review* writer also commented on a game reported in the *Pacific Commercial Advertiser* between the Muhocks and the Palamas: "The men on the Muhock team …Wong, Hook, Aylett, Xavier, Peterson and Tin. The Palama stars were Harvey, Kuue, Rice, Moses, Lozog and Brito. If anybody wants to guess the nationality of the men on those teams it is his turn next."³⁸

The other *Decatur Review* article pointed out that the University of Chicago baseball team was set to journey to Asia. The writer asserted that the Chicago ballplayers would find that Asia had plenty of good ball teams, "because the American game has been introduced not alone in the American colonies but among the natives of China, Java and other Asiatic countries. Hawaii has two baseball teams, one made up entirely of Chinamen and the other in part Hawaiians and they play very excellent ball."³⁹

This team photo of a Honolulu ball club shows the diversity of baseball in Hawaii (c. 1910). The ballplayers seem to possess both European and non-European origins (courtesy of Library of Congress, Prints and Photographs Division).

In 1912, a baseball fan in Honolulu corresponded with the San Francisco Bureau of the *Los Angeles Times*. The fan told the mainland journalists that baseball attracted a fervent and multicultural following in Honolulu. The fan wrote, "The Japanese, Chinese, Portuguese, and Hawaii natives have a number of teams."[40]

That same year, Honolulu dispatched a team of Chinese Hawaiian ballplayers affiliated with the CAC to the American mainland. This contingent of superb Hawaiian athletes will be explored more in a later chapter. For now, however, we should note that in subsequent years the team would lose its affiliation with the CAC and become more multiracial and multiethnic but essentially Hawaiian. As such, its general success in defeating American mainland teams of college, semi-professional, and even professional levels proved the international popularity and the wisdom of Uncle Sam's imperial policy to baseball celebrants in the United States. During the 1912 tour, the Hawaiian ballplayers told one East Coast journalist that baseball was popular on the islands. They conceded that their homeland hosted no professional leagues, "but the Chinese players believe that in time [baseball] will become a regular profession and money paying proposition, just as it is in this country."[41]

In the spring of 1913, Ole Hanson, a well-known Seattle politician, visited Honolulu and corresponded back to a local newspaper his impressions of a game pitting the "All-Chinese" against a Portuguese Hawaiian nine. Hanson told readers in Seattle that the game was not really between one club representing Chinese Hawaiians against another representing Portuguese Hawaiians but actually was "between white men and women of Honolulu and the yellow-skinned men and women in the same city." The Chinese Hawaiians won effortlessly 14–5, and Hanson asserted that they could have won more easily "but the Chinese merchants, who do most of their business on Sunday afternoon, demanded that the ... [All-Chinese] ... quit making any more runs as it hurt business." As the Chinese Hawaiians extended their lead, Hanson insisted, the "[w]hite crowd groaned and groaned and the yellows cheered and cheered and cheered." Apparently, some white tourists vocally supported the Portuguese, "[b]ut the Chinese accepted their defiance with anger and screeched their defiance as did the Japs, and the Filipinos, and the Coreans, etc., ad nauseatenpup [sic]." Hanson speculated that if a race war ever consumed the islands, baseball would surface as the cause.[42]

Just before leaving for the mainland in 1913, the All-Chinese nine defeated on St. Patrick's Day an all African American service team representing the 25th Battalion stationed on Oahu. Lawrence Reddington of the *Honolulu Star-Bulletin* remarked, "Cosmopolitan Hawaii fittingly celebrated the Irish national holiday with an exhibition of the American national game, given by an All-Chinese team. About seventeen other nationalities witnessed the contest. Truly it was a representative gathering of the nations."[43]

Late in 1914, teams of Major Leaguers and Pacific Coast Leaguers traveled to Hawaii. The presence of such outstanding mainland ballplayers presumably boosted the game in Hawaii. However, the *Sporting News* maintained that America's national pastime did not need much boosting on the islands.

> The islands are a hot-bed of enthusiasm over the game. Nothing else is talked of. Amateur and league teams play ball on every plot of ground large enough to permit of a field being laid out. The visiting players have expressed themselves as much impressed with the class shown by some of the Honolulu players, and it is expected that a few years will see Hawaii be represented in the ranks of the major and minor leagues on the mainland.... Thousands of Honolulu citizens, of all races and both sexes, greeted the major leaguers, the crowds including every class from a judge of the supreme court to the lowliest Chinese coolie.[44]

One of the major leaguers who journeyed to the islands concurred that culturally diverse Hawaiians loved baseball and bore witness to the fact that they could play it pretty well. John Henry said that Hawaiian fans were particularly ardent about America's national pastime when one of their own teams was involved. Nines called the All-Oahus, All-Hawaiians and All-Chinese drew fervent and diverse crowds. John Henry asserted that the All-Chinese nine was probably the best Hawaiian team the major leaguers faced. This squad, many members of which had toured the American mainland together in previous years, lost to the American Leaguers 5–2. It is not clear whether Henry referred to the Chinese Hawaiian ballplayers in particular or Hawaiian ballplayers in general, but he declared that the "players are small, [but] very active, fast on the bases and have the real inside game very well in hand." Still, somebody on the mainland must not have been happy about the social composition of Hawaiian ballplayers. According to a piece published in the *Honolulu Star-Bulletin* in July 1914, Organized Baseball would never give the Oahu Baseball League "Class D or any other rating." The reason given was the "color line." Oahu's baseball players were "the Chinese, Japanese, and the colored soldiers." And Organized Baseball demanded that "no negroes or Orientals be allowed."[45]

Hawaiian enthusiasm for baseball as a spectator sport seemingly dimmed around 1915. Orientals, according to army officer G.L. Van Deusen, were Oahu's best baseball fans in 1915. Serving as the Oahu League's president, Van Deusen maintained that "about the only good fans left here are the Orientals." However, Van Deusen insisted that ethnic nationalism rather than love of America's national pastime inspired Oahu's Orientals: "They will always get out to support one of their own teams, but their motive is more that of patriotism than a true love of the sport."[46]

When the Portland Beavers of the Pacific Coast League trained in Honolulu in spring of 1917, a Portland sportswriter observed to the *Sporting News* that American minor leaguers "bask ... in the sun and smiles of hula girls." They also "take regular beatings from Chinese, soldiers, black and white, and so on for all races and manner of men play ball in Honolulu." To be fair, the Beavers did manage to eke out a 4–3 victory over the All-Chinese before returning to the American mainland.[47]

Baseball's acceptance among Hawaiian Orientals was noted by the *Sporting News* William Peet in 1926. Peet observed that thriving Japanese and Chinese leagues started their schedules earlier in the year than Honolulu's "major league." He wrote, "The Orientals all speak the same language when it comes to baseball. They read the newspapers, the *Sporting News*, and keep in touch with the major leaguers." Peet claimed he knew of a "little Chinese shortstop" attending Punahou School. The Chinese Hawaiian memorized "the batting average of every American Leaguer, can tell what Ty Cobb batted back in 1916, and Walter Johnson's strike out record. Cobb is his ideal and Johnson his idol."[48]

John Heydler, president of the National League, confirmed the imperial reach of baseball in the early 1930s. Observing its popularity in Japan, Heydler acclaimed baseball's hold on Filipinos and Hawaiians. In all three places, Heydler maintained, "baseball has made rapid strides. In fact, it has displaced popular interest in all other outdoor sports in these countries."[49]

Tellingly, despite at least four decades of experience with America's national pastime, Asian Pacific Hawaiians were still portrayed in the 1930s as relative novices at the game, patronized as capable of mastering baseball only surprisingly well. One mainland journalist wrote in 1932 that "Hawaii is *beginning* to feel the lure of American sports and ... now [has] many crack baseball teams" (my emphasis). He added that "the chinks are better players than the Japs.... They are better hitters and I wouldn't be surprised to see the name of a Chinese player in the box score of a big league game some day. The Hawaiians are taking to the game with real enthusiasm and some of the teams that played on the island compare favorably with American semi pro clubs."[50]

On the eve of America's military engagement in World War II, syndicated columnist Bob Considine reported that baseball in Hawaii attracted considerable support. He informed readers that the Hawaii League, headquartered in Honolulu, included teams representing the rival races such as Hawaii's Portuguese, Hawaiian, white, Chinese, and Japanese populations. He added that Japanese Hawaiians had organized their own inter-island series.[51]

By the onset of World War II, elite teams had long been generally organized along ethnic and racial lines. In the 1930s, the Honolulu-based Hawaii Baseball League (HBL) included teams such as the Japanese Hawaiian Asahis, the Chinese Tigers, the Portuguese Braves, the Hawaiians, and the haole Wanderers. Players of mixed ancestry such as John Kerr might move about from team to team. But it was widely believed that ethnic teams generated interest in the league.

During World War II, American servicemen, including magnificent baseball players such as Joe DiMaggio, would play with and against teams of local, talented, and culturally diverse players. By this time, the war had pushed racial tensions close to the forefront of island life. The idea of teams representing separate Hawaiian ethnic groups became unfashionable and perhaps dangerous as anti–Japanese animosity gained disturbing strength after December 7, 1941. Thus, elite Hawaiian teams became more racially and ethnically integrated than ever before. Japanese Hawaiians were placed on the Braves, a team long associated with Portuguese Hawaiians. The Japanese Asahis became the Athletics and team management was turned over to notable non–*Nikkei* such as future Honolulu mayor Neil Blaisdell and Hawaii's future governor John Burns, while Japanese Hawaiians competed alongside players of varied racial and ethnic backgrounds. Even after World War II ended and anti–Japanese sentiments subsided, elite interethnic and interracial teams continued. For example, Wally Yonamine, a multitalented Japanese Hawaiian athlete, suited up for both the Athletics and the Wanderers after World War II.[52]

Wilfred Rhinelander, a *Honolulu Advertiser* sportswriter, and Arch Ward, a nationally syndicated sports columnist, both claimed that the dilution of "racial rivalry" during World War II had hurt the HBL attendance after the war ended and great ballplayers such as DiMaggio had returned to mainland glory. Ward believed that the effort to revive ethnic-based teams stimulated greater passion for the HBL by the end of the 1940s.[53]

Hawaii also launched multiethnic, multiracial all-star teams toward North America. In large measure, these teams were intended to showcase Hawaii as both exotic and loyally American to prospective mainlander tourists and investors. There was nothing new in this. The Hawaiian Travelers in the 1910s seemed to serve the same purpose as did an All-Hawaiian team in 1913 and Buck Lai's Hawaiian All-Stars in the 1930s.

In 1913, mainland baseball entrepreneur Guy Green brought an all-Hawaiian nine to the mainland. On his way to the islands, Green told the *Los Angeles Express* that he wanted to organize a contingent of "full-blooded Hawaiians." He was convinced that such a team would be a good drawing card. Hawaiians did not play very much baseball, Green mistakenly insisted, but Hawaii had "several fast teams."[54]

Once on the islands, Green attracted attention from the Honolulu press. He originally gathered a team that included not only players of indigenous Hawaiian ancestry such as the Desha brothers — Alex, William and Edward — but also Japanese Hawaiian standout Chinito Moriyama. Others included Willie Williams, the brother of Johnny who at the time was an ace pitcher in the Pacific Coast League, E.D. Hamauku, and A. Lota. Green assured the players and their friends and families that he would pay for their round trip to the mainland in order to allay fears that the Hawaiian ballplayers would be left high and dry somewhere in Kansas. He added that the tour would begin in Nebraska. The All-Chinese Hawaiian traveling team had opened the 1913 tour against St. Mary's in California before only 350 paying customers. Green insisted that imported teams did not draw well on the West Coast and that it was a good idea to skip it entirely. He promised that a "team of ball players from Hawaii will be a big drawing card and, incidentally, a big boost for Hawaii." The *Honolulu Star-Bulletin* was not certain how competitive the team would be. It also seemed to fear that the ballplayers would have to parade before games in grass skirts and perform the hula "for those who remember Green's Nebraska Indians, say he is great national color." As it turned out, Moriyama would stay home and the *Star-Bulletin* advised that Green would bill the nine as a team from Hawaii and not as a team of Native Hawaiians. Thus, the ballplayers would supposedly not have to dance the hula or "gobble poi" to satiate the curiosity of mainlanders eager to witness supposedly exotic natives in action.[55]

Once on the mainland, William Desha corresponded with the *Star-Bulletin*. The team's first game was not a great deal of fun for the Hawaiians. It took place in Brush, Nebraska, a town which Desha declared was well named. The Brush contingent edged the visitors 4–3, "but when it is considered that the grounds were nothing but an alfalfa field surrounded by country roads from which the dust was carried by a gale of wind, this isn't surprising." The Hawaiians could not practice, the umpires were incompetent, and the weather was cold, Desha further explained. Still, the team gave a concert of Hawaiian music at the opera house that evening "and made quite a hit." Desha assured Honolulu, "We are all boosting Hawaii and think that we will make good in this department." After beating a team in Akron, Nebraska, 27–7, Desha confided that the team was getting along well and the players had no complaints—"Good quarters, good grub, and a general good time."[56]

A few days later, Desha lamented that two of the Hawaiian players, including his brother, Ed, were hurting. The team could use a little depth, he admitted, and could use better umpiring just as much. However, the Hawaiians were hitting well. In particular, Desha praised his brother Alex's pitching and Hamauku's base running, which he likened to the great Ty Cobb's. Thus far, the travel had not worn the ballplayers' down. They particularly enjoyed a forty-one-mile auto trip from one Midwest town to another. Usually, they slept in one town and then bright and early caught a train for another the next day, arriving just in time for lunch. Then in the evening they staged a Hawaiian-themed show. Moreover, "People hereabouts are crazy to see us in action, but they certainly can ask some fool questions about Hawaii and the way we live here. The islands are being advertised alright and a lot of people have talked about spending next winter there. The boys are doing good publicity work by giving concerts, and singing all the Hawaiian songs." Indeed, according to Desha, "Hawaiian music is all the rage here and we give the people all they want." Eventually, the Hawaiian team was joined by three Native Americans — not all that surprising given Green's earlier management of an All-Indian barnstorming team.[57]

We will discuss the Hawaiian Travelers in a later chapter as well as the nine headed by a former Traveler standout, Buck Lai's Hawaiian All-Stars, which played on the American mainland from 1935 to 1937. Moreover, after World War II, Hawaiian All-Star nines promoted the idea of Hawaiian statehood as they took on various mainland-based teams and even toured North America with the Harlem Globetrotters baseball team.[58]

While such promotional efforts perhaps helped prepare American mainlanders for Hawaiian statehood, there seemingly were some glitches — that is, Hawaiian baseball was still thought of in the 1950s as separate from that of the United States. For example, a Global World Series was held in Milwaukee in the mid–1950s for non-professionals representing various baseball playing nations such as the United States, Japan, Canada, and Mexico. Hawaii was represented by its own team. This was not necessarily bad because Hawaiian ballplayers competed effectively against a nine representing all of the then forty-eight states as well as teams representing other nations. If Hawaii was not permitted a separate team, it is unlikely that any of the players would have been permitted to participate on the U.S. national nine. Still, if Hawaii was American why did Hawaii retain its own team?[59]

By 1960, Hawaii had become a state. Hawaiian-born citizens could now vote for president and send folks like Daniel Inouye and Patsy Mink off to Congress. Honolulu soon was the site of a minor league team in the venerable and talented Pacific Coast League. Baseball rivalries based on ethnicity no longer seemed in style, although Americans of Japanese Ancestry baseball leagues continued to engage the passions of Japanese Hawaiians.

Conclusion

To be sure, other Pacific Island territorial acquisitions of the United States were introduced to baseball than the Philippines and Hawaii. Commander W.M. Crowe, naval commander of American Samoa, bragged that the "the white man had made [Samoan males] stow away their war clubs." However, thanks to the introduction of baseball to Samoa these Samoan men were using their "war clubs" as bats. They were capable, Crowe insisted, of playing "rattling good baseball." During the summer of 1913, a syndicated story ran in several newspapers pointing out that two villages in Samoa opposed one another in a game that seemed to blend baseball with cricket. The game, readers were told, lasted over a week.[60]

While both possessions of the United States in the early twentieth century, the Philippines and Hawaii differed significantly. The Philippines were brought into the U.S. empire as a protectorate and its people considered

U.S. nationals ineligible for American citizenship. The Hawaiian Islands, because its elite was substantially American-born or descendents of American-born whites, were granted territorial status and its residents U.S. citizenship. However, from the perspective of the American mainland, baseball in the Philippines and the Hawaiian Islands was seen through lenses forged by a race-based colonialism. On the one hand, it was just not flattering to Uncle Sam that the non-white inhabitants of the Philippines and Hawaii took up baseball with at least some enthusiasm. Baseball served an apparently important role of helping to gain assent for colonization from the colonized. But baseball could also serve as a source of agency for the non-white people of the Philippines and the Hawaiian Islands.

C.L.R. James's *Beyond the Boundary* powerfully illustrates the point. A Marxist scholar and anti-colonial activist, James was born into a relatively privileged West Indian family under Great Britain's colonial flag. English imperialism generally countenanced a colonial strategy that sought the cooperation and creation of middle and upper strata among the colonized. This meant educating the children of privileged families in either their own lands or packing them off to the colonizing country. It also meant socializing these children in the benefits of English culture. In James' case, he not only went to English-influenced schools in his West Indian home, but he also learned a favored sport of the English elites — cricket.[61]

The sport of cricket rose to dominance in the United Kingdom as Great Britain rose to world domination in the eighteenth and nineteenth centuries. British supporters of competitive team sports such as cricket and rugby claimed that they trained middle and upper class participants to internalize the discipline, ingenuity, and comradeship necessary to conquer much of the world and contain the often-troublesome working classes of England, Scotland, Ireland, and Wales. By teaching sports such as cricket to colonized youth, colonizers hoped to teach them the benefits of Anglo culture. In other words, to borrow from Italian social theorist Antonio Gramsci, the colonizers sought through cricket to achieve cultural hegemony over the colonized.[62]

But as theorists such as Raymond Williams and Stuart Hall have pointed out, achieving cultural hegemony is no easy matter as subordinated or subaltern groups employ creative and often effective means of resistance. Nor are those in power insincere in their desire to do well by those over whom they rule. James offers a vivid example of this as he points out that West Indians of African ancestry might have internalized the fundamental rules of cricket because the game in itself represented the possibilities of fair play. Moreover, they mastered the game in such a way as to defy racist colonial ideologues who argued that the colonized natives lacked the intelligence and discipline to play cricket as well as the colonizers. West Indians of African ancestry not only played cricket well, but throughout the twentieth century defeated teams representing England and the white colonizers. In so doing, they reinforced an anti-colonial ideology that clearly recognized imperialism's fallibility.[63]

Thus cultures move and get moved, as well as travel in different directions. Afro-Caribbean people, as well as South Central Asians, joyfully took up cricket not necessarily because it Anglicized them, but because it was fun and they could beat the English and other nations at it. Cricket shaped these colonized people in part, but they shaped cricket as well — transforming it from a rather staid, white supremacist and elitist Victorian sport to something more exciting, controversial, multicultural, multiracial, and international.[64]

Filipinos and non-white Hawaiians took up baseball with similar things in mind. Undoubtedly, many appreciated much of what the United States represented, but they did not play baseball necessarily to become auxiliary Americans. They enjoyed the sport and could often master it as well as any white American. And they helped make baseball, perhaps not quite as staid as cricket, more exciting, controversial, multicultural, multiracial, and international.

Chapter II

Baseball and Asian Pacific American Communities on the Hawaiian Islands

Baseball constituted a visible and important way for culturally diverse Hawaiians to express a sense of ethnic community. Nearly all of the major ethnic groups on the islands organized their own baseball teams and leagues for much of the twentieth century. Nines representing Portuguese and other European Hawaiians, as well as African Americans, competed with Chinese, Japanese, Filipino, Korean, and Native Hawaiian teams. Hawaiians across racial and ethnic lines have frequently taken baseball very seriously and occasionally too seriously as interethnic controversy and violence sometimes flared at early twentieth century island ball games.

Native Hawaiians

Hawaiians of indigenous ancestry continued to excel in baseball for Kamehameha and community-based teams and leagues into the twentieth century. In 1912, Kamehameha fielded players such as W. Apau, Noah, G. Bush, and G. Kaonohi. In 1915, the Kamehameha baseball team included players surnamed Akana, Shipman, Correa, Makanani, Cockett, Werner, Bertelmann, Mitchell, and Pekelo.[1]

All-Hawaiian teams existed in Honolulu in the early 1900s. Late in 1911, the athletically versatile Desha brothers, Dave, William, and Alex, played for the All-Hawaiis. Henry Kuali, who also joined the Traveling Chinese, appeared on the team as did other talented players of Chinese and Hawaiian ancestry such as clever shortstop Vernon Ayau and Kan Yen Chun, who was called "the plucky little Chinese pitcher" by the *Commercial Advertiser* but later starred as a catcher for the Travelers. In September 1915, the Hawaiis beat a nine from Japan's Meiji University in Honolulu. Appearing for the Hawaiis were players such as Dave Desha and William Apau, as well as E. Noa, Peterson, White, Amoy, Brito, N. Noa, Mahaululu, and J. Hoke. In the late 1940s, an All-Hawaiian baseball league existed. Bob Naki served as its president and the Kealoha Hawaiians, managed by David Kealoha, won the league championship in 1949.[2]

Chinese Hawaiians

Asian Pacific Hawaiian ethnic communities consistently supported baseball for much of the twentieth century. Honolulu sportswriter Loui Leong Hop maintained in the 1930s that Chinese Hawaiians were especially well ensconced in island baseball in the early decades of the twentieth century: "During the period between 1910 and 1925, baseball teams representing this race ruled supreme in the territory. The aggregations were so successful that they sought new worlds to conquer. Starting in 1912 and through 1916, Chinese diamond squads annually invaded the mainland, returning each time with impressive records.... That these trips, five in all, contributed much valuable publicity for the Islands need not be repeated here."[3]

In the first decade of the twentieth century, Chinese Hawaiian teams were organized and American mainland newspaper readers learned about Chinese Hawaiian ballplayers. In September 1906, the *Pacific Commercial Advertiser* reported that Honolulu's Chinese Athletic Club's (CAC) nine beat the Palamas to win the Riverside League championship. Shortstop Sing Chong, P. Wong, John Lo, H. Aki, Hang Chack, Ed Ayau, En Sue, Mon Yin, and Ching Yet took the field for the "Oriental Nine." The daily claimed that the "game was witnessed by a large and enthusiastic Chinese delegation sporting flags, colors, brooms, ribbons and honors. They seem to have a hunch that their representatives would win and the hunch made good." In 1907 readers of the *Decatur Review* discovered that a Chinese Hawaiian baseball team thrived in Honolulu. The article in question declared, "Although Chinese baseball players are mighty scarce in this country, over in Honolulu there is a team composed exclusively of Chinese, and they play good baseball. The team is called the Chinese Alohas." On the team were such players as F. You, catcher; Cang Yen, pitcher; N. Sheng, first base; Ah Yap,

II. Baseball on the Hawaiian Islands

Chinese Hawaiians enthusiastically played and supported baseball in the early decades of the twentieth century. This team photo (c. 1910) is of a group of ballplayers representing Honolulu's Chinese Athletic Club (courtesy of Library of Congress, Prints and Photographs Division).

second base; Yuan Chaw, third base; Hoi Sing, shortstop; Ho Tong, right field; Ah Sam, center field; and Hung Nyam in left. In 1908, the *Washington Post* none too humorously quipped, "The batting order in that recent Chinese game in Honolulu looked like the police roster of the captured in a tong riot."[4]

A few years later, word reached the mainland of a Chinese Hawaiian team possibly touring the United States. Walter Eckersall, a University of Chicago football All-American turned sportswriter for the *Chicago Tribune*, claimed that he was in correspondence with Charles Quigley, a soldier stationed in Hawaii. Inspired by the American tour of Japanese university teams in 1911, Quigley said that he was trying to bring eastward a "Chinese team," that would feature some of the finest players on the islands, including a "crack pitcher." But Quigley complained he had been undermined by rumors that he was unwilling to pay what the Chinese Hawaiian ballplayers deserved. Moreover, the "managers" of the Chinese Hawaiian ballplayers had proven unreliable, according to the soldier. Quigley insisted that Chinese Hawaiian ballplayers possessed great potential in America's national pastime and that he hoped to bring over a team of "juniors" in 1912 and briefly put them on display in California in 1912, while planning a more sweeping 1913 tour of elite Chinese Hawaiian ballplayers.[5]

By 1912 the CAC was clearly represented by one of the best teams in Honolulu. Among the players on that nine were Ping Kong, Sing Hung Hoe, Kan Yen, Hoon Ki, Tin Yen, Chun Duck, Ed Lin, Tan Lo, Ah Hong, and Luck Yee. Ping Kong, Sing Hung, Kan Yen, Hoon Ki, Tan Lo, and Luck Yee were considered some of the best ballplayers on the islands. The CAC consequently served as one of the prime movers behind the organization of an elite team of Chinese Hawaiian ballplayers that barnstormed the American mainland beginning in the spring of 1912.[6]

By 1914, however, leaders of the Honolulu's Chinese Hawaiian community voiced unhappiness over the failure of the Hawaiian barnstorming team to properly represent the community. Too many team members no longer possessed Chinese ancestry, they complained. Thus, a presumably truly All-Chinese team was organized, representing the Chinese Athletic Union (CAU) and fielding some of the better Chinese Hawaiian ballplayers. Led initially by the talented Buck Lai Tin, who had decided to remain in Honolulu in 1914 after touring with the Travelers for two years, a potent Chinese Hawaiian team greeted a University of California nine in June 1914. The CAU's team success against Cal inspired an article featured in the *New York Times*. Headlined "Baseball Popular Sport in Hawaii," the article declared: "As an American possession it is natural that the Hawaiians should have taken most kindly of all the Antipodean countries to our national game—baseball. They seem to have taken it with their Americanism, play it cleverly, and have developed an army of 'fans' that would do any American possession credit." However, according to the article, Chinese Hawaiians were truly enthusiastic about the sport: "They are an athletic-loving lot and play the game with much skill and thorough understanding of its fine points." In particular, the CAU team, which the article incorrectly pointed out, consisted entirely of "full-blooded Chinese," proved itself against Cal.[7]

The CAU ballplayers defeated the Cal nine twice—the first game by a 6–4 score and the second, in a nail-biter, 8–7. In the latter game, Cal went ahead in the top of the ninth. "But the Celestials showed plenty of sand" and eventually eked out a victory. The Chinese Hawaiian fans arrived for the second game prepared for victory, according to the *Times* piece and celebrated their team's triumph with a large firecracker display. The CAU's star was "Captain Lai Tin," who displayed leadership, speed and flawless fielding.[8]

In 1915, a CAU team, minus Lai Tin, headed west to Asia while the

Hawaiian Travelers, managed by Lai Tin, took off on their fourth journey to the U.S. mainland. Upon the CAU team's departure for Asia, the *Pacific Commercial Advertiser* hailed the squad as a "Great Aggregation of Diamond Stars, Every One a Citizen of Hawaii." According to the *Honolulu Star-Bulletin*, the Chinese Hawaiian ballplayers who had not accompanied the Travelers were anxious to make the CAU team in order to see the "land of their ancestors." At the same time, commercial interests in Hawaii were anxious to use the CAU team to market the islands in Asia. Moreover, Honolulu dailies such as the *Star-Bulletin* and the *Advertiser* were anxious to promote the trip. The *Star-Bulletin*, for example, urged Honolulu baseball fans to attend benefit games staged to finance the CAU team's trek to Asia. One such game was scheduled between the CAU team and the Japanese Hawaiian Asahi nine. The daily promised that fans would not be disappointed if they emptied their pockets to watch the game: "This ought to be a thrilling affair, for neither of the Oriental teams has much love for one another." Because of some disagreement, this game did not take place. But one game that did put the CAU team against an All-Army nine. The *Star-Bulletin* dutifully reported that the CAU team won and that for the first time Honolulu's Chinese consul had attended a baseball game.[9]

Late in March, the *Star-Bulletin* publicized the impending departure of the CAU team to Asia. Under the headline, "Chinese Players Leave Friday on Tour of Orient," the *Star-Bulletin* reported that the troop would take plenty of promotional material along with them such as canned pineapples and pictures exhibiting the beauties of the islands. Indeed, Hawaii's Promotion Committee had supplied team manger King Tong Ho with significant support. Consequently, the *Star-Bulletin* predicted that China's president, Yuan Shih-Kai, would receive a box of pineapples from the contingent of Hawaiian ballplayers, as would other Chinese supporters of international athletic competition. The *Star-Bulletin* expected that the itinerary would include Hong Kong, Manila, Shanghai, Beijing, Tientsin, and Hankow, as well as that dignitaries would greet the Hawaiian ballplayers at every stop.[10]

Honolulans learned from *Star-Bulletin* details about the team's trip to Asia. On board the *Yokohama*, the Chinese Hawaiian ballplayers and those accompanying them seemingly had a good time and helped to entertain the other passengers. One evening's entertainment was called "China Night." The ballplayers sang a Hawaiian ditty called "Ahi Weia." Team manager Kim Tong Ho took part in a skit, while players William Apau, Kam Fat, and E.S. Kong demonstrated their musical talents. The players also won three indoor baseball games against passengers, as well as competed in deck games and relay races. Writing to the *Star-Bulletin*, Ho guaranteed, "I can say that all our boys have entered into everything with the right kind of spirit, with absolutely no grumbling nor kicks and this is what makes friends. Thus in all the concerts, entertainments, our boys have volunteered and have taken turns with the ukuleles and songs. There has not been a single incident to mar the trip."[11]

Although it did not complete the original itinerary, the Hawaiian Chinese nine represented and won the championship for China in the Far Eastern games held in Shanghai. Then, it competed in the Philippines before returning home. Interestingly, the Shanghai promoters thought this team was the same as the one that excelled on the American mainland. A few of the players had, indeed, played with the Hawaiian Travelers in previous years, but most had not. Moreover, Yuan Shih-Kai, China's president, donated five hundred dollars to the Hawaiian ballplayers in the hopes they could help develop baseball in his country.[12]

A report printed in a Pennsylvania newspaper in June 1915 confirmed that China's government had a hand in supporting the Hawaiian team's trek westward. Wu Ting Fang, described as a former Chinese ambassador to the U.S., declared that the Chinese government financially assisted a "team of American-born Chinese" in journeying from Honolulu to Asia. Moreover, the Chinese government apparently covered the expenses incurred by the Hawaiian ballplayers in China. Wu Ting Fang expected that the Hawaiian team would tour China's principal cities and "introduce American athletics for the physical improvement of the youth of China."[13]

While it turned out the Chinese Hawaiian team did not linger long in China, the Hawaiian Chinese team apparently made a positive impression on observers in the Philippines as they handled the best that the Manila Baseball League could offer. One of their games against an American army nine moved a *Manila Bulletin* (reprinted in the *Honolulu Star-Bulletin*) writer to gush, "The contest was a manly exhibition for supremacy on the diamond. The *Bulletin* takes this opportunity of praising the Chinese visitors for the excellent sportsmanship they exhibited on the field during the game yesterday. We hope such behavior will prevail as the standard during the entire series and in the games to come in the league." The Chinese Hawaiians were not just "gentlemen," exhibiting "excellent deportment." They could also play good baseball. Apparently, Manila baseball fans expected the visitors to swing weak bats. However, the *Bulletin* pointed out that the Chinese Hawaiians rapped out ten hits. The Chinese Hawaiians were not as fast as anticipated but they were crafty base runners. Indeed, a CAU player forced an army pitcher to balk him in for a run from third by effectively bluffing an attempt to steal home. The visitors were good fielders, especially in light of the fact that they just finished a long voyage. The losers, the *Bulletin* contended, had no reason to complain: "They were outplayed, outbatted, outrun and outfielded by the invading

Hawaiians." The Manila sportswriter was particularly taken with catcher Kan Yen, who purportedly possessed major league skills as a hitter, third baseman, and catcher. As a whole the Hawaiian team was composed of "cool and brainy ball tossers," who potentially could become "wonderful players."[14]

A few days later, the Hawaiians endured an extra-inning game against a team called the Filipino Cits, composed of American citizens. According to the *Manila Bulletin* (reprinted in the *Honolulu Star-Bulletin*), the Cits were able to hold the "brainy youngsters from the Hawaiian Islands to a 5–5 score in one of the most exciting games ever played in Manila." While the Hawaiians did not win, the *Bulletin* called them "the cool but aggressive ball tossers from the Paradise of the great Pacific." The *Bulletin* boasted that the tie game meant that "[t]he honor of Philippine baseball still stands on the balance, but the invaders have been checked and the flower of the American civilians have demonstrated that the Chinese from Hawaii have nothing on them in so far as inside baseball is concerned."[15]

A major reason why the Manila based team was able to tie the Chinese Hawaiians was that the normally reliable Kan Yen fell for an old trick. While catching with base runners on first and third in the seventh, Kan Yen tried to throw out a base runner apparently stealing second. Instead, the bluffing base runner allowed himself to get caught in a rundown, permitting the base runner on third to scamper home with a key run. At the same time, Kan Yen's battery mate, Luck Yee, did a good job, according to the *Bulletin*. He struck out nine and showed "remarkable endurance, control, and steady head work."[16]

The All-Chinese won the Oriental Cup in recognition of the Hawaiians' dominance in Manila. The islanders competed so well against Filipino and U.S. military nines that they were asked to remain in Manila and constitute the foundations of a hopefully prosperous baseball league. In particular, according to co-team manager W. Tin Chong, "Chinese merchants and businessmen" in Manila expressed a desire to see the Hawaiians stay and play in their city. They even promised the Hawaiian players good jobs if they would put off returning to their Honolulu homes. "But," Chong maintained, the Philippines "is too hot. We were there during a hot spell of the hot season and we were mighty glad to get away on that account. After cool Hawaii the Philippine climate doesn't stack up very well." Still, one prominent member of the Chinese Filipino community in Manila hoped that with the promise of good jobs some Chinese and even Japanese Hawaiian ballplayers might be enticed to compete in the Philippines. He told the press that "they are all educated and speak and write good English perhaps better than an ordinary Filipino student."[17]

The team headed by Chong and Ho left the islands for four months and it won all but two of the many games it played. Hawaiian baseball fans, according to the *Honolulu Star-Bulletin,* welcomed back the Chinese Hawaiian team. In particular, the Oahu League was glad to see the squad return. Its games had not been drawing well and talented Chinese Hawaiian teams had long attracted paying customers to Oahu League games.[18]

Indeed, Honolulu-based sportswriter Herbert G. Lowery, in correspondence with the *Sporting News*, lamented in May, 1915 that baseball in Hawaii was in sad shape. The major reason, he concluded, was the departure from Honolulu of many of the islands' better ballplayers. First, the All-Chinese headed to the U.S. and then another All-Chinese dealt Honolulu baseball another blow by trekking to the Orient.[19]

Stanford, for example, had dispatched its baseball team westward and found Hawaiian fans not particularly excited about seeing the California nine compete until the Honolulu Chinese nine returned. The *Honolulu Star-Bulletin* declared, "Everyone wants to see the boys who walk off with the championship of the Far East, and the fact that the Stanford team is here to furnish an unknown opposition will stimulate the returning Chinese to their best efforts and will provide grounds for speculation among the fans." As for the Chinese Hawaiian ballplayers, they wanted to make a "clean up" of the Stanford nine, which, in turn, wanted to do the same to the locals.[20]

A game between the Californians and the All-Chinese was scheduled for Moiliili Field. According to the *Star-Bulletin,* the game attracted a great deal of interest from local fans. Moreover, En Sue Pung and Lang Akana, neither of whom made the trek to Asia on the one hand or the mainland, on the other, strengthened the Hawaiian Traveler nine with their speedy outfield play. A reported record crowd saw the Honolulu Chinese beat Stanford 3–1. Pitcher Luck Yee kept Stanford at bay, while En Sue Pung, who had earlier in the day played for another nine in a game against a military team, made a typically thrilling catch in center. The *Star-Bulletin* reported, however, that "[a] fat Chinaman in the left field bleachers threw a bunch of lighted firecrackers to the third base coaching line just as Pitcher Hayes of the Stanfords was about to deliver the first ball of the ninth inning." On deck to bat in the ninth, Lang Akana heard his name chanted from the stands as "Chinese, Hawaiians, and haoles contributed to the medley." Akana responded by delivering a key hit.[21]

On July 4, St. Louis played the All-Chinese nine. The game drew well and the *Star-Bulletin* reported, "There was more noise at the baseball park than at any other place in town yesterday. Several Chinese rooters came well supplied with firecrackers, but even this bombardment didn't bring success to the Orientals." The All-Chinese lost to the multiracial, multiethnic St. Louis nine 3–1.[22]

Kim Luke replaced Chong as manager of the All-Chinese team that competed in the Oahu Baseball League. Before stepping down, Chong thanked those who helped make the All-Chinese team's trip to Asia "a success." In particular, he acknowledged the Hawaiians of diverse ethnic backgrounds who raised and donated money to the cause — Reverend H.D. Weserveldt, "Chinese merchants and friends," the proprietors of Honolulu's Athletic Park, the All-Army baseball teams, local newspapers, and Honolulu's baseball fans. Chong added, "We hope that our trip will result in great benefit to Hawaii from a publicity standpoint. It has always been the aim of our boys to boost Hawaii whenever opportunity permitted. The results of our trip are now known to the public. We won the championship both of Manila and China and the Chinese of Honolulu are now the undisputed champions of the Far East."[23]

The CAU team, reinforced with a returning Lai Tin, engaged in a fierce rivalry against an African American nine composed of soldiers stationed in Honolulu. Members of the 25th Infantry, this team included one of the great African American pitchers of the first half of the twentieth century, Wilbert "Bullet" Rogan. Late in October 1915, the CAU nine beat the 25th Infantry contingent 5–4 in a game which thrilled a legion of Honolulu baseball fans. A few days after the game, the *Advertiser* urged the powers-that-be in the Oahu League to arrange another contest between the All-Chinese and the 25th Infantry nine. The previous game turned out "to be the talk of balldom," at least in Honolulu. And the daily said that local fans wanted a rematch. In late November, the CAU lost to the military nine 3–2 in what the *Advertiser* called a "hotly contested game," after which both teams were anxious for a third game, as apparently were Honolulu baseball fans.[24]

Certainly, there was no shortage of Chinese Hawaiian ball clubs and fans in the 1910s beyond the Travelers and the CAU nine. The Canton Athletic Association fielded a nine in 1912, as did the Chinese Youth Association (CYA) and the Chinese Hawaiian Association. The Honolulu Crackers constituted another formidable Chinese Hawaiian nine. Games between Chinese Hawaiian nines aroused the arrogance typical of young men and their supporters in general after a victory. The Honolulu Crackers nine had their bats working when they beat CYA 28–2 in May 1912 at Aala Park. After the game, supporters of the victors rubbed it in just a bit by writing to the *Pacific Commercial Advertiser,* "We got their goats." In June 1912, the *Pacific Commercial Advertiser* insisted, "Chinatown turned out in full force" to watch a game between Chinese Hawaiian students from Jackson and Wah Mun schools at Aala Park. All of this baseball action meant that Chinese Hawaiians could organize an amateur league in 1912 with teams such as the Wah Muns, CAU, CYA, Kukuis, and Man Luns.[25]

In September 1912, the *Commercial Advertiser* headlined an article about the Wah Mun–Man Lun game with "Chinese Rooters Shine at Aala Park." According to the daily, thousands of Honolulu Chinese showed up to watch "rival factions" play. That is, the Wah Muns represented the "Chinese revolutionary faction," which supported the emergence of the Chinese republic. The Man Luns represented the Chinese Emperor Reform Association, which backed the continued dynastic rule of China. Since both sides attracted vociferous rooters, it appeared to the *Commercial Advertiser* that a riot was about to break out at any time. Fortunately, nothing of the sort happened.[26]

A month later, the *Commercial Advertiser* reported a "merry war" taking place in the Chinese Amateur League. Apparently, scorer Po Chin had abandoned his duties during a close and tense game between CAU and Man Lun. And no one knew for sure which team had officially won. The "affair," according to the daily, had "turned Honolulu Chinatown upside down and downside up." Po Chin tried to explain his behavior by pointing how team managers were not telling him about lineup changes. He wondered, what could he do "when them change lineup and no tell official officer ... I resign just now because anyhow no pay for me and darkness make impossibility keep tallies and score them right." Umpire Yew Char accused Po Chin of not only acting irresponsibly but also compounding his error by lying to the press about why he left the ballgame. For example, Yew Char said, Po Chin maintained he had not been paid for his services. However, Yew Char insisted that Po Chin was voted fifty cents a game and that he refused payment. "Now he comes complaining about his pay business," a disgusted Yew Char lamented. A little too obviously amused *Commercial Advertiser* suggested, "This will be easy for the celebration of the Manchu overthrow being over now, Chinatown has nothing in the way and can take up in full Po Chin's explanation and recital of his wrongs."[27]

The Po Chin incident was not the only fallout from the CAU–Man Lun game. A fight flared between a Chinese Hawaiian fan and a Filipino Hawaiian spectator. Reportedly, the Filipino Hawaiian was trying to compliment a Chinese Hawaiian player using a Chinese phrase that in reality was an insult. A fracas ensued and the *Commercial Advertiser* concluded, "For his compliment, the Filipino got a beating from the Chinaman. The police let it go at that."[28]

As the 1912 Chinese Baseball League's season ended, one community leader protested that Honolulu's Chinese community took the sport too seriously. Sang Loy, a league leader, lectured the league's players: "You have taken too much pride in yourselves. You have never for a moment considered the welfare of the league. In short, you have never played against each other for sports sake." Despite the competition in baseball, Sang Loy maintained that the players on the various teams needed to evince a greater unity in purpose and "play against each other for the sake of fun."[29]

Chinese Hawaiian community involvement in baseball scarcely abated. Early in 1913, a CAU nine captured the junior crown in Honolulu, prompting the *Star-Bulletin* to wonder how the Japanese Asahi juniors had managed to take a game from such a potent team. A Chinese Athletic Club nine competed effectively in the Oahu Junior League in 1915. In 1915, Sam Hop organized his own All-Chinese team to participate in a series of games with Meiji University and other Hawaiian nines. Noted Traveler outfielder En Sue Pung suited up for Hop, as did well and lesser known ballplayers such as Albert Akana, Ching Pui, Ah Hook, Ping Kong, Vernon Ayau, Ah Leong, Ah Pui, W. Aku, Kim Kui, Ah Toon, and Ah Long. In one matchup against Meiji, Hop's team was on the short end of a 9–3 game. The Japanese students were not expected to hit well but they hammered Ching Pui's pitches. Hop's team prompted consternation among leaders of the CAU, who insisted that they sponsored the only real All-Chinese team that had triumphantly toured Asia. In 1919, an All-Chinese team played in an Oahu Senior League against military nines and ethnic teams such as the Portuguese Braves. The *Pacific Commercial Advertiser* referred to the All-Chinese as "the Celestial hosts." In 1920, the All-Chinese knocked off a visiting University of Chicago nine 4–3. The same year, the University of California nine came to the islands, where it opposed "the local Chinese team." But, according to one Hawaiian chronicler of the time, the mainlanders "gained no victory, honors being even." In 1922, Honolulu's All-Chinese nine beat a visiting Stanford squad in extra innings. Luck Yee and Kan Yen, old Chinese Traveler hands formed the winning battery.[30]

In the 1930s, according Loui Leong Hop, Chinese Hawaiian ball clubs persisted in representing the ethnic community very well. Hop wrote, "The Chinese is still feared in the national pastime here, winning as many senior league pennants as teams of other racial groups and making jaunts to the Orient and the mainland." While Earl Vida, who possessed indigenous Hawaiian but seemingly no Chinese ancestry, managed the All-Chinese HBL nine in the 1930s, Chinese Hawaiian Harry Yim owned the franchise. Raymond Victor was one of the key players on the HBL's Chinese Tigers in the late 1930s and early 1940s. The U.S. Census manuscript describes Victor as a thirteen year old Asian Hawaiian in 1930. It claims his mother was racially Portuguese and his father an Asian Hawaiian and a stock clerk in an oil company.[31]

Before and after World War II, Honolulu's Chinese Baseball League served as a feeder of talent to the senior Chinese Tigers. In the late 1920s, it had teams such as the Chungshans, Chinese Amateurs, Rural Chinese,

Honolulu Chinese, and Quality Dairy. In 1928, an article in the *New York Times* informed readers that a Chinese League had just begun play in Honolulu, "numbering five purely Chinese nines." When the league season opened in 1936, Honolulu's Chinese consul was in attendance as was Buck Lai, in Honolulu to assemble a barnstorming team to journey North America. Lai also donated a trophy to the league's winner. After World War II, the Chinese Baseball League included teams such as Kam Express, Mandarin A.C., Rico Ice Cream, Chinese Amateurs, Chings Contractors, and Acme Mattress, while playing at Cartwright Field, named for Alexander Cartwright.[32]

Japanese Hawaiians

Japanese immigrants and Hawaiian born people of Japanese ancestry formed community teams in the early 1900s. Throughout the twentieth century and into the twenty-first, Japanese Hawaiians have remained steadfast in their belief in baseball as an important expression of ethnic identity on the islands.

In 1940, Japanese Hawaiian baseball celebrated the eleventh annual interisland tournament held at Honolulu Stadium. The Waialua team out of rural Oahu defeated a Kauai nine before 5,500 people. Coached by Tamatsu Horii, the victor's catcher, Sakae Higuichi, won the MVP award. Prominent Japanese Hawaiian pitcher Lefty Hirota performed for the Kauai nine. Also in the tournament were teams from the islands of Hawaii and Maui. The latter nine was coached by Ichiro Maehara, a veteran of *Nikkei* baseball on the islands and an inspiration to one of Hawaii's greatest ballplayers, Wally Yonamine.[33]

Americans of Japanese Ancestry (AJA) assembled well-supported teams and leagues on the islands. In Honolulu, AJA teams represented neighborhoods such as McCulley, Kakaako, Moiliili, Kalihi, Kalihi Valley, and Waialae. Apparently, the Japanese Hawaiian enthusiasm for baseball somewhat dimmed during and just after World War II. In January 1951, the *Hawaii Herald* claimed that baseball had recovered its "top spot" in the hearts of Japanese Hawaiians. What helped, according to the *Herald,* was that a team of collegiate all-stars from Japan had toured the islands in 1950 and "generated interest" among Japanese Hawaiians in baseball "to a high degree."[34]

AJA baseball proved an enduring assertion of Japanese Hawaiian community development. Masa Yonamine, a coach and athletic director for Waipahu High School, explained to the press how for years AJA baseball was played: "People like to see the ball go into the stands, but when you small, you got to push the ball here and there, play defense and get good pitching to win." AJA rivalries could be intense. Long time pitcher Mayo Uyehara remembered for the *Star-Bulletin* that "[w]hen Moiliili played McCully, it was dog eat dog." Les Murakami, who played and coached AJA baseball, stressed the issue of ethnic pride: "When a group of people can last and hold a league together for this many years without major struggles, you know the organization is good and the guys are high class." Moreover, Murakami pointed out to a *Star-Bulletin* reporter, AJA games frequently drew well. For one Sunday contest at Honolulu Stadium, he recalled, an AJA game attracted 5,000. And Jimmy Miyasato, who managed the Palama team, remembered that one of the games his team played lured 7,000 to the old stadium.[35]

Of course, Hawaiian *Nikkei* have been supporting baseball for a long time. Probably growing out of the Excelsiors, a nine representing the Japanese Athletic Club (JAC) was active in Honolulu baseball circles in the early 1900s. In March 1906, the *Pacific Commercial Advertiser* published a condescending account of a game between the JAC nine and the Tenth Infantry team. The daily announced, "It was anything but 'banzai' for the little brown men" as they lost 20-2. According to the *Advertiser*, the winners "allowed the Japs to get a couple of men home in order that they might 'save face' and go home and boast of having scored against Uncle Sam's mighty ballplayers." Soon, the Honolulu-based Asahi team fielded highly competent Japanese Hawaiian ballplayers and eventually competed against the best teams on the islands by the 1910s. Among the leaders of the Asahis were Steere Noda and Andy Yamashiro. Noda was a son of a plantation worker and starred as an all around athlete at Mid-Pacific Institute. Eventually, he would become a territorial legislator. According to Arthur Suehiro, Noda had suggested the name of Asahi to his teammates and helped them out in 1912 and 1913 by batting a very impressive .579 and .517 respectively. The talented Moriyama brothers, Tom and Chinito, also played on the Asahis in 1912 and 1913.[36]

While admired for their baseball ability, the Asahis were racialized and exoticized by *haoles* and the *haole* dominated press. In 1912, the Honolulu-based Oahu Senior Baseball League considered including the Asahis. However, doubts, according to the *Hawaiian Star*, persisted: "The Asahis are a fast little team and have made a mighty good reputation in the junior league, winning last year's pennant hands down. They are speedy as the proverbial greased lightning in fielding and on bases, they play well together, and they are full of snap. But here are the lamentable weaknesses, they are not strong on stick work and the pitching staff." The team needed a good battery but the *Star* doubted a Japanese battery would help much. The team could not recruit non–*Nikkei* as "[i]t is a law under the Asahis that only Japanese shall play on the team." A few months later, the *Pacific Commercial Advertiser* maintained that the "little Japs are fast and quick players, especially on base." Both the older and younger players were all "island boys," although apparently one Asahi ballplayer had played for the Keio University team when it had previously visited the islands. When the Asahis took on an All-Service team in 1914, the *Advertiser* referred to them as "little brown men." A cartoon printed in the March 22, 1914, edition of the *Advertiser* depicted the figure representing the Asahis with racialized features and as by far the smallest of the figures representing other ethnic teams on Oahu.[37]

Interestingly, one of the elite Honolulu teams the Asahis played in 1912 was a nine called the Japanese Athletic Club. While this nine fielded a junior team composed of Japanese surnamed players, the senior team that contested the Asahis on May 19, 1912, did not have a single Japanese surnamed player. A few months later, the emperor of Japan died. Baseball was cancelled in Honolulu out of respect for the islands' *Nikkei* mourners in general and the Asahi and JAC baseball teams in particular. When the Japanese Hawaiian nine beat the more experienced and not very Japanese Athletic Club in 1912 some doubted if the results were honest—that the JAC had thrown the game for some mysterious reason. Nevertheless, the manager of the Portuguese Athletic Club tried to rescue the Asahi team's reputation by remarking, "The Asahi is a fast little team and I don't care which team it is that goes against it, but it has to play real hard to beat the Asahi bunch."[38]

In the fall of 1916, the Asahis challenged "any team" in Honolulu in a letter published in the *Pacific Commercial Advertiser*. The Asahis especially wanted to play the presumably Chinese Hawaiian Canton nine. According to the letter, the Asahis had previously scheduled a game with Canton at Aala Park, but the contest was cancelled because of contruction work to the park.[39]

The next year, the Asahis' Lefty Maesaka hurled a one hitter against the local Young Men's Buddhist Association nine. Yoshikawa, Yasunaga, Mamiya, Miyhahara, Murakami, Zenimura, Murshige, Nushida, Yamashiro, and Maesaka played for the Asahis. The YMBA team included Yosu, Osaki, Hamano, Mitsumoto, Uyemori, Naomura, Mityaguchi, Miragichi, Doi, and Kobayahsi.[40]

The Honolulu Japanese were represented by junior nines in the early decades of the twentieth century. In 1915, with a *Nikkei* lineup, the JAC junior nine competed in the Oahu Junior League. In 1916, the Nippons comprised a competitive junior team in Honolulu. One of the big stars of the Nippons was, according to the *Commercial Advertiser*, "little Nushida, the midget wonder.... For his age and size he is a marvel." Just a teenager, Nushida was, according to the Honolulu daily, only four and half feet tall and "will not be old enough to vote for seven years or more." Asao, Komeya, Fukushima, Ueno, Araki, Okano, Yamaguchi, Doi, Tsukiyama, Murashige, and Iwanaga also played for the Nippons. Competing at the same time was a team representing Honolulu's Japanese High School. It fielded athletes surnamed Yujutako, Kinoshita, Zenimura, Sasaki, Suzuki, Tsukamoto, Kozuki, Tani, and Manbu. In 1919, the junior Asahis were called "pert Nipponese" by the *Pacific Commercial Advertiser*, Managed by George Murakami, the junior Asahis included Zenimura, perhaps the Kenichi Zenimura who moved to California where he helped develop Japanese American community baseball in the 1920s and 1930s. Yamashiro and pitcher Nushida were his teammates.[41]

Beginning in 1915, the Honolulu Asahis made the first of three trips to Asia. Late in August, the *Honolulu Star-Bulletin* announced that Steere Noda would lead a "team of star players among the local Japanese" to Japan. Invited by Keio University, they would board a steamer to Yokohama. Among those going were K. Araki, Y. Uyeno, and K. Iwasaki, pitchers; K. Nishi, S. Uyeno, S. Itamura, N. Amano, Y. Nakamura and Yamanaki. They were expected to play first in Yokohama and then move on to Tokyo and Osaka. They anticipated a three month journey and if they were financially able, the Asahis hoped to travel to Manila. The Keio University baseball team had reportedly been impressed with the Asahis' "snappy play" when it previously toured Hawaii. The *Star-Bulletin* declared, "It will be interesting to see what a picked team of the local Nipponese can do to the offerings of their fellow countrymen on their home soil." Previously, Japanese teams had done well against Hawaiian Japanese nines. Perhaps, the *Star-Bulletin* speculated, this was because the Japanese were better and had played longer together. But the locals had done plenty of practicing together and were improving. "Above all," the *Star-Bulletin* concluded, "it would be worth a trip across the water to hear rooting in pure Japanese and read a score kept in the same language."[42]

In Japan, according to Kerry Nakagawa, the Honolulu Asahis won eight of fourteen games in 1915. Folks back home kept track of how the "Hawaiian Japanese" team did. The *Star-Bulletin* reported that a cable had been received in Honolulu by the *Hawaii Shinpo*. The cable observed that the Hawaiians had defeated Yokohama Commercial School 4–3. Another cable informed Honolulu that the Japanese Hawaiian team beat the Hosei University nine. The cable added, "It was the Hosei University whose scalps now hang on the Honolulu boys pagoda." Upon the team's return, the *Pacific Commercial Advertiser* asserted that the Japanese Hawaiians had "enjoyed a successful invasion of the Far East." According to the *Advertiser,* the Japanese Hawaiian ball team's effectiveness in Japan piqued the interest of Japan's consul general in Honolulu. The diplomat believed that the Hawaiian *Nikkei* merited continued representation by a worthy team. Subsequently, the Hawaiian Asahis would return to Japan in 1920 and 1940. In 1940, the team competed as well in the East Asian Games against nines from Japan, Manchuria, and Korea.[43]

The Asahis became a prominent fixture in the most prominent leagues active on Oahu such as the Hawaii Baseball League. Moreover, they played touring teams from the mainland and Japan. In 1921, the Waseda University nine visited Honolulu and opposed the Asahis. Readers of an International News Service (INS) account of the game learned that baseball fans in Hawaii deserved sympathy from mainland sportswriters in that they had too many hard names to pronounce. It was bad enough that Hawaiian baseball fans had to deal with teams consisting of Chinese, Japanese, and Portuguese surnamed players. With the Waseda team arriving from Japan, their tasks grew even more arduous. The INS writer claimed that when Waseda played the Asahis, it was "Jap meets Jap ... under the American flag at Moiliili field, under the frowning fortifications of Diamond Head." The home team won 8–3 with a lineup of Miyahara at third base, Hirano at shortstop, Nushida in right field, Moriyama at second, Yamashiro in center field, Tokuda in left field, Kozuki catching, Iwata pitching, and Suzuki at first. Yamashiro, probably the former Traveler, hit a homer. When Stanford's team arrived on Oahu in 1922, it took on, according to the *Daily Palo Alto,* a nine called the "Asalie." The success of the Asahis and the backing given them and other Hawaiian Japanese nines on the island led George Gene Sakamaki to write in the late 1920s, "Athletes of Japanese descent have been particularly conspicuous in baseball—probably because more than 75 percent of the fans are of the race."[44]

World War II changed the Japanese American community's involvement with Hawaiian baseball, but certainly did not end it. During World War II, anti-Japanese sentiment forced the Asahis to change their name to the Athletics. Ironically, team owner Dr. Katsumi Kometani was serving in the U.S. military in Europe. Thus, Honolulu police captain and future governor John A. Burns took over as the Athletics' owner. After World War II, the team became known as the Asahis again. And clearly, it continued to serve as a source of pride among Honolulu Japanese. Jimmy Wasa, who managed the nine, remembered, "One year we lost to the All Hawaiians who were in last place and people started hitting me on the head with (rolled up) newspapers, calling me *bakatare* and telling me I should quit.... They even called my mother to get me to quit. But when we were winning, you could go into restaurants and eat for free." In the 1970s, the Asahis, with the help of non–AJA players, went to Japan, where they beat a world champion Cuban squad 5–3 before 70,000 in Tokyo. Making the trip were AJA ballplayers such as Clyde Hirata, Clayton Fujie, Jimmy Itamoto, and David Kitamura. Eddie Hayashi served as coach, while Masa Yonamine managed.[45]

In 1923, Hawaiian Japanese were represented by an all-star squad that traveled to the American mainland. The *San Francisco Chronicle* announced its arrival with the headline, "Foreign Ball Club." *Issei* Kenichi Zenimura managed the team and one of his stars was Kenso Nushida, portrayed by the *Chronicle* as a "diminutive pitcher" and by the *San Jose Mercury* as a "boy wonder." This Nushida was clearly the youthful pitcher hailed several years earlier as a Japanese Hawaiian ace. Another star was Y. Okina, described in the *Mercury* as "the Babe Ruth of Hawaii." The *Chronicle* added that the team was composed of English speaking American citizens. In the Bay Area, the Hawaiians beat the Alameda Athletic Club and then the San Jose Asahis. Apparently, the Hawaiian ballplayers intended to stick around the mainland. An unnamed Japanese American newspaper was going to sponsor the players on the mainland, arrange for jobs in Fresno and Stockton, and try to keep the team together. The infusion of Hawaiian talent such as Zenimura and Nushida undoubtedly helped make California's Central Valley a hotbed of Japanese American baseball, as will be examined in the next chapter.[46]

Other islands than Oahu nurtured Japanese Hawaiian baseball. In 1912, some Hilo residents complained that *Nikkei* on the island had transformed a local cemetery into a baseball diamond. It was lamented that "[t]ombstones are being used as seats and on the whole the doings are very much out of keeping with the character of the place." In 1915, a pitcher named Doi hurled a no-hitter for Hilo's Japanese Athletic Club's nine against the Chinese Athletic Club. On Kauai, Japanese Hawaiians formed a league. The "little fellows," according to the *Pacific Commercial Advertiser*, played on teams from island communities such as Kekaha, Kolea, Makewili, and Hanapepe.[47]

Japanese Hawaiians passionately supported Japanese national teams as they visited the islands in the early twentieth century. Lacking fondness for Hawaiian *Nikkei*, the *Pacific Commercial Advertiser* observed that when the Keio University nine played a series of game in Honolulu in 1911, the local Japanese population could not be dissuaded from attending their games. It complained, "It was a bad day for Japanese house help for they all went to the game and there was many a late dinner on Sunday evening in consequence."[48]

When Keio took on the All-Chinese, Honolulu's Japanese and Chinese communities were stirred. Before Keio beat the All-Chinese 6–3, fans were warned in Japanese, Chinese, and English that the police would not tolerate any fighting and, indeed, enthusiastic spectators kept their emotions in check. However, the second game proved another matter, as the Keio nine stalked off the field in protest of an umpire's decision as the All-Chinese held a seemingly commanding 5–2 lead. According to the *Pacific Commercial Advertiser,* the police were called in to stem a brawl between irate *Nikkei* and happy Chinese spectators. Still fuming over the perceived mistreatment of the Japanese ballplayers, Honolulu *Nikkei* boycotted future games involving Keio and Honolulu nines. The *Advertiser* responded that "aliens" seemed to be ruining America's national pastime in Honolulu. It called upon "Europeans" to take back "the best game on earth."[49]

Filipino and Korean Hawaiians

Filipinos began to arrive on the islands in significant numbers in the second decade of the twentieth century and they formed Hawaiian community teams about the same time. On Oahu, the Filipino Association team lambasted a nine representing the Chinese Youth Association at Aala Park 14–1 in late May 1912. On Kauai, a team of Filipino in 1915 edged a German nine on Lihue diamond 9–8.[50]

A Filipino nine competed in a series of games in Honolulu with Meiji University, an All-Hawaiian, and a Chinese Hawaiian team, run by Sam Hop. Players surnamed Tibong and Batung were among the best on the Filipino team. Ortiz, Maqueen, Reyes, Luis, Marcial, and Ramos were also on the nine. According to the *Honolulu Star-Bulletin,* the Filipino team usually played well for seven innings or so but managed to lose the game in the end: "You can't beat those Filipino players in a seven inning game but when you call the game in nine innings it is a different story." Against the Hawaiians, the Filipinos, the *Star-Bulletin* reported, took on a ten-man team as umpire Joe Fernandez apparently "played a great game for the Hawaiian team." Ortez and Batong formed the Filipino battery.[51]

In 1916, the *Honolulu Star-Bulletin* announced an upcoming game between the C Troop of the Fourth Cavalry and the Filipino Houseboys. Ramos, who would supposedly pitch for the Filipinos, was called "one of the cleverest baseball artists in the archipelago." The lineup would include Pedro at third base, Mariano in center, Adecir at shortstop, Ramos at pitcher, Francisco in left, F. Pedro in right, Aguinaldo at first base, Filippe at second, and Lopez catching.[52]

In the 1910s, Korean Hawaiians organized their own baseball teams and established their own baseball grounds in Honolulu. Early in 1912, a Korean Hawaiian nine engaged in a bitterly contested game against a Japanese team at Aala Park, resulting in a post-game riot. A few months later, however, an unnamed Korean Hawaiian pitcher struck out twelve batters and led his team to a victory over a Chinese Hawaiian nine. In the following months, the Korean Boarding School nine defeated Iolani. Pitching for the winners was Ah Foon Nan, who struck out fifteen Iolani batters. The *Commercial Advertiser* observed that Ah Foon Nan "was truly great since none of the opposing batters will admit any of them struck out on purpose." The daily claimed that Honolulu Koreans had become increasingly interested in baseball since they had heard of a team of Korean nationals playing baseball in Japan. They wanted to organize a good local team that would go to Korea and show "their stay-at-home compatriots that the locals are truly and really being Americanized in the proper manner." In December, the Korean Boarding School team beat the Kahamanu nine at Aala Park. In 1915, a Korean Hawaiian team lost to the Beretainia Juniors. The *Star-Bulletin* snidely observed that the Korean Hawaiians lacked two necessary things: "The first is rooting and the second is practice, and the [Korean Hawaiian] team ... would do well to get on speaking terms with both."[53]

In the 1930s, both Korean and Filipino ethnic groups celebrated their communities through baseball. In 1936, Honolulu hosted a Korean Baseball League with teams representing the Korean Athletic Association, the Delta Frats, and Wahiawa. Meanwhile, Filipino Hawaiians honored Jose Rizal Day with baseball, as well as other sports. At the same time, a Filipino scholar noted in the mid–1930s that *Pinoy* plantation workers liked baseball but playing it was difficult for them because the sport was too time consuming and costly for poorly paid agricultural workers. Moreover, he contended that only a few plantations laid out suitable grounds for the game.[54]

After World War II, ethnic community based teams continued to exist on the islands. The HBL teams no longer were exclusively ethnic based, but teams like the Tigers and the Asahis remained rooted in Honolulu's Chinese and Japanese communities respectively. In the HBL in 1949, Richard Ching owned the Chinese Tigers, Lang Akana ran the Hawaiians, and John Kometani owned the Athletics-Asahis. In 1951, Honolulu's noted sports entrepreneur, Mackey Yanagisawa, bought the Athletics-Asahis. The Asahis in 1951 were managed by Takeo Fats Nakamura and included top-notch Hawaiian Japanese players such as catcher Jyun Hirota and infielder Jimmy Wasa. However, by this time Oahu's rural Japanese Americans were represented in the HBL by a team called the Rural Red Sox. The Red Sox, who used more than a few non–Japanese Americans, became one of the best teams in the HBL, winning six straight league championships. In the process, they became the Asahis' arch rival. In 1947, the San Francisco Seals of the Pacific Coast League trained on the islands. The PCL team was able to defeat all of the local nines, except for the Rural Red Sox. Lawrence Kunihisa served as the team manager for years. Among the Japanese Americans to play for the Red Sox were Toku Tanaka, Masa Gunda, and Victor Mori. In the 1950s, *National Geographic* bore witness to Hawaiian baseball. The writer claimed that the HBL "benefit[ed] from the Japanese enthusiasm for the game" and noted that the Rural Red Sox were not only a league powerhouse but regularly traveled to Japan.[55]

Post World War II Filipino Hawaiians organized baseball leagues. On Oahu, they formed a league that included teams such as Young Americans, Hawaii Fil Vets, Wahiawea Fils, Waialuu Filipino Community, and the Filipino Federation of America. Arch Ward, noted *Chicago Tribune* sportswriter, informed readers that Filipino Hawaiians assembled a winter league in Honolulu as did Chinese Hawaiians and the AJA. The Fil-Americans competed in the HBL in the 1950s. Pitcher Crispin Mancao was one of the team's stars. Pitcher and infielder Fred Daguma and catcher Ming Panerio were other standouts.[56]

Conclusion

Despite the fact that racism may have been less pervasive on the islands than in many other parts of the United States, it still existed. To sustain them, under sometimes arduous circumstances, Asian Pacific Hawaiians needed to develop strong and durable community institutions. Baseball teams were considered, if not the most important of such community institutions, consequential enough to attract considerable support. This was true not only of Hawaiians of Japanese ancestry, about whom much has been written, but other Asian Pacific Islander ethnic groups as well. For instance, for years the most famous baseball team to emerge out of the islands was organized by leading members of Honolulu's Chinatown and included many top athletes from that Chinatown and Chinese communities on other islands. The existence of such teams calls into question baseball's power to aid the assimilation process in America. Seemingly, as will be discussed more in the next chapter, something more complicated was going on.

Significantly, controversy has surrounded Japanese Hawaiian community baseball in Honolulu in recent years. In the 1990s, a white Hawaiian ballplayer sought to join an AJA team. However, the AJA league denied him that opportunity, citing "cultural traditions." Hawaiian scholar Jon Okamura has been critical of the AJA leadership, while pointing out that maintaining ethnic cultural traditions merits respect. Okamura adds, however, that sharing cultural traditions across racial and ethnic boundaries has been as well a worthy aspect of Hawaiian ethnic history.[57]

Putting the matter into historical perspective, Okamura informs readers that Robert Kaneko became the first *hapa* to play AJA baseball in the 1950s because his father was a *Nikkei*. However, *hapas* with white fathers were not permitted to compete in the AJA league for years. Okamura notes, moreover, that a non–*Nikkei* had been playing AJA baseball in the late 1900s but provoked concern only when he wanted to switch teams. And Okamura adds that Japanese Hawaiians involved in the AJA were not all of one mind about the matter. For example, *Yonsei*, or fourth generation *Nikkei*, were more likely to accept inclusion of whites than the third generation *Sansei* and the second generation *Nisei*.[58]

However, Okamura argues that neo-conservative whites in Hawaii exaggerated the importance of the AJA racial exclusion issue. Institutional and personal racism, he maintains, remains alive and well in Hawaii. And by transforming a white athlete into a victim of "reverse discrimination," neo-conservatives could divert attention from the racism confronted in Hawaii by indigenous Hawaiians, Filipinos, and Samoans.[59]

Chapter III

Baseball and Asian Pacific American Communities on the American Mainland

The relationship between baseball on the American mainland and Americans of Asian Pacific Islander ancestry has only sporadically been tension-free. For example, the *Sporting News* in 1965 traced the origins of the derogatory term "Chinese homer." According to the "Baseball Bible" the term was first applied in early twentieth century San Francisco to a home run barely making it over the fence. The reason, the *Sporting News* explained, was that San Francisco was home to a large Chinese community, but the weekly publication failed to mention that San Francisco embraced for decades a fervent anti–Chinese movement.[1]

Baseball became a way for Asian Pacific Americans to build and shore up cultural bridges to non–Asian Pacific Americans. Yet the road to Asian Pacific American assimilation via America's national pastime was for decades barred by institutional and personal forms of racism. Thus, baseball also became a way for Asian Pacific Americans to assert community pride.

Japanese Americans

Much has been written about Japanese American community teams and leagues. Indeed, they thrived wherever Japanese American communities resided on the mainland. Gary Otake, a historian of Japanese American community baseball, has written:

When we see the photograph of the all–*Nisei* Alameda Taiku Kai team in the 1920s, we must not only recognize the creative adoption and adaption [sic] of America's national pastime by the Japanese American community, but we must acknowledge the discrimination and segregation from the larger society that forced the Japanese American community to build leagues of their own.[2]

For Otake, Japanese American community baseball expressed something akin to a desire for cultural citizenship. "Excluded from mainstream life," Otake maintains, "Japanese Americans created their own baseball institutions in response to the discrimination and hardship they faced in their daily lives."[3]

Eighty-eight-year-old Jack Kunitomi told the press in 2003 that baseball's roots were sunk deeply in the hearts of many Japanese Americans. He said that prior to World War II Japanese American community baseball teams were abundant: "Before the evacuation, there were leagues all over California. It was very important for the young people. What else could they do, besides work?"[4]

Japanese immigrants organized teams upon their arrival in the United States, according to Otake, because at least some had already taken joy in baseball back in Japan. Moreover, the *Issei* believed that through baseball they could build cultural bridges to European Americans. The first *Issei* nine in California was the Fuji Club, organized in 1903. Artist Chiura Obata was a founder of this organization. Subsequently, *Issei* formed community teams in Colorado, Washington, and Wyoming, as well as California. In the summer of 1908, "a Japanese baseball team," according to the *Los Angeles Times*, would play the Ezperanza nine at the Simon Brick's baseball grounds in Los Angeles. In April 1909, readers of the *Los Angeles Times*' sports section discovered a headline reading: "Japs Will Play." The accompanying article announced that "the Japanese baseball team" would face the Los Angeles Giants, "a colored team," at Joy Park. The *Times* predicted, "Fans will be treated to an exhibition of the national game by the best talent of the black and brown races." The powerful daily added that many of the "Jap" players had previously competed for teams in Japan and planned to barnstorm the East Coast once the game with the Giants was over. The *Nikkei* players were Maeda, Saiho, Tojo, Hashido, Sonara, Kitsuse, Suzuke, Ki Kicuchi, and Shira.[5]

Ten years later, a story dispatched from Brawley, California, reported that a game had been scheduled between the "Japanese Nippon baseball team" and an El Centro nine. Because they alleged that New Year's Day was one of their sacred holidays, members of the *Nikkei* team refused to play El Centro. The two teams belonged to the Imperial Valley Winter League and were supposed to play a previously postponed game.[6]

In the early 1900s, according to historian Gail Nomura, *Issei* assembled baseball teams in the Seattle area. Within a few years, they had organized a league. In 1910, 500 people attended a game between the Mikados of Seattle and the Columbias, a Japanese American nine from nearby Tacoma. The game for the Japanese American Northwest championship was won by the Mikados. Nomura maintains that Japanese American community nines were formed for many of the same reasons other community athletic teams were formed — to furnish a healthy alternative to gambling, prostitution, and other forms of recreational vice that had long plagued working class, ethnic communities, regardless of race.[7]

In the Pacific Northwest, the Seattle *Nisei* became the first *Nisei* nine to play in Japan. In 1914, the Seattle club, headed by future banker and teacher Frank Fukada, trekked westward to Japan. After the initial tour, Fukada's team traveled to Japan five more times until 1923. Fukada declared his objectives: "One is to make our young players understand their mother country more deeply. And the other is to introduce them to Japan and also study the current situation of Japanese commerce, which the president of the Seattle Chamber of Commerce strongly recommended." The Seattle Asahis won sixteen of twenty-five games in Japan in 1914. One Asahi player explained the purpose of the trip was to learn how to combine the best of both the Japanese and American cultures. A *Seattle Post-Intelligencer* sportswriter declared that the Asahis could compete "well with the American players. While a little weak in batting, the little fellows are wonderful fielders, fast, and good base runners."[8]

Nomura examines the experiences of Japanese American community baseball in Washington's Yakima Valley. Unlike some analysts of ethnic baseball of both the European and *Nikkei* variety, Nomura discovers little generational tension in Yakima Valley over the issue of baseball. She writes, "Baseball served to bring together the two generations and lessen the generation gap between the immigrant fathers and their American-born sons. In baseball, the immigrant fathers could come together with their sons in a shared passion." She reports that the Wapato Nippons were organized in the valley in 1928. Largely a youth team at the outset, the Wapato Nippons participated in the Mt. Adams League, winning championships in 1934 and 1935. Subsequently, the Wapato Nippons were invited to play in the faster Yakima Valley League.[9]

Between World War I and World War II, Japanese Americans transformed California's Central Valley into a hotbed of community baseball. Kenichi Zenimura was an *Issei*, brought to Hawaii as a child. On the islands, he learned and mastered baseball. In 1920, the twenty-year-old Zenimura moved to Fresno, California, where he preached the gospel of Japanese American baseball and founded the Japanese American Fresno All-Stars and established a ten team *Nisei* League. The Fresno team established by Zenimura from the ranks of top *Nikkei* ballplayers from Hawaii and the American mainland took on local nines such as the white Fresno Tigers. In beating the Tigers 9–8 in one game, the Fresno *Nikkei* pulled off a triple play. Zenimura's team also crossed the Pacific to play in Japan. Returning to the American mainland from Honolulu on the *Taiyo Maru*, Zenimura was described in the ship's manifest as a twenty-seven-year-old salesman, racially Japanese, born in Hiroshima, and possessor of an Alien certificate, allowing him to return to the United States. Among the ballplayers traveling with him were Katsuro Hirokawa, a twenty-three-year-old Honolulu student; Satoru Iwata, a twenty-four-year-old Fresno farm laborer; Satoshi Kawasaki, a twenty-four-year-old Honolulu student; twenty-six-year-old Anthony Kunitomi, a student from New York City; and Kazuro Mizmura, a twenty-one-year-old farm laborer from Honolulu.[10]

Sacramento and Stockton bred plenty of *Nikkei* baseball in the 1920s. In Sacramento, the Nippon Stars competed in the city's 1922–1923 winter league. In 1924, the Nippon Nine beat the Marysville Giants in what the *Sacramento Bee* described as a "hotly contested game." The *Bee* depicted "the local Nippon nine" as "one of the fastest Japanese clubs in this part of the state." And a team called the Nippon Cubs played in Sacramento's Municipal Baseball League in 1927. Led by Tar Shirachi, the Stockton Yamatos competed as one of the more talented Japanese American nines in California. The Japanese American Yamato Colony was represented by a ball club. In 1926, it lost to the semi-professional Lodi nine 1–0.[11]

As early as 1923, Japanese Americans in Sacramento and Stockton could boast of their own baseball parks. A few years later, Marysville's Japanese American community petitioned the city council for help in constructing a second ballpark. The petitioners claimed that one park would not suffice for European American and Japanese American ballplayers. The petitioners, however, assured the council that the second park would not exclude whites.[12]

In the 1930s, according to historian Samuel Regalado, a Central Valley Japanese Association had eight teams, sponsored by churches and businesses and located in places like Walnut Grove, Lodi, and Livingston. The Church Division of Sacramento's Twilight League included nines called the Japanese Baptists and the Japanese Presbyterians. And in 1935, a team of Japanese All-Stars from the Central Valley left on June 5 to barnstorm the East Coast.[13]

But there were other Japanese American baseball teams and leagues throughout the Golden State that were just as skilled and just as able to summon community pride. In the early 1920s, a Japanese Baseball League started in the San Francisco Bay Area. The opening day ceremonies took place at St. Ignatius Field in San Francisco. The game pitted the San Francisco Japanese Club against the Oakland Japanese Students' Club. San Francisco's Japanese consul attended the contest and threw out the first ball.[14]

By the early 1920s, the *Los Angeles Times* noted the existence of a team it called the Los Angeles Japanese. Team members included T. Ikasaki, Mori, Miyahara, Isozaki, Oshio, Matsuda, Shimomura, and M. Igasaki. Subsequently called the Los Angeles Nippons, the team fielded talented players such as Sammy Takahashi, a "flashy shortstop" who earned a tryout with the Los Angeles Angels of the Pacific Coast League in the 1930s. The Los Angeles press recorded the team's many triumphs, such as the 1930 victory over a Baldwin Park nine. On December 7, 1941, the Los Angeles Nippons were playing Paramount Studio. The FBI reportedly turned up at the game and waited for it to end in a 6–3 Paramount victory. Then, according to the *Hollywood Reporter,* the FBI "rounded up the Jap contingent."[15]

Indeed, the Los Angeles Nippons opposed the Paramount Cubs several times in the previous decade, as well as other Los Angeles semi-pro nines. In March 1937, the Nippons lost to Paramount 10–5 with Matsura and Harris, one of the European Americans on the nine, as the battery. A few months later, Matsura pitched much better but lost 3–2 at Cole Field in Hollywood. In late 1938, the Nippons edged Paramount 2–1 in what the *Times* called a "thrilling game." Okuda, the Nippons' pitcher, struck out ten Paramount batters at a new field built for the studio nine at Culver City. In 1930, the *Times* reported that the new innovation of night baseball had become quite popular among Los Angeles's "foreign element." The Mexico–El Paso nine had just beaten the Nippons 7–5 at Wrigley Field, the beautiful downtown home of the PCL's Los Angeles Angels. The game attracted 10,000 fans of both Mexican and Japanese ancestry. It was well played, according to the press account, and featured several double plays and sound hitting. In 1931, the Nippons tied the UCLA nine 8–8 in a game at the school's Westwood campus — a game that was ultimately called on account of darkness. Playing for the Nippons were Kondo, Kobayashi, Nomura, Takahashi, Horio, and Matsura, as well as European American players Harris, Crandall, and Frazier. After the UCLA game, the Nippons sailed for Japan. In 1938, the El Centro All-Stars beat the Nippons 11–7. The game took place in El Centro and served as a fundraiser for infantile paralysis in honor of Franklin D. Roosevelt's birthday. The next year, the Los Angeles Nippons beat the San Pedro Nippons 9–4 at Terminal Island. The *Times* asserted that a "record crowd of Japanese fans" showed up.[16]

The San Fernando Aces competed as another talented *Nisei* team. Pitcher Pete Matsui told baseball historian Jay Feldman that the *Issei* took great pride in the team's success. "It was all community oriented," he said.

"The communities didn't intermingle like they do now, you see, and the ballclub was an important part of community identity, so they really wanted us to do well."[17]

The San Jose Asahis achieved a reputation as one of the best semi-pro teams in the San Francisco Bay Area in the 1920s and 1930s. In 1922, the *San Jose Mercury*'s Jack Graham could only gush about the nine that played on San Jose's "Jap diamond." The Asahis attracted "the biggest bunch of rooters behind them of any team in the city, their diamond is probably the best in town and fast games are the rule." Graham added that if anyone wanted to see good ball they should "witness the Japanese team play." In 1923, the Asahis hosted a contingent of all-star Hawaiian Japanese. Before what the *San Jose Mercury* called the largest crowd to attend a game at the "Japanese diamond" the Hawaiians, led by future PCL pitcher Kenso Nushida won, 1–0. According to the *Mercury*, the San Jose Asahis were managed at the time by a white man named Ray Chittick. Moreover, "[t]he Japanese boys have proved themselves to be thorough sports and are highly spoken of among the other teams playing in the winter league." The San Jose Asahis were so good that they were organized into two teams. The second was talented enough to compete against *Nisei* nines such as the Berkeley Japanese in 1925. In 1929, the San Jose Asahis hosted the Waseda University nine. After spotting the visitors six runs in the first inning, the Asahis lost to Waseda 9–0. In 1935, the San Jose nine downed the visiting Tokyo Giants professional contingent 3–2. Asahi standout Russ Hinaga furnished the game-winning hit. The San Jose Asahis continued to earn positive publicity from the city's most prominent newspaper, the *San Jose Mercury*. In 1932, the *Mercury* informed readers that the "invincible Asahi team" will take on "the strong Japanese team from Salinas" led by Tar Shirachi—"one of the best pitchers in California."[18]

There were, indeed, plenty of good Japanese American teams in the San Francisco and Monterey Bay areas between World War I and World War II. Not far from Salinas the Watsonville Japanese, also known as the Watsonville Apple Giants, competed in the 1920s and the Watsonville Kasels excelled in the 1930s. The latter team was led by a formidable shortstop named Chick Ogi. Just a bit north of San Jose, Japanese Americans in Mountain View supported a baseball team in the mid–1920s. In the Bay Area's Alameda County, the Oakland Merrits and the Alameda Taikos were strong Japanese American nines, while San Francisco's Japanese YMCA had a baseball team. Meanwhile, college students of Japanese ancestry organized their own teams on in the Bay Area. In 1930, the Japanese Club won Stanford's intramural league.[19]

To be sure, Northern California in general was so alive with *Nikkei* ballplayers that a Japanese All-Star team was formed out of teams in the region in 1937. In the spring, this nine played the San Francisco Seals rookie team, featuring a young outfielder named Dom DiMaggio. A crowd of 2500 attended the game at Seals Stadium and saw the home team win 11–6 and Joe's younger brother go one for three with three RBIs.[20]

The importance of baseball to Japanese American assembly and concentration camp internees has been well documented. At the Fresno assembly center, Kenichi Zenimura got busy organizing baseball teams and leagues, which helped supply a sense of continuity to often-traumatized internees. Two of Kenichi's sons, Harvey and Howard, played at the Fresno assembly center. At the Topaz camp, internee leaders requested the construction of thirteen baseball diamonds. At the Gila River camp, "Baseball Crazy" *Issei* raised money for camp teams and avidly bet on games. Kenichi Zenimura helped organize baseball at the camp. At one time, the camp buzzed with thirty-two baseball teams, fitted out with equipment shipped in from Fresno. Reportedly 4000 to 5000 people watched games at Gila River. Camp teams ordered uniforms from Sears, Roebuck and at Tule Lake baseball supporters removed canvas covers from government issued mattresses and sewed them together. A skilled Japanese American pitcher, Henry Honda, told a *San Jose Mercury* reporter, "When I think about the camp, the baseball and softball games are what I remember most.... It was the only thing that gave us enjoyment." Jack Kunitomi remembered that baseball in the camps helped restore a needed sense of community but also showed America how American Japanese Americans were.[21]

The camps, however, were not always filled with baseball games. "Teddy Bear" lamented in the *Manzanar Free Press* in July 1944 that the boys in the camp had allowed the baseball grounds to become home to numerous ravenous gophers. To be fair, by this time, many Japanese American young men had been either inducted into the military or faced the possibility of induction. The *Free Press* hoped that furloughed young men could get a league going in the winter.[22]

Japanese American community teams continued to flourish after World War II. In 1947, noted Japanese American journalist Bill Hosakawa observed that evacuees to Idaho's Boise Valley were assiduously starting *Nisei* teams and had engaged the skills and experience of players and coaches from the state of Washington. A Northern California *Nisei* Baseball League included the potent San Jose Zebras, as well as teams from Lodi, Monterey, Richmond, Suisun, Florin, Stockton, and Madrone. In 1953, the Zebras took part in a doubleheader in Santa Clara, California. In the first game they opposed the Berkeley *Nisei* and in the second they played a nine representing a local auto dealership. In 1954, the Zebras competed in the Santa Clara County Summer

Night League. Up the peninsula, San Francisco's *Nisei* Clippers were in action in 1951. In Monterey, an all Japanese American baseball team called the Presidio Monterey All-Stars was active after the war. The team's ace pitcher was Harry Kitamura, the "boy wonder" of Hawaii. To the south, the Santa Barbara A.C. was, according to the *San Jose Mercury*, "a *Nisei* crew from Southern California Semi-pro league" and apparently the only non-white team in the league. The Santa Barbara athletes had played at Arizona's Gila Relocation Center and, in the process, established one of the best amateur teams in the southwest. In Los Angeles, the *Nisei* Vets competed in 1947. Moreover, the San Fernando Aces nine was still active, hailed by the *San Jose Mercury* as the "powerful Southern California *Nisei* baseball champions" in 1949. In Utah, the Japanese American Athletic Union organized a league with teams from Honeyville, Syracuse, Murray, Ogden, Davis, Garland, Corrine, and Salt Lake. A major goal of this league was to nurture "good will." In 1951, the Japanese American Citizens League (JACL) of Penryn, California, had a team in the Placer Nevada League. According to the *Pacific Citizen*, most of the team's players competed at one time for Placer Union High School and Placer Junior College. The team's home games took place at the JACL's own field. In Sacramento, in 1953, a six team Japanese Rural League used three of the city's fields.[23]

Racism's "traveling eye" appeared, as it did for the Zebras in the early 1950s. The team was invited up to Humboldt County to go up against a strong semi-professional nine known as the Crabs. However, when the Humboldt team discovered the Zebras were Japanese Americans the invitation was rescinded. Zebra player Frank Shimada told author Ralph Pearce, "That was probably the lowest point we ever had."[24]

In the early 1960s and 1970s, Japanese American nines competed in California. Auburn's Japanese American Citizens League, for example, had a team in the Foothill Baseball League. In the 1970s, Japanese Americans in California organized teams in Alameda, Oakland, Florin, Los Angeles, San Fernando, Lodi, and Northwest Fresno. In 1974, Southern California Japanese Americans staged the Harry Ota Memorial Baseball tournament. Teams invited included the Spartans of Gardena, the Kono Hawaii Dolphins, the Reedley JACL, and the Selma *Sansei*.[25]

Before and after World War II *Nikkei* communities welcomed Japanese baseball teams to the American mainland. In 1905, *Issei* enthusiastically followed the tour of the Waseda University team of the American mainland. In San Francisco, the Waseda nine took on Stanford. A crowd of 2,000 showed up and the *San Francisco Chronicle* pointed out that two-thirds of those in attendance were Japanese, who transformed the crowd into a scene from a "holiday in Nagasaki." A few weeks later, "hundreds of Japanese," according to the *Los Angeles Times*, attended a game between Waseda and Los Angeles High School. The *Times* wrote of the fans "carrying bright color banners": "It was the firm conviction of the Japs that the 'white boys' could not play ball with the men from Tokio." The next day the *Nikkei* fans outnumbered the white fans at a game between Occidental College and Waseda. The Waseda rooters, the *Times* asserted, "made quite a deal of noise, but it was less effective than the concerted music of the college supporters." The *Seattle Times* maintained that during a game between Waseda and the University of Washington, "the sympathy of the crowd was all with the Japs and there was an oriental tinge to the grand stand, given by a few hundred Seattle Japs, who smoked cigarettes, cracked peanuts, and rooted for the Waseda bunch." In 1911, Waseda returned to the American mainland. According to a report published in the *San Francisco Chronicle*, many *Nikkei* living in Salt Lake City showed up to cheer the Waseda nine's victory. To the American press, it was not a matter of insulting the people of Japanese ancestry who rooted for the Waseda nine. Rather, the press declared what many European Americans took for granted, that, in the words of Ronald Takaki, Japanese immigrants and their progeny were "strangers from a different shore."[26]

When the Tokyo Giants arrived in San Francisco in 1935, sportswriter Ed Hughes predicted, "The visitors from Nippon will get enthusiastic support from Japanese of this city and surrounding territory." And when the Giants played their first game against the Pacific Coast League's San Francisco Missions, Ed Hughes acknowledged, "[T]here was a big outpouring of Japanese to greet the Giants, and there were branches of bright colored flowers in front of their bench, as they lined up to have their pictures taken." After the Giants took on the San Francisco Seals, Hughes estimated that about 2000 spectators attended the game "with a large sprinkling of Japanese who were there to watch their first professional ball club and saw a snappy game of baseball and a team of boys from the orient that seemed to know what the national pastime is all about." In 1953, the Tokyo Giants, with Japanese Hawaiians Wally Yonamine and Bill Nishita on the roster, arrived in Santa Maria, California, to train with the San Francisco Seals. Sportswriter Jack McDonald noted that the "Japanese citizens of the Santa Maria Valley hosted the team at a chicken barbecue." In 1960, the Japanese Maruzen traveling team arrived in California's Orange County to play the Orange Coast Community College nine. Greeting the Japanese ballplayers were members of the Japanese American Interclub Council of Orange County. The council members presented the ballplayers a plaque and two crates of oranges.[27]

Japanese American community support for minor and major league teams has also been noticeable on the mainland. In 1947, the *San Francisco*

Chronicle's Harry B. Smith observed that the Pacific Coast League's Sacramento Solons achieved a large following among Japanese American fruit pickers working on a farm outside of California's state capital. Twenty years later, the California League's Lodi Crushers reached out to the local Japanese American population. The team was owned by a Japanese national and another Japanese national stood out as one of the team's ace pitchers. The Crushers' program featured an advertisement for Japan Air Lines, reserved a large box section for the local *Nisei* Society, and held a Japanese night.[28]

Chinese Americans

Japanese Americans were not only the only Asian Pacific Islanders organizing community nines on the mainland before and after World War II. In 1900, the *New York Times* reported that a team of soldiers was scheduled to play a Chinese contingent in a New York City armory. The daily also announced that a "Chinese band" would entertain spectators. In 1912, Chinese Californians in the state's Central Valley celebrated the new the Chinese Republic. A baseball game between Chinese American residents of Colusa was part of the festivities. In 1918, San Francisco's Chinese Athletic Club possessed a baseball team. A "Chinese team" from the University of California was battered by the semi-professional San Jose Bears in 1919 11–0. The team was called the Sing Fats and was led by a former Cal football player, Son Kai Kee. An unimpressed *San Jose Mercury* could only conclude, "The Chinese made a poor showing" against the Bears.[29]

In 1908, the *Chicago Daily Tribune* ran an entire article devoted to the Hip Lungs, the new "Chinese team" in the city's First Ward league. The team consisted of Paul Sun, pitcher; Paul Lee, shortstop; Henry Moy, catcher; Willie Sun, first base; Charley Moy, second base; Joe Moy, third; Wong Moy, center field; Lee Moy, right field; and Tom Moy, left field. The First Ward's alderman claimed that if the league's games were held on the ward's Clark Street, there would be "no doubt that the Hip Lungs would win the championship." The Hip Lungs had been practicing on Clark Street, day and night, for the previous month, according to Alderman Kenna. And they had proven quite adept at playing baseball on a very busy urban street. With streetcars running along Clark Street every few minutes, practicing baseball on the thoroughfare was no easy matter. However, "the Chinese boys" had become skilled at chasing balls under passing streetcars, catching them, and then throwing runners out at first or home. At the same time, the Hip Lungs had managed to knock out a few windows with their hitting. Captain Henry Moy agreed with Kenna that if the Hip Lungs could choose their home grounds, they would win: "It takes nerve combined with rare skill to chase a hot one under rapidly moving streetcar and that's where the China boys have the beat of it. We have done all our practicing on Clark Street and I think we ought to play some of the games there." To prove the talent of his players, Captain Moy pointed out that Joe Moy had stopped a hit ball headed in the direction of a Wentworth Avenue car. The ball had apparently come within six inches of the motorman's head before the intrepid fielder snatched it and threw the runner out at first.[30]

In 1922, the *Los Angeles Times'* Joe Bush noted an upcoming game between two "Oriental" teams at Los Angeles's White Sox Park. The Los Angeles Chinese would play against the Los Angeles Japanese. Both teams were members of the Greater Southern California Baseball Association and Bush expected they would draw a good crowd of Chinese and Japanese Angelenos anxious to support their "countrymen." Bush declared, "Many large bets have been wagered on the game and so each of the squads will enter the fray with blood in the eye." Tommy Lee managed the Los Angeles Chinese, while the Los Angeles Japanese nine was declared by Bush as the best "Nipponese" team in California — a team apparently strengthened by relatively new arrivals from Fresno. The Chinese Angeleno team included A. Chung, left field; Jimmy Kai, center field; G. Don, right field; J. Chung, first base; D. Lee, second base; Kam, third base; V. Chung, shortstop; Philip Lowe, catcher; and T. Lee and F. Don, pitchers. The next year, the Los Angeles Chinese Baseball Club occupied first place in the Greater Southern California Baseball Association in early February. In 1924, the Los Angeles Chinese nine lost to the Willard Battery team 9–2 at the Salt Lake Playground. On the team, according to the box score printed in the *Times,* were A. Chong, left field; Kam, third base; J. Chung, first base; Kai, center field; Lowe, shortstop; and Lee, catcher. Two presumably European American players surnamed Maier and Cahn were also in the lineup. In 1925, the *Times* reported that the Los Angeles Chinese had easily defeated the City Merchants 14–5. By 1927, team members included Kenny Ung, Willliam Chan, Ray Lue, Walter Chung, Willie Chung, James Chan, Victor Wong, H. Chu, Charles Lee, and George Lee.[31]

The Los Angeles Chinese contested tough semi-professional opponents. They played nines such as Pacific Clay, Palm Merchants, and the Redondo Beach Merchants. One player remembered, "One time we played the Japanese Junior Championship team of Southern California and we beat them! That was the best we ever did." Most of the games the Los Angeles Chinese played took place at Echo Park. No admission was charged but a hat was passed around to reward players for their trouble. Ray Lue said that all the team players spoke Chinese. Thus, they signaled to one another in Chinese in order to confuse opponents. The Los Angeles Chinese relied on more than deception. James Chan boasted that the team possessed a great deal of speed and used that speed to force errors on the part of their opponents.[32]

It was not always easy for players. They maintained a rigorous playing schedule while dealing with the taunts of bigoted fans. Chinese school and work cut into practice and playing time. William Chan recalled, "In certain seasons, there were many times I couldn't play. In the summertime, it was cauliflower. Our farm was down in Vernon. We had another farm in Downey." At the same time, Kenny Ung remembered, players heard spectators calling them "Chinks!" Ung told oral historians, "The younger people who played ball with us were o.k. The older people thought we still wore pigtails. They would yell at us from the stands." However, he claimed that he and his teammates won local fans over by 1930.[33]

The Los Angeles Chinese seemed to draw better outside of Los Angeles's Chinatown than inside. Player James Chan admitted that many of Chinatown's old timers did not understand baseball and could not understand any more why the community's youngsters wanted to play it. Even if the Los Angeles Chinese did not inspire hostility, they piqued inquisitiveness. Chan stated that outside of Los Angeles, semi-pro baseball fans "were curious in those days — they wanted to watch a Chinese team play."[34]

The Chinese Angeleno ballplayers knew they were not exactly the New York Yankees. The Los Angeles Chinese wore makeshift uniforms bought at Goodwill Stores. And while everyone had a glove, the team was forced to use secondhand baseballs and bats. One player remembered, "When we hit the ball over the fence, the game was stopped while everyone looked for the ball so we could start playing again." Exacerbating the equipment and uniform issue was that the team received little or no financial support from merchants in Los Angeles's Chinatown.[35]

In the San Francisco Bay Area, Chinese American nines were active between World War I and World War II. In the 1920s, San Jose's Chinese Americans established a baseball team which played, among other opponents, the San Jose Asahis. More notably, Chinese Americans in Oakland organized the Wa Sung club. The Bowen brothers, Al, Henry, and George, along with Al Huey, Lock Kai-Kee, Ed Chan, Allie Wong, and Gay Wye were the founders of the team that ranked among the most feared in Bay Area semi-professional circles and was a member of the Northern California Baseball Managers Association. In 1930, the Wa Sungs beat the Japanese American Merritt Athletic Club. Pitcher Al Bowen struck out eleven. Al Bowen, whose real name was Lee Gum Hong, pitched in the Pacific Coast League, and shortstop Ed Chan was rumored to be sought by PCL clubs. Other team members in 1934 included Ed Bowen, Key Chinn, Joe Lee,

Playing out of Oakland in the 1930s, the Wa Sung baseball team was considered one of the best semi-pro nines in the Bay Area (courtesy of Betty Wong, published in *Images of America: Oakland's Chinatown* [Arcadia, 2004]).

Arthur Chinn, Ed Hing, Frank Dun, Al Wong, and Hen Lum. The Bowens, in particular, attracted the attention. The *San Francisco Examiner* called them a "splendid attraction." However, the nine disbanded in the late 1930s.[36]

In the 1940s, the San Francisco police department organized a Chinatown youth team called the Chinese Dragons. The motivation, according to the organizers, was to stem Chinatown juvenile delinquency and "to inculcate in the minds of American boys of Chinese extraction, through the medium of baseball, the ideals and principles of American citizenship." Will Connolly of the *San Francisco Chronicle* thought the San Francisco police were on to something. In 1945, he wrote: "Chinese boys are going in for baseball in a big way, if only in the spirit of perversity to prove they can eclipse the Japanese heretofore the prime exponent of baseball, outside the continental U.S.A. ... Chinese should make excellent ballplayers. They are nimble of foot and quick of hand, and unlike the Japanese, grow big enough to hit a ball hard." Chinatown businesspeople Harry Yip and Joe Shoong would sponsor the team and Richard Tam would serve as coach.[37]

After World War II, Chinese American nines remained active on the mainland. In San Francisco, the police department abolished its "Chinatown detail." This meant, according to the *Examiner*'s Carl Reich, that white police officers could no longer watch after the Chinese Optimist team whose origins were described in the previous paragraph. Thus, Reich complained that only four players showed up for a game in 1947. However, the Chinese Optimists apparently survived the lack of supervision from white police officers. The team beat the Booker T. Washington nine in March, the Presidio Boys Club 14–4 in June, and the Napa Optimists 8–6 in late July.[38]

Chinese Americans on the mainland organized other teams after World War II. In 1946 a *San Francisco Chronicle* writer observed two Chinese American teams playing each other every Sunday. In a game between the Bears and the Cobras, the "Bears got but 2 hits, while their opponents got five, and the youngsters played good ball all the way." The Chinese A's comprised another team active in San Francisco in 1950. According to the *Chinese Press*, this team was co-sponsored by the Red Dragon Cocktail Club and Universal Café. In 1951, San Francisco's Chinatown was represented by the Cathay Post American Legion team with players such as Kim in left field; Lui at first base; Gee, center field; Eng, shortstop; Lee, pitcher; Woo, at third base; Wong at second; catcher Chin; and Chan in right field. The Chinese Merchants competed in San Francisco at about the same time. In Sacramento in 1950, the *Sacramento Bee* announced "try outs for a Chinese baseball team" and that Jack Fong would serve as manager. The team would subsequently be known as the Monarchs. And in Stockton, a Chinese American baseball team competed in 1950.[39]

Mainland Chinese American communities showed support for elite ballplayers of Chinese ancestry such as the All-Chinese nine from Hawaii. For example, when the Hawaiians first arrived in San Francisco in 1912 they were met by a local delegation from San Francisco's Chinatown, as well as a Chinatown band. A few days later, the *Sacramento Bee* reported under the headline, "Orientals Await Opening Game," that local Chinese were interested in greeting and watching the All-Chinese nine. In particular, the Young Chinese Association planned on giving the Hawaiians a reception. While on their initial tour, the Chinese Hawaiian ballplayers were honored with two trophies, one bestowed by former Chinese Hawaiians living in San Francisco and the other by Chicago's Chinese American community. In 1913, the Hawaiians beat Stanford 7–3. The next day the *San Francisco Chronicle* announced, "Suppers were late on the Stanford campus and in Palo Alto due to culinary celebration and kitchen fannings over the Chinese victory." A year later, the Hawaiian Travelers were in Los Angeles to play Occidental College. The *Los Angeles Times* predicted that when the game took place, "Every Chinese laundry and vegetable wagon in the city will be out of commission." As it turned out about 150 Chinese Angelenos showed up for the game, won by the Hawaiians.[40]

Filipino Americans

Filipino community teams were organized before and after World War II. In 1922, the Filipino Association of Chicago formed a baseball team with players who had competed in the Philippines for different schools and colleges. In San Francisco, the Filipino All-Stars played in 1927 in the Class B Spalding and Brown Midwinter League. The Filipino Merchants team competed in the city's large semi-pro circles in the 1930s, as did the Filipino Athletic Club. In the 1940s, San Francisco's Mango Athletic Club organized a baseball team.[41]

Lyrical Filipino American writer and labor activist Carlos Bulosan recounted the importance of baseball to Filipino cannery workers on an Alaskan island during the early 1930s:

> It was only at night that we felt free, although the sun seemed never to disappear from the sky. It stayed on in the western horizon and its magnificence inflamed the snows on the island, giving us a world of soft, continuous light, until the moon rose at about ten o'clock to take its place. Then trembling shadows began to form on the rise of the brilliant snow in our yard, and we would come out with baseball bats, gloves, and balls, and the Indian girls who worked in the cannery would join us, shouting huskily like men.[42]

Major League Baseball and Asian Pacific American Communities

Major League baseball teams have, in recent years, attempted to promote ties to Asian Pacific Islander American communities. The Los Angeles Dodgers were receptive to Southern California's urban Asian Pacific Islander American communities. Former Japanese American residents of Terminal Island held annual Dodger nights at the team's Chavez Ravine stadium. The Dodgers agreed to sell community members $5.00 tickets at a $2.50 level in 1972. Korean Americans in Los Angeles followed Chan Ho Park's career as a Dodger closely. The Dodgers cultivated this relationship by instituting a Korean American night, distributing Chan Ho Park street banners, and setting up a ticket kiosk in the city's Korean American community. Indeed, Park's popularity among Korean Angelenos was imposing. Richard Choi of Radio Korea told the press, "When Chan Ho is pitching there are not any customers in Korea restaurants. There are no customers in Korean markets. They're listening to the radio or going to Dodger Stadium. Chan Ho is — what can I say?— he's a big shot now." Sadly, the right-handed pitcher was not all that excited by the interest Korean Angelenos expressed in him. In 1997, he complained that because of the close scrutiny of the Korean American press and local Korean American fans, he had lost his chance at a social life in Los Angeles.[43]

The Dodgers were not the only major league team building bridges to America's Asian Pacific American communities. The San Francisco Giants tried to connect to Bay Area Asian Pacific Americans. In 1983, the franchise held a Japanese American Day–a day on which Atlee Hammaker, a *hapa* of Japanese ancestry, was scheduled to pitch. In 1996, the franchise honored Japanese Americans such as Henry Honda who played semi-professional and amateur baseball in Northern California. Even though the New York Mets did not have a player of Asian Pacific Islander ancestry on their roster in 1997, the franchise still wooed the city's large Asian Pacific American communities. For example, the Mets sponsored an Asian American night that featured the sale of Asian food and the performance of Asian dancers. Moreover, a Korean American sang the national anthem. To publicize the event, the Mets ran spots on Chinese and Korean language television stations, as well as circulated flyers in New York City's Asian Pacific American communities.[44]

In the early 2000s, a leader of Hmong Americans in Minnesota spoke out for keeping major league baseball in the state. At the time, it appeared that the Minnesota Twins might move out of not only Minneapolis but the state in general. However, Mee Moua, the first Hmong American elected to a state office, supported as a state senator the effort to keeping the Twins in Minnesota. Moua hoped, nevertheless, that the team would relocate to St. Paul, which happened to be her home town.[45]

Still, Asian Pacific American communities have not always demonstrated support for mainland professional baseball. In 1981, Oakland Athletics catcher Mike Heath upset Asian Pacific Americans in the Bay Area by lamenting that opponents had been getting "chink hits" off Athletics pitchers. A letter writer to *East/West* declared, "I don't want an apology. I just want to make sure that nothing like that happens again." In 2000, Chinatown merchants in Philadelphia threatened a community-wide business shutdown to protest a plan to build a new baseball park in their neighborhood.[46]

Conclusion

The forces of racial exclusion were so powerful on the American mainland that Asian Pacific American ethnic groups needed durable community institutions. Japanese and Chinese American mainlanders, for example, developed venerable athletic organizations and leagues. While baseball was not the only sport in which they engaged, Asian Pacific Americans clearly saw in swinging a bat and chasing a fly ball meaningful ways to strengthen and represent their diverse ethnic groups.

Yet Asian Pacific American community baseball on the mainland and the Hawaiian Islands has represented something more complicated than a need for assimilation. Asian Pacific Americans used baseball as a way of defining themselves as both ethnically distinct and yet a part of a larger American culture. That is, through baseball Asian Pacific Americans have asserted their cultural citizenship.[47]

CHAPTER **IV**

Asian Pacific American Amateurs and Semi-Pros

Even as they faced substantial racial exclusion, people in the United States of Asian Pacific Islander ancestry played baseball with and against persons of non–Asian Pacific Islander ancestry. Elementary and high school, youth, semi-professional, and college teams offered an occasional roster place for generally young men of Asian Pacific Islander ancestry over fifty years ago and in Hawaii more than an occasional roster place. In more recent years, Asian Pacific Islander American young people of both sexes compete with non–Asian Pacific Islander Americans on many levels. This demonstrates progress in the campaign for more racial democracy in American baseball. However, as we will find, bigotry persistently shadows the Asian Pacific Islander American experience with American baseball.

Japanese American Border Crossing

Despite the prevalence of anti–Japanese beliefs in California, Golden State *Nisei* played with white and other non–Japanese Americans before World War II. In 1915, Los Angeles High fielded "Sangi ... the Japanese pitcher." Early in the 1920s, Kenjo caught for Poly High School in Los Angeles. Up in San Jose, Jutato Nushida played for Orchard Grammar School's nine in 1922. In Washington's Yakima Valley, several Japanese Americans played on the Wapato High School team with whites. Earl Tanaka captained the Occidental College nine in the mid–1920s. According to social scientist

Russell Mears, one of Tanaka's teammates remarked, "T — may be yellow on the outside, but he is white on the inside." Across the continent, Arthur Matsu, a Canadian born son of a Japanese immigrant father and white mother, played baseball, as well as football and basketball, for William and Mary. In Fresno between World War I and World War II, *Issei* baseball pioneer Kenichi Zenimura competed in the racially integrated Fresno Twilight League. Zenimura, Johnny Nagakawa, and Harvey Iwata joined a Fresno All-Star team that met Babe Ruth and Lou Gehrig's barnstorming teams after the 1927 season. In 1930, Harry Kawata patrolled center field for the Berryessa nine in Santa Clara County, while a Kawamoto played for the Milpitas club along with Russ Hinaga, who served as captain of the multi-ethnic squad. In 1931, Otani roamed left field for UCLA while Okura fielded grounders at second base. In the early 1930s, Harada was in the St. Mary's of California lineup. In the mid–1930s, Kiyoshi Nogami lettered as a shortstop for the University of California. When Cal took on USC in 1936, the *San Francisco Chronicle* reported that "Nogami, Japanese shortstop" batted three for four. In Hood River, Oregon native Kay Kiyokawa pitched for Oregon State before the government ordered Japanese Americans to assembly centers and the concentration camps.[1]

In 1938, a *Sporting News* correspondent observed that Philadelphia Athletic standout Jimmy Dykes was doing his preseason warm-ups with a "Japanese schoolboy named Yoshi Wawno at the Pasadena, Cal., training camp." Apparently, the Japanese American youth had previously helped another Athletic, Mule Haas, to limber up "before complications set in the Far East." Getting its Asian stereotypes mixed up, the *Sporting News* correspondent warned Dykes to "watch his chow-mein."[2]

Meanwhile, Alice Hinaga, Russ's sister, was a top hitter and pitcher in San Jose's Night Ball Association in the 1930s. Popular in Great Depression California, Night Ball employed a ball that was larger than the one used in baseball but smaller than the one used in softball. Along with Hinaga, Asaye Sakamoto also competed in San Jose. Over in Fresno, Vicki Kawakami starred as first sacker and top hitter for the Golden State Bakery team.[3]

During World War II, a number of Japanese Americans played with and against non–Japanese Americans on the American mainland, despite the internment of over 100,000 Pacific Coast *Issei* and *Nisei*. Even after the attack on Pearl Harbor, Modesto and Placer Junior College nines suited up so many Japanese Americans that when these ballplayers were relocated from California the schools had to cancel their baseball seasons. Keo Nakama, a magnificent world-class swimmer of Japanese Hawaiian ancestry, was also a good enough baseball player to captain the Ohio State nine. Meanwhile, George Shimizu pitched for Washington of St. Louis and Kay Kiyokawa moved on to the University of Connecticut, where he played both baseball and football.[4]

In the late 1940s and into the 1950s, Japanese Americans showed up on a variety of youth and adult teams. In 1946, Tetsu Kaneko played the outfield for Southern California's Inglewood High School. At the same time, Shig Tachebana played shortstop and starred as a pitcher for Mountain View High School in Santa Clara County. Henry Honda, a talented pitcher for the San Jose Zebras, was picked to perform with the largely white semi-pro Valley All-Stars team in 1946. During World War II, Honda had gotten a try-out with the Brooklyn Dodgers. The Dodgers were interested in Honda but held off on signing him because they knew he would probably be drafted. In 1947, Honda was offered a chance to pitch in the Cleveland Indians organization but turned the offer down because of a torn tendon in his arm. Santa Clara County's Southside Market was one of the top semi-pro teams in the state in 1947 and fielded two gifted *Nisei* ballplayers—George Hinaga and Babe Nomura. In 1950, Eddie Hiramoto competed for Lodi High School in California's Central Valley. In 1955, Dick Tsuji suited up for a "bush team" known as the Seattle Savoys, while Ken Sakamoto took the field for a Seattle American Legion nine. In 1959, Robert Sumida pitched Auburn, California, to a victory over Gadsden, Alabama, in the Little League World Series. Not all of these cultural borderlands crossers were male. Nancy Ito played baseball in the late 1940s, according to the *Pacific Citizen*, with a team called the Denver Tivolis.[5]

During the next two decades, Japanese Americans continued to compete for diverse teams. In 1960, George Kuagami played for La Habra High School in Southern California. In San Francisco, Jack Suguwara's feats as a pitcher for George Washington High School inspired the *Nichi Bei Times* to call him "the most outstanding *Sansei* athlete in San Francisco since the end of World War II." In 1973, Japanese American Mike Otsuji helped California's Santa Clara Mission Pony League All-Stars win the Pony League World Series.[6]

George Abo and other Japanese Americans competed in post–World War II college baseball. Abo pitched and played outfield for Fresno State, starred for the Japanese American Fresno All-Stars and, subsequently, the San Jose Zebras. Although he had apparently received several professional offers, Abo decided on a career in education. In 1950, he joined the teaching staff at Fresno's Memorial High School, where, according to the *Pacific Citizen,* he became the first *Nisei* baseball coach in California. Tommy Ogaki played regularly for San Jose State in 1950. Howard Zenimura, one of Kenichi's two baseball playing sons, batted over .400 for Fresno State in 1949. Hawaiian Henry Tominaga became a star pitcher for Springfield College in Massachusetts. After seeing

Tominaga compete in the NCAA baseball tourney, his coach said, "Tominaga has a world of slow stuff and is one of the smartest southpaw pitchers I've seen in the college ranks."[7]

In 1951, Hawaiian Bill Nishita displayed his talents as a pitcher for Cal in the early 1950s after an impressive stint with Santa Rosa Junior College, where he achieved a 16 and 1 record in 1950 and where skilled Hawaiian catcher George Fujishige also suited up in 1951. The *Pacific Citizen* hailed Nushita as the most outstanding pitcher in junior college ranks and publicized his Cal debut against a Camp Pendleton nine. Nishita hurled five innings of effective baseball against the Marines in a 7–2 victory. A couple of months later, the *Los Angeles Times* reported that Cal beat UCLA behind the "nifty pitching of their nipponese right hander." Jim Scott in the *Los Angeles Times* claimed that major league scouts were swarming over Nishita. His Cal coach, Clint Evans, reputedly had to shoo scouts away from the "the 6-foot Japanese pitcher." Scott wondered, "Could be that he'll be the first Nipponese to make the big time." Nishita subsequently pitched in the Armed Forces League for Fort Shafter in Hawaii. Another notable Japanese Hawaiian, Andy Miyamoto, played on the same army team. Moreover, Nishita's former teammate, George Fujishige, starred for a Fort Hickham nine in the mid–1950s.[8]

In 1951, Fresno State suited up an impressive team and a couple of impressive Japanese American players. Fresno State fielded Harvey Zenimura, who batted a whopping .436, and Fibber Hirayama, who hit a solid .288. This 1951 Fresno State team achieved an enviable 36 and 4 record. A long time follower of Fresno State baseball asserts that Harvey Zenimura and Fibber Hirayama helped make the outfield defensively imposing, although neither was a power hitter.[9]

There were other Japanese American college standouts after World War II. Lefty Fujioka pitched for Fresno Junior College after World War II. Ben Yano also suited up for Fresno Junior College. Yuba College had pitcher Haki Yokama, shortstop Jimmy Yokota, as well as outfielders Tom Yego and Ed Miyamoto. In 1956, Maka Takajima played for Coalinga Junior College, which won the Northern California Junior College championship. In Southern California, Bob Kiyamoto starred as a hitter for Reedley College, David Fukumoto was a catcher for Whittier College in the early 1970s and Japanese Hawaiian Glen Goya became his home state's only NCAA batting champion while starring for Pepperdine in 1977. In the Pacific Northwest, Bob Uemoto was a catcher for Oregon State in the early 1970s. At the same time, Hawaiian David Kitamura starred as a shortstop for Colorado State.[10]

In the 1950s, Nancy Ito made her way from Denver to New York City, where she played baseball for the Bloomer Girls in the National Girls Baseball

Japanese American ballplayers appeared on college teams throughout the West Coast after World War II. Fresno State, which had one of the best college nines in California, had no trouble fielding key Japanese American ballplayers. Two Japanese Americans played on the 1950 squad — Fibber Hirayama and Howard Zenimura (courtesy of Special Collections, California State University, Fresno).

Fibber Hirayama starred in football and baseball at Fresno State College in the early 1950s. He subsequently played major league ball in Japan and was the subject of an intriguing *Sports Illustrated* piece by novelist Mark Harris (courtesy of Special Collections, California State University, Fresno).

Like Fibber Hirayama, Harvey Zenimura played for Fresno State College in the early 1950s. Like Hirayama, as well, this son of a Japanese immigrant baseball pioneer, Kenichi Zenimura, played major league baseball in Japan (courtesy of Special Collections, California State University, Fresno).

League, which posed as something of a rival to the better known All-American Girls Baseball League. The *Chicago Tribune* called Ito the "Bloomer Girls' Japanese shortstop." In mid–August, Ito hit her league leading ninth home run against the Maids. Several days later, on August 25, 1953, Ito led her team to a victory over the Bluebirds before 3,000 spectators at Thiliens Park.[11]

In the Great Plains, Hawaiian Japanese ballplayers were making their way into the University of Nebraska's baseball rosters during the second half of the twentieth century. David Murakami competed for the Cornhuskers from 1960 to 1962. A decade later, Ryan Kurosaki starred as a pitcher for the University of Nebraska, while in the mid–1970s Bryan Akisada played college ball in Lincoln, Nebraska. Kurosaki was an All-American talent at the University of Nebraska. Moreover, in September 1973, he was named the Most Valuable Pitcher in the National Baseball Congress tournament while pitching for a team representing Liberal, Kansas. In the late 1990s, Danny Kimura left Honolulu's Iolani High School to play stalwart third base for the University of Nebraska before transferring back home and to the University of Hawaii. And Shane Komine emerged as a top-notch pitcher for the University of Nebraska. In the early 2000s, Shane Komine was described as "one of the most dominant hurlers in college baseball today." *Asian Weekly* writer Ethen Leiser stated, "Komine has the ability to snap every ounce of his body into velocity that can reach the mid–90s. Komine also mixes in a slider, change-up and curveball to keep hitters honest." Komine was subsequently drafted by the Oakland Athletics. In 2006, Komine joined the East Bay team's pitching staff for a brief stay.[12]

In the late 1990s, University of San Francisco did well in intercollegiate baseball thanks, in part, to recruiting Japanese Hawaiians. Greg Omori, Troy Nakamura, and Ryan Yamamoto formed a nucleus of top flight Don ballplayers. One of the reasons why these Hawaiians made their way to San Francisco was assistant coach Chad Konishi. A former Cal pitcher and assistant at San Francisco City College, Konishi grew up in Honolulu and knew where to find talented AJA ballplayers. As for USF's appeal to Japanese Hawaiians, Nakamura explained, "There's a desire to get off the island and experience Division I baseball." Nakamura subsequently became an assistant coach for USF after achieving a .307 lifetime average with the Dons.[13]

Hawaiian-born Kurt Suzuki was an All-American catcher for the NCAA champion California State University, Fullerton, team in the early 2000s. As of this writing, he is playing in the Oakland Athletics organization (courtesy of David Marasco).

After the turn of

David Nakama has coached mainland college baseball for years after leaving his native Hawaiian Islands. As of this writing, he is batting coach for the Stanford University nine (courtesy of David Marasco).

the twenty-first century, Japanese American ballplayers stood out for Weber State, California State, Fullerton and USF. Greg Shimada starred as a shortstop for Weber State in Utah. His coach, Dominick Jeffries, praised Shimada as "a true baseball player.... He's a purist. He plays the game to play baseball." At California State University, Fullerton, Kurt Suzuki emerged in the early 2000s as an All-American catcher. In 2003, Suzuki won the Johnny Bench Award as the top catcher in college baseball. A native of Maui, Suzuki batted .413, hit sixteen homers and knocked in eighty-seven RBIs for Cal State Fullerton. What is more, he drove in the winning run to lead his Titans to an NCAA championship over Texas. A nearly unanimous first string All American, Suzuki was drafted in the second round by the Oakland Athletics. And one of Troy Nakamura's players, Royce Fukuroku, became the subject of a letter to *Sports Illustrated* in 2005. Written in response to an article on the five-foot, three-inch Chris Cates of Louisville, the letter protested that Cates, while good, was not "the best 5[ft] 3[in] baseball player in America." Fukruoku, who had earned All-American mention, deserved that honor.[14]

Dave Nakama has been a head coach and assistant in college baseball on the West Coast. The Hawaiian born Nakama was head coach at Mission College in Santa Clara, California, and then San Francisco State in the 1990s. In the early 2000s, Nakama assisted Mark Marquess for Stanford University, a long time national powerhouse in college baseball. Marquess maintained, "Dave is a very talented and knowledgeable coach, one of the very best infield coaches in college baseball and a good offensive coach." Nakama, in addition, head coached the Hawaii Island Movers, a team of high school and college stars from the Hawaiian Islands.[15]

Arizona's Bill Kajikawa merits special attention as a pioneer. Born in Oxnard, California, in 1912, Kajikawa's family moved to Arizona, where his mother and stepfather set up a barber's shop. Kajikawa worked on a farm as he attended Phoenix High School and played baseball as well as basketball and football. His high school yearbook states that Kajikawa also joined the Lettermen's Club, served as vice-president, of the Boys Federation, as well as home room president. He remembered, "Sports was a great vehicle for me because I could meet people and fit in.... I was the first Japanese-American to play sports at Phoenix Union, and I enjoyed it."[16]

Bill Kajikawa was a remarkable all-around athlete who coached several years at Arizona State. An assistant football coach for Arizona State, Kajikawa was head coach for the Sun Devils baseball and basketball teams in the late 1940s and 1950s (courtesy of Media Relations, Arizona State University).

A versatile athlete and coach, Kajikawa competed in baseball, basketball, and football at Arizona State in the 1930s while continuing to perform farm labor. He subsequently coached baseball at his alma mater for many years. In 1940, a syndicated feature showed a detailed drawing of Kajikawa and identified him as "the only Japanese College coach in the United States." His coaching career was delayed, however, by service in the famed 442nd during World War II. Upon returning to Arizona, Kajikawa began head-coaching duties for Arizona State's baseball team. Kajikawa also conducted a baseball school in his home state for the Brooklyn Dodgers after World War II. Kajikawa remained in charge of Arizona State's baseball program for eleven years until the legendary Bobby Winkles replaced him.[17]

Other Crossings

Other Asian Pacific Islander ballplayers competed with and against non–Asian Pacific Islander teammates. In Chicago, an All-Nations team played in the First Ward League. The team included Chinese as well as Japanese ballplayers. The *Los Angeles Times* testified to the play in California of Chinese Hawaiian Henry Pan Hoe, described by the daily in 1908 as the "Chinese Baseball Wonder." According to the *Times,* Hoe, a "Chinese student from the Hawaiian Islands," captained the Pomona prep school team. Learning baseball on the islands, the Celestial was a good infielder and pitcher, the *Times* maintained. According to a report published in the *Pacific Commercial Advertiser* late in 1912, two Chinese from Hawaii were going to play baseball the next year with the University of Southern California (USC). Called Kiura and Young, both attended USC's school of dentistry. However, the *Advertiser* corrected the report by claiming that Kiura was actually Japanese. In 1914, Hawaiian raised Chor Ou played baseball for Western High School in Washington, D.C. Dubbed the "Chinese Jim Thorpe" by a Washington, D.C., journalist, Ou apparently was indeed a talented all-around athlete. In the 1930s, Leslie Fong competed for Vallejo High School, and Wa Sung standout Allie Wong took part in an all-star game in the Bay Area — a game that consisted of some fine PCL and major league talent. During World War II, Wong suited up for the Del Rey semi-pro team based in the San Francisco Bay Area.[18]

Filipino American baseball pioneer Bobby Balcena played high school and semi-pro baseball during and immediately after World War II before turning pro. In 1942, Balcena starred as a pitcher for San Pedro High School, winning five games and losing but one. In February, Balcena pitched a one-hitter against Torrance High School. In 1947, Balcena hurled a victorious game for the San Pedro Merchants against the Yugoslav Americans, which featured future major league pitcher Erv Palica.[19]

After World War II, Asian Pacific Americans continued to cross the foul lines to play with and against non–Asian Pacific Islanders. Jack Ladro, a Hawaiian of Filipino-Portuguese ancestry, played for an American military team stationed in Hawaii. In the late 1960s, brothers Franklin and Eugene Tom stood out on San Francisco's Galileo High School nine. In the 1970s, Darryl Wong starred in baseball for San Francisco's Lowell High School.

Laurie Gouthro was a Filipino American who excelled in softball at Florida Community College and the University of South Florida. Subsequently, she became a member of the Colorado Silver Bullets, a professional women's baseball team that toured the United States in the mid–1990s. At about the same time, Hawaiian Rochelle Uwaine, a 5-foot 1, 110-pound infielder, competed for the San Jose Spitfires in the late 1990s. In 2005, the Spitfires used Misata Yamada as a pitcher. The East Bay Furies fielded Etsu Masada as both an infielder and an outfielder. Donna Moy pitched and took the outfield for the Alameda Oaks and Tammy Tam took the infield for the San Francisco Fillies.[20]

American college nines have included several notable athletes of non–Japanese but yet Asian Pacific Islander ancestry. Jack Desha, who possessed indigenous Hawaiian ancestry, competed for Harvard in 1911. William Achi played for both Stanford and the University of Chicago in the early 1900s. While more famous on the gridiron, Herman Wedemeyer played well for the St. Mary's of Moraga, California, nine during and after World War II. After World War II, Jack Ladro competed for Fresno State. Hawaiian Charley Ane, who, like Wedemeyer, was also a great football player, pitched for the University of Southern California in the early 1950s. In the 1970s, Milt Holt, who possessed indigenous Hawaiian ancestry, was known as "Pineapple Milt" when he pitched Harvard to the College World Series. Raymond Townsend, a son of a *Pinay* mother and a star basketball player himself, played shortstop for UCLA in the mid–1970s. In the 1990s, Jim Vo Parque pitched for UCLA and the 1996 U.S. Olympic nine.[21]

In the mid–1940s, Herman Wedemeyer was an All-American football player for little St. Mary's College in Moraga, California. Possessing Native Hawaiian and Chinese ancestry, Wedemeyer could also play baseball very well. He is shown here wearing his St. Mary's College baseball uniform. Later, he tried his hand at minor league baseball in 1950. (Courtesy of Special Collections, Saint Mary's College of California, College Archives.)

Buck Lai, Jr., the son of the Chinese Hawaiian baseball star, carved out an interesting baseball career himself. He had played with his father on the Hawaiian All-Star team that barnstormed North America in the mid to late 1930s. He then got a baseball scholarship to Long Island University, where he generally roamed the outfield. In March 1941, Lai broke up an eight-inning shutout hurled by a Seton Hall pitcher. Playing first and batting third, he went two for four. A month later, Lai batted second and played center field in a game against Fordham. After serving in World War II as a naval fighter pilot, Lai returned to his alma mater to coach baseball and assist the famed Clair Bee in coaching basketball. In 1952, he was named to succeed Bee as athletic director in the wake of the basketball gambling scandals that significantly damaged LIU's basketball program. Lai also was employed as an instructor for the Brooklyn Dodgers. In the early 1950s, he gained some publicity for helping coach a team called the Brooklyn Stars of Tomorrow for the Dodgers. In 1956, Lai assisted Brooklyn Dodgers manager Walt Alston in running a baseball school for Air Force members in Montgomery, Alabama. Meanwhile, Lai, Jr., wrote a widely used instructional book on baseball called *Championship Baseball: From Little League to Big League*. Lai seemingly applied his knowledge of baseball fundamentals to his college coaching job as in 1960, his LIU nine won its third league title and its fifth in seven years.[22]

In recent years, several non–Japanese Asian Pacific Islanders have made college baseball rosters and have often excelled. Kamehameha graduate Duke Sardinha was a catcher for Pepperdine in the late 1990s and early 2000s, while Marvin Wong played for the University of New Mexico. Han Yi, a son of Korean immigrants, played for Brigham Young University after graduating from West Torrance High School in California. On the same team was a Hawaiian infielder, Kainoa Obrey, who earned Honorable Mention All-American as a freshman. Obrey had arrived in Utah by way of Honolulu's Iolani High School, where Dean Yonamine coached him. Also by way of West Torrance High School, Justin Su'a was a Samoan American pitcher for BYU. His father, Martin, had also pitched for BYU in the 1960s. And pitching for Swarthmore in 2005 was Justin Chen.[23]

Hawaiian Crossings

On the Hawaiian Islands Asian Pacific Islanders playing, coaching, and managing multiethnic, multiracial teams was far more common than on the mainland. One observer noted the multiethnic, multiracial composition of a plantation team, presumably in the 1920s or 1930s. He asserted, "In the preliminary practice the captain, a hapa-pake or Chinese Hawaiian called

The son of the well-traveled Buck Lai, Buck Lai, Jr., played at Long Island University and then coached, taught, and served as an administrator at LIU for years. This photo depicts Ilene Somkin, LIU's manager and the first female manager of any college baseball team, talking it over with Buck Lai, Jr., at Ebbets Field in 1958 (Courtesy of Special Collections, Long Island University.)

Buck Lai, Jr., also served the Brooklyn Dodgers as scout and instructor. Here he is shown coaching young players at the Dodgertown Camp for Boys in Florida (c. 1950s). (Courtesy of Special Collections, Long Island University.)

A Pacific Islander, Justin Su'a pitched in recent years for Utah's Brigham Young University Cougars (courtesy of David Marasco).

out: 'Hey, Lee Hop you pitch and Fuji you catch; you Portegee, on first base; Filipino on second; Kanaka on third and you Haole — play short.' Then the captain told the social worker who was umpiring: 'All mix up like Hell.'"²⁴

As early as the late 1800s, Hawaiians organized culturally diverse teams. The Hawaii team that won the Oahu Senior League championship in 1911 included players such as the Desha brothers, Fred Markham, Hamauka, Ayau, and Kuali. The Aala nine in 1912 had players of Chinese, Hawaiian, and Japanese ancestry. Sam Hop, who managed the Chinese Hawaiian traveling team for two years, was on the team, as was Henry Kuali and players named Yoshiga, En You, Ayou Chan, Ah Toon, Marnichi, and Ozaki. The same year a team called the Barry Beauts, managed by a Sergeant Barry, competed in Honolulu and fielded talented Hawaiian players such as En Sue Pung and Fred Markham. The Pawaa nine sought a game with the Chinese Hawaiian Travelers after they had returned to Honolulu in the fall of 1912. Future major leaguer and part Native Hawaiian John B. Williams played for this team along with future Travelers James Aylett and Fred Markham. Young men named Takitani, Aki, Akana, Kilauea, G. Akana, Sam Kai, and J. Akana played for the Kauai Baseball League in 1912. Tsukiyama, Yosahachi, Tetsu, and Katsu took the field for the Kaahumanu squad. A team called the All-Students, comprising star Honolulu players competing for various schools in the city, took on the Chinese Hawaiian Travelers in January 1913. Fred Markham, Foster Robinson, and Kamehameha standout Bill Oppunui played for the student squad. Ayau, Foo You, and Fong were in the line-up for Aiea of the Oahu Plantation League in 1913. The opening of the Oahu Plantation League in 1915 saw a Waipahu team with a Yoshii on the same roster as well as Ornellas and Cordeiro, while Aiea had Keohane and Nealoha along with Cabral. Hipa, Kaopua, Nahuka, and Kahalewai took the field for the Pawaas of the Oahu Junior League team. And Anahu played third base for the Braves in 1916.²⁵

Culturally diverse ballplayers competed for Honolulu schools. Top Hawaiian ballplayers such as Barney Joy, En Sue Pung, Lang Akana, Foster Robinson, and Albert Akana played for St. Louis in the early years of the twentieth century. In 1915 and 1916, the school's ballplayers included Ting Poy, King Tan, Lai Sin, Fun Luke, Bunn Hee, Kakiipii, and Kurisaki. When St. Louis beat a team of visitors from California's Stockton High School, the mainlanders seemed surprised that the Hawaiians played so well. Punahou, an elite prep school, fielded Hong Kim Wai, Kong Tai, Napihaa, and Sahawota in 1915. The Mills School team suited up Na, Chee, Yashiga, Watase, Yamagi, Toke, Loo Sun, Sueoka, and Kurashige. McKinley High School in 1912 had a baseball team with players such as Ping Kong, Carn In, Sherry Tyau, Hoon Chong, A. Wong, C. Wong, Tachiro, Hiranaka, Kono, and

Kahalewai. The nine representing the College of Oahu, which would eventually become the University of Hawaii, included Fred Markham in 1912. The college also offered an interclass league. Possessing Native Hawaiian ancestry, Fred Markham captained the sophomore team, which fielded players such as A. Yap, J. Yap, and Sakai. J.T. Pung played for the seniors, while Alex Desha played for the juniors and W. Hong competed for the freshmen.[26]

Plantation and commercial nines were typically diverse. The Aiea nine competing in the 1912 Plantation League had ballplayers named David Liuhani, G. Wong, and David Kealoha. Yap took right field for the Bank of Hawaii team in 1915. Former Traveler and mainland professional Bill Inman organized a team for Wahiwa's Hawaiian Preserving Company in 1916. Nishi, a one time Asahi player, suited up for Inman. In 1919, the Mutual Telephone Company fielded a team that included En Sue Pung in center field, Fred Markham at first base, as well as a Tominaga at shortstop and Chang as pitcher.[27]

In the 1930s, the pattern of racial and ethnic diversity persisted. Playing for the Mutual Telephone Company in 1936 were Afo Pung, Hans Pung, Enomoto, C. Mamiya, and Shinagawa along with a talented African American pitcher, Ted Shaw. The Transits fielded Kealoha, Kanuao, and Earl Vida, a veteran pitcher of indigenous ancestry. And the Electrics included Chow, Ahue, Al Nalua, and John Kerr, a fine Chinese Hawaiian ballplayer.[28]

The fact that several of Hawaii's best players possessed mixed ancestry may have made racial and ethnic border crossing easier in baseball. In the early twentieth century, talented Hawaiians such as Lang Akana could play for a team representing Chinese Hawaiians one day and a team representing Native Hawaiians another. Lorrin Andrews, a haole official of the Oahu Baseball League in the 1910s, was not amused. He insisted, "[T]he man who pays the freight does not care to see a man playing as a Chinese one day and then as a Hawaiian the next."[29]

Lang Akana and other top Hawaiian ballplayers also played for a team composed of St. Louis College alumni. This team frequently competed in the Oahu League and against military and visiting nines such as the one representing the University of Chicago in the late summer of 1915. According to the *Honolulu Star-Bulletin,* Akana's appearance as a batter for St. Louis against the University of Chicago in September 1915 inspired a "Chinaman with firecrackers" to yell, "Hit'er Lang."[30]

The various elite and non-elite leagues on the islands promoted ethnic based teams but also racial and ethnic border crossings. When Santa Clara College traveled the Pacific to play on Oahu in 1908, it ran into the Diamond Head team that featured Sing Cong at shortstop. The *San Jose*

Mercury reported that Santa Clara had learned that "the Island teams are made up of Chinese, Japs, Americans, and Hawaiians. There [sic] were in the field is said to be inferior to the average American team's work, but they are good batsmen." On Maui, the part-Hawaiian and part-Chinese Foster Robinson played for the Paia nine in the 1910s. On Kauai, the Kilauea Plantation nine won the island championship in 1912. On the team were men named Bill Kerr, San Kai, George Akana, John Akana and Osaka Sasichi. The Japanese Athletic Club had a team included in the Oahu Senior League in 1912. However, Andy Yamashiro was the only Japanese Hawaiian on the nine along with future Chinese Travelers Henry Kuali, Foster Robinson, and Fred Markham. After they returned from their first visit to the American mainland, Lai Tin and Kan Yen joined Native Hawaiian pitcher Barney Joy on the Oahu Senior League's Star nine. On the administrative side, Japanese Hawaiian and Asahi manager C.K. Abe was chosen vice-president of the Oahu Junior League in 1912. Several years later, Earl Vida served as territorial commissioner for the National Baseball Congress in Hawaii, while Lang Akana served as president of the HBL.[31]

Possessing Hawaiian and Chinese ancestry, the Hilo-raised Kaulukukui brothers crossed cultural barriers to compete for several Hawaiian nines in the 1930s, 1940s, and 1950s. In addition to being fine baseball players, they were excellent all around athletes. Tommy Kaulukukui, for example, earned a spot on the small college All American football team in the mid–1930s while playing halfback for the University of Hawaii. In the early 1930s, he appeared in the lineup of a Hilo Senior Baseball League team that competed against a mainland team headed by Babe Ruth. Kaulukukui also played another game on Ruth's side. Later in the 1930s, Tommy and Charles Kaulukukui began competing for the All-Chinese nine affiliated with the Hawaii Baseball League — a team known as the Chinese Tigers. In 1936, Charles "hurled masterful ball" for the Machine Shop nine when it beat the Shopfitters 7–0. In 1940, Tommy Kaulukukui led the HBL's Tigers to a victory over a nine representing the island of Hawaii and the territorial championship. Kaulukukui also served as coach and assistant franchise owner until he entered the military in 1942. While in the service, he coached the *Nisei* Varsity Victory Volunteers' baseball teams. Joe and Ed Kaulukukui pitched on the 1940 Tigers team, while James Kaulukukui played second base and Charles Kaulukukui served as the team trainer. In 1947, Dick Kaulukukui pitched four shutout innings for the Tigers in an exhibition game against the San Francisco Seals of the Pacific Coast League. Later in the day, the Seals soundly defeated the Hawaiis, led by Eddie Kaulukukui.[32]

John Kerr, who possessed indigenous Hawaiian, as well as Chinese, ancestry, performed for numerous Hawaiian teams in the 1930s and 1940s and became the first person to hit a home run out of Honolulu Stadium. While touring with Buck Lai's Hawaiian All-Stars in 1935, Kerr was described by the *Helena Independent* as a "pure Hawaiian" as well as "the greatest distance hitter ever developed in Hawaiian baseball." Indeed, Kerr had reportedly hit a 451-foot home run against the visiting Philadelphia Royal Giants nine earlier in the 1930s. Kerr's performance with Lai's team attracted attention. In late 1935, the *Sporting News* announced that the Philadelphia Phillies had signed Kerr, "a Hawaiian infielder, who has no professional experience."[33]

While the Phillies seemingly lost interest in him, Kerr tried out unsuccessfully for the San Francisco Seals but apparently impressed some in the process. Kerr and another Hawaiian, Allen Andrade, appeared at the Seals' workout in San Francisco. Will Connolly of the *San Francisco Chronicle* observed that the "Honolulu boys" looked like prospects. Kerr, described by Connolly as a "speed ball specialist" tried out for Lefty O'Doul's Seals as a pitcher. He lost the first spring training game in which he pitched but according to the *San Francisco Chronicle* did not do badly as his Seals teammates made key errors behind him. Several days later, the *Chronicle* reported that Kerr "proved himself the sweetest rookie in the camp." A former Seals pitching standout, "Pard" Ballou acclaimed the "Honolulu kid" the best Seals pitching prospect he had seen in years. Ballou said Kerr was smart, had command of a variety of pitches, and fielded his position well.[34]

Kerr, for some reason, did not make it in the Pacific Coast League. A graduate of Kamehameha, Kerr played additionally for the Chinese Tigers in the 1930s, as well as managed the Chinese Hawaiian nine. In the 1940s, Kerr was on the historically haole Wanderers roster, along with players surnamed Kai, Arakaki, and Kameda.[35]

Filipino American Cris Mancao pitched for a wide variety of commercial and HBL teams from the late 1930s until the 1970s. In the late 1930s, Mancao took the mound for the culturally diverse Oahu Sugar Company team. In 1947, Mancao was an ace for the predominantly Japanese American Rural Red Sox club. In 1951, the southpaw pitched for the Hawaiis of the HBL. In 1961, Mancao, at forty-seven, got a chance to play Organized Baseball when he signed with the Hawaii Islanders of the Pacific Coast League. In 1975, Mancao played his last baseball game at Pearl Harbor. At sixty, he pitched against a team of Marine All-Stars. Mancao also served as an assistant baseball coach at Farrington High School, Mid-Pacific Institute, and the University of Hawaii. At eighty-four Mancao still played softball and won one of Hawaii's Blue Shield Association's Ageless Hero awards in the late 1990s. In 2000, Mancao remembered that unlike many present day pitchers, he had a "rubber arm" and did not worry about such matters as a pitch count. When the New York Yankees barnstormed Hawaii in the mid–1950s, Mancao recalled, "I got all those big guys out ... at Honolulu Stadium.... In five innings, they only got three hits. Then that little guy, small like me, Billy Martin, hit a home run off me. He was the only one."[36]

In 1999, ninety-two-year-old Francis Funai died. Called "Mr. Baseball in Hawaii" by Wally Yonamine, Funai coached secondary school baseball in Hawaii for more than fifty years. Principally, he piloted teams for Honolulu's St. Louis, from 1944 to 1959, and then from 1967 to 1970. He also served as an assistant coach for Iolani High School and put on several youth clinics until well into his senior years.[37]

Other Hawaiian ballplayers, coaches, and managers traversed cultural borderlands. Depicted in the 1930 census as a partially indigenous Hawaiian, Earl Vida played and coached Hawaiian baseball for years. In the mid–1930s, Vida managed the Chinese Tigers of the HBL. At the same time, Toshi Moriyama managed the Mutual Telephone Company nine, a commercial league team playing out of Hilo. The Hawaiis had *Nisei* players Tosh and Ted Kameda on the roster in 1942. In 1944, Punahou grad, Lawrence Kunihisa, was named coach of the Athletics. The one-time Portuguese Braves fielded *Nisei* standout Jimmy Wasa, along with Larry Kamishima and George Wasa. Jimmy Wasa was asked to join the Braves as a way of easing racial tensions in World War II Honolulu and got paid 900 dollars for his troubles. William De Fossett, a former Negro Leaguer serving in Hawaii during World War II, recalled that he played on a racially integrated squad in Aiea, a region of Oahu just outside of Honolulu. He called this team "a regular League of Nations." Aside from five African Americans, it also included white, indigenous Hawaiian, and Japanese American players. The team manager was a Native Hawaiian, while a Japanese American served as coach. In the spring of 1946, Mateo Higuchi, the "little Japanese lefthander," pitched effectively in an exhibition game against the San Francisco Seals for a culturally diverse team called the Hawaii All-Stars, which played the PCL nine on the islands. Later in 1946, Eddie Kitamura pitched for the Wanderers. At the same time, McKinley High School graduate Henry Kiyoshi Tominaga was chosen to represent Hawaii in a youth all-star game to be played in Brooklyn. In 1947, the Chinese Tigers had players with Japanese surnames such as Muramoto, Naito and Higuchi, while the Portuguese Braves had Percy Ching on the roster. Several years later, Chinese Hawaiian Joe Tom coached baseball at McKinley High School while competing with the Asahis.[38]

By the mid–1950s, the Hawaii Baseball League was headed toward extinction. Baseball still stood as a middle ground on which athletes of various racial and ethnic backgrounds competed with and against each other. In 1956, former Asahi great Vern Higa managed the Naval Base team — a team that included only one obvious Asian Pacific American player, Roy Nakamura. Cris Mancao managed the historically Portuguese Hawaiian Braves.[39]

In Hawaiian youth baseball, Asian Pacific Islander participation was, of course, heavy. In 1946, an American Legion team from Waipahu competed in a regional tourney in Tucson, Arizona. Japanese Hawaiian Don Sugai was one of the team's big stars. In 1959, the *New York Times'* Milton Bracker reported on a Kailua Little League team that participated in the Little League World Series held at Williamsport, Pennsylvania. Bracker wrote that the team members typically played barefooted in Hawaii and that "although their ancestry includes Anglo-Saxon, Chinese, European, Japanese, Philippine, Polynesian, and Portuguese strains they are American, they speak English, chew gum, and don't eat poi three times a day." Players included Rodney Okabayashi, Arthur Kauilani Doo, and Milton Tanaka. Alfred Chan served as one of the coaches. And Milton's father, Bracker noted, had fought in the 442nd during World War II. In 1964, an island youth team came to Southern California to play against a local team in the cavernous Los Angeles Coliseum. The star of the team was Casey Ishamoto, a female "sensation." Apparently, her success proved embarrassing to the Southern Californians promoting International Junior Baseball, Inc. Organizer Dick Pittinger said that because "we're growing up," girls would no longer be allowed to participate. In 1965, Brian Nakashima starred for the Maui Pony League team that competed in the Far Western Tournament in Santa Clara, California. Forty years later, a Hawaiian Little League all-star team won the Little League World Series. Hailing from Ewa, the contingent unsurprisingly consisted of several talented young athletes of Asian Pacific Islander ancestry.[40]

In the late 1990s, a team of youthful Hawaiian amateurs toured Japan. Called the Hawaii Movers, the team consisted of Kanoa Fong, Derek Honma, Jared Kitamura, Duke Sardinha, Scott Tajima, Marvin Wong, and Sean Yamashita. Don Takaki, who headed the team, declared that team members would be "good-will ambassadors" for Hawaii — they would help market the fiftieth state among prospective Japanese investors and tourists.[41]

After World War II, Hawaii dispatched multiethnic, multiracial teams to North America to play some of the continent's best semi-pro squads, as well as teams such as the Harlem Globetrotters, who also played baseball for many years. In 1947, the *San Francisco Call-Bulletin* acknowledged the arrival of a Hawaiian All-Star squad. Percy Ching was one player that drew the daily's attention. Only 135 pounds, Ching had earned a reputation as "the Chinese Babe Ruth" by leading the Hawaii Baseball League in homers. The *Pacific Citizen* hailed the arrival of the Hawaiian All-Star team by pointing out that in pursuit of statehood, Hawaii was determined to send athletic representatives to the American mainland. Hawaiian supporters of the visiting ball team believed that doing so helped convince mainlanders that Hawaii was "one of the most sports conscious areas under the American flag," and, consequently, worthy of statehood. The venerable Negro League Chicago American Giants beat the Hawaiian All-Stars in the late summer of 1947. The Hawaiian team finished sixth in a national semi-pro tournament at Wichita, Kansas. It, moreover, included prominent Japanese Hawaiian players such as Jun Muramoto, Jyun Hirota, Kats Kojima, Tsuneo Watanabe, Fred Hasegawa, Dick and Harry Kitamura, Bill Yasui, Lefty Higuchi, Larry Kamashima, Masa Morita, and Jimmy Wasa, in addition to Chinese Hawaiian Sal Kaulukukui. Moreover, according to the *Pacific Citizen*, Hirota and Wasa were tendered offers from professional teams. A highlight of the 1947 trip had to have been the Hawaiian All-Stars taking a doubleheader in Crossley Field from the Cincinnati Clowns, a skilled Negro American League team.[42]

In 1948, a Hawaiian All-Star undertook an eighty game tour of North America. Many of the games pitted the Hawaiians against the Harlem Globetrotters. Cris Mancao pitched for the team, as did Lefty Higuchi. Jyun Hirota, a future Japanese Major Leaguer, was on the roster as a catcher and was widely considered the team's MVP. Another Hawaiian All-Star, Jun Muramoto, recalled, "It was a dream come true.... We played a lot of baseball in small cities as well as major league parks." The tour had been put together by two cross-Pacific sports entrepreneurs, Hawaiian Mackey Yanagisawa and Abe Saperstein, who ran the Globetrotters. In June 1948, the *Los Angeles Times* announced a game between the Globetrotters and the "Honolulu Hawaiians" at Wrigley Field. The great Olympic star Jesse Owens would provide fans an extra treat by giving "a series of exhibitions." A few weeks later, the Globetrotters beat the All-Stars 7–0 in Vancouver, British Columbia, before 3500. According to the *Honolulu Star-Bulletin*, the all-stars came home with a 44–35 record. Manager George Rodriquez declared that the team tried to boost Hawaiian statehood whenever possible, "Everywhere we played ... the boys played Hawaiian music and presented their opponents with leis."[43]

In the mid–1950s, Hawaii was represented in the Global World Series held in Milwaukee. Upon arrival in the Wisconsin city, the Hawaiian ballplayers were greeted by Duke Kahanamoku, the islands' most famous athlete and widely known as "Hawaii's goodwill ambassador." Larry Kunihisa, who ran the Rural Red Sox, managed the team. Sal Kaulukukui's hitting stood out, while Cris Mancao was called by the *Official Baseball Annual 1956* "Hawaii's diminutive hurler." Although the Hawaiian nine did not win the Global Series, Kaulukukui led all other participants in runs batted in. (RBIs). Vic Mori hit two triples in the series and Mayo Uyehara stood out as a reliever.[44]

Multiethnic, multiracial Hawaiian teams hosted mainland professionals. In 1916, a team of major leaguers arrived in Hawaii after their season ended. It was not an all-star team, by any means. Pitcher Dutch Reuther was probably the best known player on the team. But the All-Americans were still major leaguers and generally treated Honolulu baseball fans to entertaining ball. Playing against the All-Americans were the All-Chinese and the African American 25th Regiment squads as well as racially and ethnically mixed nines. All-Chinese standout Kai Luke competed with the All-Oahus, while Native Hawaiian Barney Joy took the slab in the ninth, "with the results that the All-Americans got five hits and three runs in one inning." Kan Yen Chun was chosen as catcher on a Honolulu all-star team that played and lost against the All-Americans. Still, he impressed onlookers as he gunned down All-American base runners. Indeed, the team largely consisted of members of the 25th regiment and All-Chinese squads, as Ensue Pung, Ah Lee, Vernon Ayau, Fred Swan, and Yen Chin in addition to Bullet Rogan and Bob Johnson joined Kan Yen Chun. The possibility that the great Rogan would form the battery with Kan Yen Chun thrilled the *Commercial Advertiser*, and in center field Ensue Pung had "no peer in the Islands." Nearly twenty years later, Babe Ruth toured the islands and when on the island of Hawaii played for the Hilo Baseball League All-Stars against the league champs, the Waiakea Pirates, a longtime source of the small city's multiethnic, working class pride. Pitching for the Pirates was a strikeout artist named Futoshi "Taffy" Okamura. While Ruth got a single and a home run off of Okamura, the eighteen year old also struck out the Bambino. In 1947, the San Francisco Seals trounced the Hilo All-Stars 20–2. According to the *San Francisco Examiner,* "[a] little Nipponese name Yasuonari Arakaki" shut out the Seals for three innings.[45]

The University of Hawaii (UH) has typically fielded multiethnic, multiracial baseball rosters and coaching staffs. In the late 1920s, Japanese Hawaiians such as Dean Ishii and Yoshi Tanaka starred on the UH nine. In the mid–1930s, Tommy Kaulukukui, Fujishige, Katsunuma, Ahuna, Uchimura, and Furukawa suited up for UH. In the late 1940s and early 1950s, Jyun Hirota, Harry Kitamura, Richard Kitamura, Henry Tominaga, Wayne Sakamoto, Tsuneo Watanabe, Larry Matsuo, Tom Nakagawa, Sol Kaulukukui, George Okihiro, and Saburo Takeyusu competed for UH. UH graduate Tommy Kaulukukui coached the university nine for much of the 1940s, excluding his time of military service during World War II. And for much of the 1950s, Toku Tanaka served as the university's baseball coach.

Previously Tanaka had played for such HBL teams as the Rural Red Sox. Jimmy Asato, Dr. Tommy Ige, David Murakami, and Henry Tominaga also coached the UH nine after World War II.[46]

Les Murakami coached the University of Hawaii for over a quarter of a century. In 1971, Murakami began his UH coaching career. Murakami took over a university baseball program that was in sad shape. Murakami had to borrow uniforms from a local AJA team and he had no scholarships to entice promising high school prospects. By the end of the decade, UH was pulling in record breaking crowds and became a respected NCAA program. In 1981, Murakami earned the Lefty Gomez Award for outstanding contributions to amateur baseball. In 1986, he was named NCAA district coach of the year, while in 1987 and 1991 the Western Athletic Conference (WAC) honored him as coach of the year. In 1999, Murakami entered the American Baseball Coaches Association Hall of Fame. His UH team won six WAC titles and earned a College World Series berth in 1980. Among Asian Pacific American assistant coaches hired by Murakami were Les Nakoma and Dave Murakami.[47]

A number of talented Asian Pacific American athletes suited up for the UH baseball team as it went big time under Murakami. During the 1970s, Tsuneo Watanabe's son Curt was one of UH's best ballplayers. In the late 1970s and early 1980s, Derek Tatsuno put together one of college baseball's most impressive pitching records. While at UH, Tatsuno set four individual college records in recording the most strikeouts in a season, most career strikeouts, and most starts and wins in a season. Tatsuno repeatedly pitched to sold out crowds at UH's home diamond. A then collegiate record attendance of 18,348 showed up to watch him pitch in 1979. According to the *Los Angeles Times*' Elliot Almond in 1979, "Tatsuno is the talk of Honolulu. Celebrity status has come to this junior agriculture major and the Rainbows are drawing record crowds." In 1982, Tatsuno was the first draft choice of the Milwaukee Brewers. Tatsuno tried instead to catch on as a major leaguer in Japan. However, according to Dan Cisco, Japanese catchers had a hard time handling his pitches and the Hawaiian never was particularly effective. Tatsuno in later life became involved in business development for his alma mater.[48]

Tatsuno and Watanabe have not been the only UH stars in recent decades. Catcher Colin Tanabe earned All-American recognition in 1980, as did outfielder Greg Oniate in 1982. Later in the 1980s, Ross Hayashi was good enough to receive a contract bid from the Hawaii Islanders and Danny Kapea signed a contract with the Pittsburgh Pirates. In the early 1990s, outfielder Franz Yuen stood out for UH. And Paul Ah Yat was a talented left hander for the University of Hawaii in the mid–1990s before trying to carve out a professional career on the mainland.[49]

Possessing Japanese ancestry, Joey Estrella, who played for the University of Hawaii as a shortstop as well as for Japanese American nines on the islands, coached the University of Hawaii, Hilo, team for years beginning in 1977. His teams competed three times in the NAIA World Series. Outstanding Asian Pacific Islander American players at the University of Hawaii, Hilo, have included Lance Suyama, Guy Oshiro, Kaha Wong, Keith Yasui, Lance Fukumitsu, Joe Arakaki, and Eric Tanagawa. Carrying a career batting average of .339, Oshiro, became the first UH Hilo baseball player to make the university's athletic Hall of Fame.[50]

Hawaii Pacific University (HPU) has been coached in recent years by Hawaiians of Asian Pacific Islander ancestry such as Pat Kuniyoshi, David Eldredge, and Allen Sato. In the 1980s and 1990s, HPU's NAIA All-Americans included Les Akeo, Lyle Shimazu, and Ben Agbayani, the future New York Met. At HPU, Agbayani set school records in most home runs in a season with ten, most stolen bases in a season with thirty-six, and most career stolen bases with eighty-two. Eddie Hayashi, Grant Enommoto, Brian Takara, Kevin Fujioka, Mike Nakana, Gordon Ijima, and Allan Sato have been other standout HPU players of Asian Pacific Islander ancestry.[51]

Umpires, Scouts, Trainers, and Officials

Over the years, Asian Pacific Americans have served American minor and major league baseball in a variety of non-playing capacities. Joe Katsunama was a well-known umpire in Hawaii, who also chaired the Oahu Plantation Athletic Association in 1940. In 1947, San Francisco Seals manager Lefty O'Doul was reportedly impressed with Katsunama's umpiring skills. He, thus, recommended that the Pacific Coast League hire the Japanese Hawaiian. Katsunama, who played school ball in Honolulu for Punahou and Mid-Pacific, never umpired in the PCL. Hank Shimada, however, did umpire for the California League in the 1950s. A native of Vacaville, California, Shimada cut his teeth as an umpire for armed services games in Europe. And World War II veteran Yosh Kawano became a long-time trainer for the Chicago Cubs after the war.[52]

Asian Pacific American major league scouts have included Ralph Yempuku and Cappy Harada. Yempuku, a Honolulu café owner, scouted post–World War II Hawaii for baseball owner Bill Veeck. He also helped clear Hawaiian Wally Yonamine's path toward Japanese major league ball in 1951. Harada long acted as a bridge between American and Japanese baseball. In 1951, he brought three Japanese major leaguers to the San Francisco Seals training camp. For many years, Cappy Harada was a scout for the San

Francisco Giants and played an important role in luring Japanese left-hander Massanouri Murakami into the organization. In 1964, Murakami became the first Japanese player to make the American show. The San Francisco Giants also employed Clarence Chun Hoon as a scout for the Hawaiian Islands in the early 1960s. In the 1970s, Keo Nakama was hired as a scout for the Detroit Tigers.[53]

Cast in a supporting role in Michael Lewis's *Moneyball*, Eric Kubota served as the Oakland Athletics' scouting director in the early 2000s. Lewis calls Kubota a "brainy graduate" of the University of California, Berkeley. Moreover, "[t]hat Eric had never even played high school baseball was, in Billy Beane's mind, a point in his favor. At least he had not learned the wrong lessons." Thus, Beane, considered a controversial but successful general manager, trusted Kubota more than retired ballplayers, who, according to Beane, were beguiled by the wrong things in prospects.[54]

Asian Pacific Americans have served in the front offices of minor and major league teams. When the PCL planted a franchise in Honolulu in 1961, Lang Akana became one of the Hawaiian Islanders' directors and Bill Kim was a vice-president. At the same time, Chinese Hawaiian capitalist Chinn Ho helped to finance the Islanders in the franchise's early years in Honolulu. According to journalist Wells Twombley, the very wealthy Chinn Ho was "practicing to be the Oriental version of Howard Hughes."[55]

In the early 1990s, Duane Kurisu initiated the Hawaii Winter League. The idea was to provide a useful competitive situation for top professional prospects and, indeed, the league originally comprised four teams with young hopefuls from American, Japanese, Korean, and Taiwanese professional leagues. The league opened play in mid–October and ended its season in mid–December. Later in the league's existence, the Maui Stingrays made baseball history by becoming the first professional team to field women alongside of men. Kurisu promoted the league by proclaiming, "And where else in the United States could fans watch baseball under swaying palms, have an ice cold beer and a red hot or a teriyaki plate or sushi? Both the fans and the players represent a diverse range of cultures with one thing in common. They all love baseball." The league reflected Kurisu's vision of Hawaii as "where the world comes to play baseball." However, the refusal of American major league baseball to help Kurisu pay the bills inevitably pushed the league toward extinction by the end of the 1990s.[56]

In 1997, Kim Ng was named assistant general manager for the New York Yankees. In the process, she became the second female and the youngest person to attain such a high administrative position for a Major League Baseball (MLB) team. A former high school athletic star in New Jersey, Ng had interned and then earned a salary in administration for the Chicago White

Sox. Ng hoped that she would encourage more Asian Pacific Americans to seek careers in sports management. However, she added in the late 1990s, "[J]udging from my own family and friends, I don't think the sports industry is the industry of choice."⁵⁷

In 2001, Ng moved on to the Los Angeles Dodgers where she also served as assistant general manager. However, while with the Dodgers, Ng was stung by racially insensitive remarks made by former major league pitcher and New York Mets' scout Bill Singer. While attending a league meeting, Singer confronted Ng at a bar. Singer asked Ng questions about her background and then proceeded to talk in gibberish in order to ridicule his notion of the way Chinese speak. Ng informed the New York Mets' general manager, Jim Duquette, about the incident. Duquette then fired Singer. The Dodgers general manager, Dan Evans, told the press that Singer's "conduct was inexcusable and extremely disappointing" and that "Kim handled the entire situation in a professional manner."⁵⁸

Some wondered what went on behind the scenes when Kim Ng was passed over for the Dodgers general manager position after Dan Evans was fired. Reporter Ryan Leong noted, however, that the person chosen instead of Ng was the seemingly quite qualified Paul De Podesta, who as assistant general manager for the Oakland Athletics was mentored by the astute Athletics' GM, Billy Beane. Ng told Leong that not getting the Dodgers GM job "happens in baseball as well as other industries quite a lot. I don't know that it's necessary for me to comment any further than that." Nevertheless, a few years later, De Podesta was fired and once again Ng was passed over — this time for Ned Colleti, a longtime assistant to the San Francisco Giants' GM, Brian Sabean. Colleti, however, kept Ng on as the Dodgers' assistant GM.⁵⁹

For *Asian Week* editor Samson Wong, nevertheless, Kim Ng signified the future of Asian Pacific Americans in big time American sports. Wong acknowledged in a 2004 editorial that more Asians are playing in the MLB, but the next step was to gain greater access to coaching, managing, and front office jobs. Wong wrote, "Ng represents a potential breakthrough. Her future will set the bar as more APAs and women enter the ranks of sports leadership and other fields in which they are underrepresented."⁶⁰

Ng has not been the only woman of Asian Pacific Islander ancestry to face bigotry in Major League Baseball. A recent employee of MLB, Juri Morioka, accused her employer's business arm of encouraging anti–Asian bias. In October 2003, she filed a multi-million dollar suit in Manhattan's U.S. District Court. She contended anti–Asian hostility was evident while she worked as an administrative assistant in the MLB's broadcasting department. Apparently, the situation grew worse while she worked in the MLB's

International Department. Morioka contended that she was regularly subjected to racial abuse until she was terminated in May 2003. She maintained that "unreasonable, offensive and demeaning anti–Japanese and anti–Asian hostility ... pervaded the entire International Department." Moreover, she complained that one executive repeatedly referred to people of Japanese ancestry as "Japs." Another executive told her he hated the "Japanese more than the Koreans." Morioka protested these slurs. However, she lamented that her protests encountered retaliation and her ultimate termination.[61]

Conclusion

Racism's traveling eye clearly has followed Asian Pacific Islanders as they have traversed baseball's racial and ethnic borderlands. Nevertheless, the sport has proven something of a middle ground for diverse Americans of Asian Pacific Islander ancestry. The ability to hit a ball hard and throw strikes has historically allowed Asian Pacific Americans to play with and against people of different racial and ethnic backgrounds. In recent years, more and more Americans of Asian Pacific Islander ancestry have made their way on to Little League, high school, and college baseball rosters. Yet as Kim Ng's experience shows, racism's traveling eye may only be better hidden. It has not disappeared.

CHAPTER V

Barnstorming the Mainland with the Hawaiian Travelers, 1912–1916

Supported by Chinatown business interests in Honolulu, as well as the Hawaiian Merchants and Advertiser's Club of Honolulu, a baseball team of Chinese American citizens was dispatched in 1912 to the mainland. The nine's backers hoped the athletes would pump up mainland tourism and investment in the islands, as well as erect a cultural bridge between European Americans and Chinese Americans. The 1912 and 1913 squads largely consisted of players of Chinese ancestry, although several athletes such as Buck Lai Tin, Vernon Ayau, Kan Yen Chun, Apau Kau, and Lang Akana also possessed indigenous ancestry and Fred Markham, added to the team in 1913, possessed indigenous Hawaiian and haole backgrounds. In subsequent years, the team became more ethnically diverse, but essentially remained Asian Pacific Islander. Thus, by 1914, the team fielded several players possessing Japanese and indigenous Hawaiian ancestry. The local press initially called the nine the All-Chinese but eventually took to referring to the Hawaiian ballplayers as the Travelers, the Hawaiian Travelers, or the Chinese Travelers.[1]

Making the issue of naming the team even more complicated was that the mainland press frequently publicized the barnstormers as representatives of the Chinese University of Hawaii. Still, there was no Chinese University of Hawaii. Red McQueen, veteran Honolulu sportswriter, maintained in the 1960s that the team's management encouraged the fiction that baseball fans at Stanford and Penn State were watching a college team in action. McQueen claimed that team management wanted to schedule college teams and believed doing so would be impossible unless mainland colleges were persuaded that the Hawaiian visitors represented a college. However, mainland college nines regularly played independent amateur and professional teams and it is hard to believe that administrators at Stanford, for example, would not know that Chinese University of Hawaii was a fiction. Yet it probably would have been easier to find mainland college teams to schedule if the Hawaiians were effectively represented as "well-bred" and college educated.[2]

The players composing the Hawaiian Travelers could claim varied social and economic backgrounds. Infielder Buck Lai Tin's Chinese father was a merchant, while his Hawaiian mother was a temple priestess. The 1900 manuscript census reported that shortstop's Vernon Ayau's father was a Chinese immigrant salesman, while his mother was Hawaiian. The 1910 manuscript census declared that outfielder Lang Akana's name was actually Fong Lan Akana. His Chinese born father, C.T. Akana, was a physician and his mother was Hawaiian. The 1890 Honolulu City Directory shows that C.T. Akana was not only a physician but a merchant tailor and livery stable owner as well. In 1910, the twenty-two-year-old Lang Akana worked in Honolulu as a bookkeeper. The 1930 census manuscript claimed that Lang Akana was racially an Asian-Hawaiian and worked in Honolulu as a public school secretary. First baseman Albert Akana, Lang's brother, worked as a title searcher in Honolulu in 1930. Forty-seven years old in 1930, the one-time speedy outfielder En Sue Pung was a son of a Chinese immigrant and a Native Hawaiian. Racially described as Chinese, Pung sold hardware. Hawaiian born catcher and third baseman Fred "Denny" Markham was described in the 1910 census as an eighteen year old Caucasian-Hawaiian. Both of his parents were born in Hawaii. His father, who was a prominent Honolulu politician, had parents born in Hawaii as did Markham's maternal grandmother. However, his paternal grandfather was born in Germany. The 1930 census claimed Markham worked as a territorial clerk. In 1930, thirty-seven-year-old utility player James Aylett was unemployed. He was racially described as an Asian Hawaiian and a son of Hawaiian born parents. A son of Chinese immigrants, Hawaiian born Sam Hop, who managed the team in 1913 and 1914, was employed by a soda company in 1910. He operated a chop suey shop in Honolulu in 1930. Hop was born in Honolulu in the mid–1880s of Chinese immigrant parents. Outfielder Andy Yamashiro was thirty-six years old in 1930. Both of his parents were Japanese immigrants. His father ran a Honolulu hotel, where Andy apparently worked. Pitcher Luck Yee, racially depicted as Chinese, had a Chinese father and a Hawaiian mother in the 1930 census, which also indicated he worked in a Honolulu auto shop.[3]

The recruitment of players possessing little or no Chinese ancestry and surnames such as Markham, Robinson, Moriyama, and Yamashiro posed a problem for the creative team manager Sam Hop. When Markham joined the team in 1913, the *Pacific Commercial Advertiser* wondered, "What Chinese name Markham will take is undecided but the manager of the Travelers will no doubt find something to meet the emergency."[4]

As it turned out, Markham was frequently listed as Mock or Mock Ham in the box scores. Foster Robinson was transformed into Ah Heong or Foster Heong. Once the Moriyama brothers, Chinito and Tsuneo, joined the team, they became J. Chin and T. Chin. Meanwhile, Andy Yamashiro was known as Andy Yim. And Native Hawaiian Luther Kekoa, a fine pitcher and hitter, turned into Ako.[5]

This use of non–Chinese Hawaiian athletes eventually got Sam Hop into hot water with Honolulu's Chinatown's commercial interests and baseball fans. Clearly, Chinese Honolulans expected the ballplayers to represent them on the American mainland. At least, according, to one mainland press

Emerging out of Honolulu's Chinatown, the Chinese or Hawaiian Travelers barnstormed the American mainland annually from 1912 to 1916. In this photo, the ballplayers (c. 1913) may not know where their eyes should be, but when the game started their eyes were usually on the ball. (Courtesy of Library of Congress, Prints and Photographs Division.)

report, Chinese Honolulans hoped that the Hawaiian barnstormers would do away with the vicious overgeneralizations many mainlanders entertained of the Chinese living in America. In August 1912, readers of Ohio's *Elyria Evening Telegram* learned Honolulu's Chinese merchants wanted the traveling team to show the "people of the United States that all Chinamen are not laundrymen or cooks." This is why, the article went on, each player possessed at least a secondary education and why they all spoke "English, in addition to the four other languages which are commonly heard on the Hawaiian Islands as fluently as they play baseball." The then manager, Edward Yap, moreover, told the press late in the 1912 tour much the same thing—that the team he ran would demonstrate to the American mainland that not all Chinese operated laundries or chop suey restaurants.[6]

The Hawaiian Travelers' trek through the American mainland inspired a certain amount of confusion. For one thing, the marketing of the team as representative of the non-existent Chinese University of Hawaii proved perplexing to the island press. Nevertheless, mainland sportswriters continued to refer to the nine's association to the Chinese University of Hawaii or the College of Hawaii even through 1916. Indeed, Sam Hop was misidentified as a student of the College of Hawaii by a Philadelphia daily.[7]

Confronting Stereotypes

Mainlanders responded to the arrival of the Hawaiian athletes by frequently dredging up pernicious stereotypes regarding the ability of Asian Pacific Islander people to compete effectively in a tough, physically strenuous game such as baseball—stereotypes that, more importantly, denied Asian Pacific Islander people the ability to lead multifaceted lives. Mainlanders often, however, recognized that the Travelers were able to transcend those stereotypes. In May 1912, the *New York Sun* account of the Hawaiians' defeat at the hands of Seton Hall claimed that a large crowd was attracted to the local minor league park in Newark, New Jersey, "by the reputation of the Orientals that had preceded them." Once in the seats and in the bleachers, "the multitude derived much amusement from the antics of the Mongolians, particularly the celestial coachers." In Grand Rapids, Michigan, in 1912, Bill Gilbert, who managed a professional nine, said, "Little did I ever think, when I used to take my father's shirt to the little laundry around the corner, that I'd ever be out watching Chinamen play baseball." Another local manager responded, "Sure, I never dreamed they had it in them.... Did you see that now?" as shortstop Vernon Ayau raced around the base path to score for the "Yellow Peril."[8]

Much of the mainland press did not intend to malign the Hawaiian visitors but they still managed to deprive them of their human complexity. In announcing the Hawaiian team's arrival on the American mainland, the Associated Press noted that the "Celestial Ball players" possessed "unmixed Oriental blood." While they were all U.S. citizens, they retained the "Hawaiian love of music and skill in singing." They were, moreover, proud of their ability to "talk United States." Very early in the Hawaiians' 1912 trek, a *San Francisco Call* account was headlined "Chinese .900 in Baseball Slang." The reporter observed that "the Celestials displayed an astonishing knowledge of the game." Moreover, they showed a "surprising mastery of baseball slang such as 'On your toes, boys,' 'peaches and cream,' 'good night' and numerous other kindred phrases were frequently used to the great delight of the fans."[9]

A writer for the *Arizona Daily Star* insisted in April 1915 that "[t]he introduction of Celestials into the great national pastime will undoubtedly tend toward the moral uplift of the game." Sally Jacobs additionally asserted that the visitors' "polite and courteous manner was contagious," leading to not one sign of ill-temper directed toward anyone, including the umpire.[10]

"A Snappy Brand of Ball"

The Hawaiian barnstormers earned not always grudging respect from the mainland press. In May, 1912 the *New York Sun* declared, "The Oriental aggregation showed a keen knowledge of baseball, having the ability to play the national game in a manner that amazed the hundreds of [Fordham] rooters." In the November 1913 edition of *Current Opinion*, a journalist maintained, "We were startled by the announcement that a club of Chinese students was on its way from the Chinese University in Hawaii to play our college clubs. It was still more startling to find, when the Chinese club came, that its members were wonderful base-runners, that in the tricks of the game they had nothing to learn from Americans, and that in many cases they were victorious over our college teams."[11]

The Hawaiians' speed and fielding provoked the most praise. After beating Stanford, the university's newspaper claimed, "The Mongolians had a fast infield and put up a snappy brand of ball." In 1914, the *Fort Wayne Journal-Gazette* noted that the Indiana University nine "repelled the invasion of the fast Chinese players ... defeating the brown skin men, 9 to 5." Upon defeating a semi-pro team in Adrian, Michigan, the *Detroit Free Press* in 1915 claimed that the "Chinamen ran the bases a la Ty Cobb" and fielded in a "sensational manner."[12]

The Hawaiians seem to have mastered the "inside game" that prevailed in pre–Babe Ruth baseball ninety years ago. Bob Shand, a San Francisco sportswriter, wrote in 1913 that "the Chinese know how to play ball. They are fast as lightening [sic] on the bases and toss in bunches of inside ball. They have the delayed steal and the double steal down pat and they know how to acquire base hits when such things are necessary." Two years later, a Texas sportswriter noted of one Hawaiian ballplayer that "Mr. Yap showed that he knew some inside ball." First baseman Albert Yap, with two men on and no outs in the ninth, bunted the runners over into better scoring position. The next Hawaiian batter drove in the two runners with a single, thus giving the Travelers vital insurance runs in their victory over Rice.[13]

At their best, the Travelers combined athleticism with guile. In West Philadelphia in 1914, 4,000 fans showed up to watch them play a local semi-pro Victrix nine. According to one mainland account, the spectators displayed "no little surprise" at seeing the Victrix team downed by the "Yellow Peril." A presumably knowledgeable observer told the press that it was doubtful if the Victrix ballplayers had ever been subdued by "such a display of Inside Baseball." The Hawaiians dropped fly balls intentionally in order to make double plays, while using the suicide squeeze bunt effectively. Moreover, "the baserunning of the Chinamen was to many an enigma, the cunningness, speed and agility bewildering at times the players and spectators." The fact that a good number of the Travelers were no longer "Chinamen" in 1914 slipped the notice of many mainland sportswriters and fans.[14]

Mainlanders frequently asserted that the Hawaiian ballplayers' multilingual facility afforded them an edge over ballplayers who knew only American English. In July 1912, readers of the *Sheboygan Press* discovered, "Those Chinese ball players who in our midst are not setting the world afire by their playing, but their language gives them a great advantage over their American brethren in jawing at the umpire." In August 1912, the *Elyria Evening Telegram* asserted that the Hawaiians had defeated a Cleveland semi-pro outfit because their coaches did not have to use English to impart strategy. The Ohio daily added, "The members of the team all speak, beside their native tongue, Japanese, Portuguese and the conglomerate languages of the Hawaiian Islands. What they do to those on the coaching lines is simply shameful and no team is said to be able to withstand the bombardment of gutturals and exclamations." Nearly three years later, the Travelers apparently puzzled the University of Missouri nine when their coaches shouted out instructions in Hawaiian and Chinese.[15]

The Hawaiian pitchers, especially Foster Robinson, Apau Kau, and Luck Yee, more often than not did their job. As mentioned earlier, the Maui born Robinson possessed Chinese and European ancestry. Still, the *Washington*

Post hailed him as "the Matty of the Far East." The fact that the right hander was not Ah Heong gained recognition over time. A Reading, Pennsylvania, daily called him "[t]he Chinaman with the American name." In 1914, Robinson performed a stunt generally associated with Satchel Paige and other talented Negro League pitchers. Pitching against Occidental College in Los Angeles, Robinson got himself into a two out jam, with runners on second and third. Robinson then ordered all of his fielders off the field and proceeded to fan the Occidental batter for the third out.[16]

Apau Kau pitched more games for the Travelers than anyone else. Born in Hawaii in 1893, Apau Kau was depicted as a twenty-one-year-old Chinese in the S.S. *Honolulan* manifest as it embarked for the mainland in early March of 1914. However, he was racially described by his 1917 draft registration card as Malaysian, although the word Mongolian was struck out. Thus while I have not been able to find any census data on him, Apau Kau most likely possessed Hawaiian as well as Chinese ancestry.[17]

Apau Kau commanded respect as the Travelers' primary hurler, except in 1913 and 1914 when he shared the ace's mantle with Robinson. When the Hawaiians beat Penn State, Apau Kau's pitching "proved an enigma" to the losers in June 1913. A week later, the Holy Cross learned to their dismay that "Apau was the master of the situation in every inning."[18]

Apau Kau apparently was no Walter Johnson. He could throw hard but concentrated on control and consistency, as well as a curious windup which deceived batters and base runners alike. According to observers, he stopped his windup prematurely and then suddenly threw the ball. Some complained that he uniformly balked with men on base. In 1912, the *Grand Rapids Times* maintained that even though the "Chinese pitcher Apau Kau" was pitching his third game out of the last six the Hawaiians played, he still managed to fool Grand Rapids batters with regularity. Making Apau Kau even harder to hit was that he reportedly picked up the spitball with the help of Hall of Fame pitcher Ed Walsh. In 1914, the *Indianapolis Star* speculated that Apau Kau might make it to the big leagues thanks to his "elusive shoots and smoking speed."[19]

Perhaps the highlight of Apau Kau's career with the Travelers came in 1915 when he hurled a no hit game against Baylor in Waco, Texas. A clipping from the *Waco Morning Star* published in the *Baseball Monthly* reported that the "clever young American citizen of Chinese descent" struck out twenty and did not seem to know he was pitching a no-hitter until the seventh inning. Albert Yap, who was the regular first baseman for the Travelers for much of the year, wrote home by way of the *Honolulu Star-Bulletin*. Yap claimed that Apau Kau's spitball worked fine, while his other offerings were too puzzling for the Baylor batsmen: "All they did was to go up to the batter's box, take the count and slip back to the bench."[20]

A son of a Chinese immigrant father and a Hawaiian mother, Luck Yee had plenty of talent, although probably not as much as Foster Robinson or Apau Kau. In the spring of 1915, the *Pacific Commercial Advertiser* pronounced him "by far the best Chinese pitcher hereabout." Yet pitching in the Travelers' first game in New York City against Fordham in 1912, Luck Yee's wildness, according to the *New York Times*, might have cost the Hawaiians the game. Yet the next year, he two-hit a professional nine in Ogden, Utah.[21]

A number of the Travelers' position players attracted praise. Lai Tin, who generally played third for the Travelers, was often singled out for his fine fielding, swift base running, and timely hitting. Lai Tin's skills would eventually gain him notice from mainland professional teams. According to the *Pacific Commercial Advertiser* in 1913, Lai Tin was one of Honolulu's favorite ballplayers: "Among the crack players of the All-Chinese baseball team, now on the eve of a second trip to the mainland, there is probably no one better liked by the fans and fanettes who have made Athletic Park there [sic] Sunday afternoon home than Lai Tin, third baseman and all around athlete." The *New York Times* noticed that in the previously mentioned 1912 Fordham game that Lai Tin "grabbed hard grounders of the most puzzling variety" just as former big leaguers Art Devlin and Jimmy Collins once did. Lai Tin had his bad days at the hot corner. His errors probably cost the Hawaiians victory in their extra inning game against Georgetown in May 1912. Lai Tin was one of the Travelers' more consistent hitters. Not generally known for his power, Lai Tin still crushed two grand slam home runs against the University of Utah in April 1912 as the Hawaiians beat the Utah nine 22–15.[22]

Although only twenty-one years old in 1915, Lai Tin emerged as the team's field commander. Sally Jacobs reported that Lai Tin became a fan darling in Arizona. She wrote, "He has the most marvelous way of doing things getting a great deal out of nothing, you know. He made a single and stretched it into a three-bagger just on account of a little home grown error." Then, he sped home on an overthrow. In the midst of the team's Eastern swing, the third baseman was laid up with a "charley horse." Albert Yap conceded that Lai Tin was missed as a player. Still, the Chinese Hawaiian did a good job of coaching from the sidelines. Yap observed that Lai Tin possessed plenty of "pep."[23]

Shortstop Vernon Ayau was one of the smaller players on the team but his sure hands, strong arm, and speed won admirers and interest from professional teams on the mainland. Early in the 1912 tour, one mainland daily called Ayau a "little, wiry youth" and "the fastest and most accurate fielder" on the team. A Binghamton, New York, daily said Ayau could become a star if he added some weight. The *Detroit News* was more impressed with Ayau than any of the Hawaiian Travelers in 1912, pointing out that he was the team's best hitter, possessed good range at shortstop and a good arm. The Detroit daily predicted that he would be a "sure-nough star."[24]

Lang Akana was an outfielder with both speed and relative power. The Chinese Hawaiian, whose brother Albert played first base and wielded a valuable bat for the Travelers, went three for three in a 1912 game against Chicago's Uncle Sams, a reputedly talented semi-pro squad. Moreover, according to the *Chicago Tribune*, Akana performed an unassisted triple play after catching a shallow fly ball. A report in the *Oakland Tribune* declared that Akana's only real weakness as a left handed batter was that he could not lay off the high and tight fastballs.[25]

A son of Chinese immigrants, Kan Yen Chun was a small but skilled catcher. He also knew what to do with a bat. In March 1913, the *Pacific Commercial Advertiser* called him the Travelers' best hitter. While Kan Yen Chun's defensive skills generally warranted praise, the *Washington Evening Star* conceded that while his arm was strong it also was erratic in the 1912 game against Georgetown. Later in the 1912 tour, however, Kan Yen "proved a wonder at cutting down men on bases" in a game against a Chicago semi-pro squad in September.[26]

Three Japanese Hawaiians, Andy Yamashiro and the two Moriyama brothers, helped the Travelers as nimble fielders, quick base runners, solid hitters, and occasionally effective pitchers. Tracking their exploits is not made easier, however, by the fact that they played under supposedly Chinese names. Yamashiro was Yim, while the Moriyama brothers were J. Chin and T. Chin. Late in the 1916 tour, the *Indianapolis Star* reported on the Travelers losing both ends of a doubleheader against the African American Taylor ABCs. However, the *Star* pronounced Yim and J. Chin as two of the "Celestial" standouts because of their "clever" base running. All three Japanese Hawaiians pitched. Tsuneo Moriyama, or T. Chin, was called the team's "spitball artist" by Albert Yap in 1915. Yap reported that "Chin" hurled a steady game as the Travelers defeated West Virginia's Marshal College in 1915. However, both of the Moriyama brothers were in the box when the Portland Beavers of the Pacific Coast League slugged their way to a 19-4 victory over the Hawaiians.[27]

Team Finances

The Hawaiian Travelers may have furnished the islands with good publicity and hopefully inspired mainlanders to think twice about the stereotypes they may have entertained about Asian Pacific Islanders. However, it is unclear as to how successful they were at making money for their promoters. They did not seem to have made much money themselves. Because they were promoted as amateurs, the ballplayers at any rate could not pocket the revenue made at college games. Moreover, there is some evidence that at least their 1912 tour was mismanaged as the destitute team was stranded for awhile in New York City.[28]

The tour was initially arranged by Robert Yap, a Chinese Hawaiian musician living in Chicago. Yap was apparently at least an acquaintance of Pat Page, who coached the University of Chicago baseball team and had previously helped schedule games played by Japanese university teams on the American mainland. Page, according to the *Washington Post*, was expected to advise Yap on booking games throughout the country. Yap's brother, Edward, meanwhile managed the team on a daily basis.[29]

But very early on in the 1912 tour Honolulu dailies expressed concern about the lack of games played by the All-Chinese. The first two games of the tour were played a week apart and the *Pacific Commercial Advertiser* complained that the team better play more games if they were going to make it financially. A month later, however, the *Advertiser* appeared more content as games came "thick and fast" while the Hawaiian ballplayers moved eastward. However, the bookings seemingly did not come "thick and fast" enough. Players expressed dissatisfaction with the Yap brothers. Eventually, the well known and not always well liked Nat Strong took over the scheduling and promotion of the Hawaiian team sometime in 1912. Once the Brooklyn-based Strong began handling the bookings, the *Advertiser* maintained, the controversial baseball promoter "did well by the local boys."[30]

Hurry Up and Play

Traveling about the mainland, trying to get to bookings on time, sometimes proved challenging for the Hawaiian Travelers. The *Baseball Monthly* published an article by Sing Hung Hoe. The Chinese Hawaiian outfielder said he and his teammates, while appreciative of the courtesies extended to them by many mainlanders, were glad to return to their "home burg" of Honolulu after the 1913 trek. In Honolulu, the ballplayers felt "safe and free — safe because we no longer have to jump on moving trains with our heavy suitcases and baseball paraphernalia in order not to disappoint our white cousins in the different cites." In Honolulu, as well, "We can take all the time we want for our meals, instead of the quick-order dinners at the crowded railroad stations and 'dog houses,' with many curious eyes staring at you.

We have as much sweet sleep as we please and find more comfort on our cozy little beds than those of the noisy night trains or on the twelfth or fifteenth story of some hotels."[31]

In 1915, Albert Yap's correspondence to the *Honolulu Star-Bulletin* frequently described the sometimes harrowing and sometimes tedious treks from one small town to another on the American mainland ninety years ago. After losing to a Stockton ball club early in the 1915 tour, Yap informed *Star-Bulletin* readers that before the game his team had traveled on a "train for three and a half odd hours and this had a bad effect on many of the boys, besides a few have been slightly laid up from the game before."[32]

Once in the Midwest, the team's schedule became more hectic, although Yap did not seem overly stressed by it all. On April 26, the team was in Missouri, taking in the sights of St. Louis before heading to Ames, Iowa, where the Hawaiians played Iowa State on April 27. They had an "easy time" in the game, winning 6–2. Then they "made a rush to the 7:05 train for Vermillon S.D.," where the Hawaiians were scheduled to play the University of South Dakota on April 28. Once in Vermillon, the Hawaiians defeated the University of South Dakota 5–2, but, according to Yap, "it took 10 thrilling innings to fight for this supremacy." On April 29, the Hawaiians left Vermillon at 4 A.M. in order to return to Iowa. Nineteen hours later they arrived at Decorah, Iowa. Yap could only exclaim, "Some jump!" The next day, they beat Luther College 7–1. Yap wrote, "The mayor of the town threw the first ball. The attendance was very good and was chiefly made up of the town's ball fans." At 11:05 A.M. on May 1, the Hawaiians departed Decorah for Prairie du Chien, Wisconsin.[33]

On the way to Prairie du Chien, the team "jumped off at North McGregor's Landing, then took a gasoline launch across the Mississippi." The Hawaiians arrived at 3:15 P.M., May 1, for a game with Campion College. The game was supposed to have started at 2:45 P.M.. While they "went into the game without any batting practice," the Hawaiians still won 12 to 3.[34]

In New England, travel did not get much easier. Furthermore, according to Yap, making onerous train connections did not help the Hawaiian ball club's winning record against very tough competition. On the way to Lewiston, Maine, where they were scheduled to oppose Bates College, the Hawaiians discovered that taking a train to Lewiston from Hanover, New Hampshire, was no simple matter. The team had to leave its hotel in Hanover at 3:30 A.M. to catch the train. Then the Hawaiians suffered through five transfers to arrive at Lewiston at 12:30 P.M. Yap understandably maintained, "Though we lost to Bates College it was fairly excusable." Indeed, Bates won 14–6, but Yap would not concede anything: "[W]e hit the ball almost as hard as they did, though we were fatigued. We had many chances to score through a number of consecutive hits, but our poor tired legs couldn't carry us any faster." Luther Kekoa hit well and Markham managed a home run. Still in Maine, the Hawaiians traveled to Bangor to play the University of Maine nine. The Travelers won 8–3, thanks to timely hitting. Yap reported, "The game was witnessed by a fairly large crowd, who applauded the different good plays throughout the entire game."[35]

Controversy

The barnstormers aroused controversy on occasion. In August 1914, Sam Hop brought his team into Gettysburg, Pennsylvania. According to the *Gettysburg Star and Sentinel*, "Sam Hop and his yellow warriors" had just arrived after losing badly to a Chambersburg nine. Then, the "Chinks" departed before playing their scheduled game in Gettysburg. Hop explained that he did not think the game would draw because of inclement weather. Nor, according to the Gettysburg daily, did he think that lingering would reap any profit. Locals apparently sought to change Hop's mind but to no avail.[36]

The barnstormers got into trouble with some pious North American ethnic Chinese. In the summer of 1912, the All-Chinese nine was scheduled to cross the border into Canada. The *Honolulu Star-Bulletin* reported that the ballplayers' venture into international baseball proved less than a grand success. It told readers that the All-Chinese had gained Honolulu and Hawaii a bad reputation among Canadians, most particularly the Chinese Canadian community of Montreal. That is, the All-Chinese were "advertising Hawaii as a land of howling savages and ungodly heathens. Even their own countrymen in Montreal have turned from the Chinese ball-tossers in holy horror." What the All-Chinese had done to damage the Hawaiian image was that apparently Nat Strong or Robert Yap had scheduled a game on Sunday in Montreal. Making matters worse was that the team arrived in and departed from Montreal on the Protestant Sabbath day.[37]

The *Star-Bulletin* cited a report published in a Montreal daily to prove its point. The *Montreal Witness* reported that the "Chinese Christians of Montreal" did not approve of the Hawaiians' Sunday game. They would have gladly welcomed the game on any other day. But Montreal's Chinese Christian Association issued a protest, maintaining that the "Hawaii University Team" played baseball on Sunday "to the dishonor of God and the discredit of the new Republic of China."[38]

Two years later, according to the *Pacific Commercial Advertiser,* the team was waylaid at Angels Island in San Francisco Bay. The U.S. government had installed an immigration center on the center to detain and investigate Chinese immigrants it believed wanted to get into the country using false documents. Apparently, "the citizenship of Sammy Hop's artists was put in question." The Hawaiian ballplayers might have had to wait on the island for twenty-four hours. However, Albert Taylor, a former employee of the *Advertiser* and at that time the San Francisco representative of the Hawaii Promotion Committee, made the necessary calls and the ballplayers were permitted on shore.[39]

Regardless of the obstacles, the barnstorming Hawaiian team put together an impressive record on the mainland against an assortment of college and semi-professional teams as well as against prominent African American professional nines such as the Philadelphia Royal Giants, Lincoln Giants, and the Taylor ABC's. In 1912, the Hawaiians won sixty-six games, lost forty-nine, and tied four. The next year, the Hawaiians won 103 and lost forty. In 1914, a team weakened by the loss of Akana and Lai Tin still managed to win 131 of 157 games. Its last season on the mainland saw the Travelers playing 135 games, winning 77 and losing 56.[40]

While generally praised on the islands for their ability to more than hold their own against mainlanders, the Travelers, especially while managed by Sam Hop, were not universally loved at home. After the 1912 tour, the team, known in Oahu as the All-Chinese, was challenged by several island teams. However, Sam Hop did not want to put the team on display unless it was properly compensated. For example, the Travelers were expected to oppose a military nine at Oahu's Schofield Barracks. They did not show up and Hop explained that the team would not appear unless it was guaranteed 60 percent of the gate, regardless of which nine won. Hop was rumored to have boasted that the Travelers were like heavyweight champion Jack Johnson, who, the Chinese Hawaiian said, did not fight unless he was guaranteed a majority of the receipts. Critics complained that Hop was making an outlandish comparison. The *Commercial Advertiser* complained, "The All-Chinese baseball nine is as far from reaching [Jack Johnson's] station, as the north is from the south pole, if not a little further."[41]

Playing Professionals

The Hawaiian Travelers usually did not disgrace themselves against high level white and black professional teams. However, there is no evidence they played against any white major league team. Early in the 1915 tour, the Travelers appeared in San Jose to oppose the Pacific Coast League's Salt Lake City team. Articles in the *San Jose Mercury* promoted the game, the Hawaiian athletes, and American imperial ambitions. The articles the *Mercury* printed undoubtedly stretched things a bit in the effort to lure paying customers to the local ballpark. One article declared that the Hawaiian club "is without doubt the greatest drawing card playing baseball in the United States." More realistically, it maintained that the Travelers were a good team — the equivalent of many American minor league aggregations. In another article, *Mercury* readers were told, "Uncle Sam is pulling another of his wise old tricks in sending these boys around the country" and that "Our Uncle is showing off his ability as a developer of races and as a teacher in this baseball trip." There was nothing exotic about the ballplayers in that the "most interesting thing about these young fellows is that they are regular — not different, not unusual." However, they were also "refined gentlemen of the highest type." And they reminded the writer of typical American "college boys." In other words, "They speak English, spend rainy afternoons around the piano, ragtime music and Hawaiian songs are popular with them. 'Ring, Ring Hawaii, ring/Swell the chorus of our song.'"[42]

At San Jose's Luna Park, the PCL team edged the Hawaiians 3–2. The *San Jose Mercury* boasted that the game drew the largest crowd ever to the San Jose ball grounds. The Hawaiians, furthermore, pleased observers with their command of "inside baseball." And the *Mercury* contended that the "clever Chinese" performed with the "aplomb of major leaguers." The game, however, could have been marred when Lai Tin aggressively knocked down a Salt Lake infielder while sliding into second. A bit of a commotion stirred in the stands apparently at the sight of a non-white player forgetting his racial manners. Still, according to a press account published in the *Los Angeles Times*, the fans in the bleachers "unmistakably root[ed] for the Chinese to win." The game was well played on both sides and the "University of Hawaii showed that they knew the American game." Apau Kau's pitching, in particular, proved impressive. A few weeks later, the Hawaiians did much less well against the Portland Beavers of the Pacific Coast League. According to one press account, the Beavers beat the "China boys" 20–4.[43]

The Hawaiian Travelers often played formidable black teams such as the Chicago American Giants, the Lincoln Giants, and the Taylor ABCs. In 1912, however, the Hawaiians had reportedly refused to play the Lincoln Giants. In late July, the *Decatur Review* published a wire story on the matter under the headline "Chinese Draw Color Line." The story declared, "The color line has been drawn in a great many cases but this one may be tied, but not beaten. The Chinese baseball team that came over here with a great reputation was challenged by the Lincoln Giants of New York recently. The answer came back from the yellow boys that they drew the color line and would not mingle." However, the fact that Nat Strong took over management of the Hawaiian baseball tour some time in 1912 might have changed matters. Strong, who both notoriously exploited and openly boosted African American baseball teams, may have convinced the Hawaiians that playing black nines made monetary sense.[44]

In Chicago in 1913, the Hawaiians opposed the famed Chicago American Giants, a pioneering black team headed by Rube Foster. The *Chicago Defender*, an influential black newspaper, publicized the game by telling readers that the American Giants would take on a "crack Chinese team." Yet despite the fact that the home team won by only 3–2, the *Defender* insisted that the Giants "had easy pickings and played horse with the little men from the University of Hawaii and the best the brown men could do with curves of Lindsay was to connect twice."[45]

In New York City, the Hawaiian Travelers played elite black professional nines such as the Lincoln Giants. In 1914, the African American *New York Age* noted that the Hawaiians' "star pitcher" Apau Kau shut out the Giants 2–0. However, the Giants also beat the Hawaiian team 5–4 in 1914 before a packed crowd at New York City's Olympic Field. The *Age* noted that despite losing the "Orientals" played "sensational" ball.[46]

In promoting an upcoming game between "the Chinese University team" and the "Lincoln Giants World's Colored Champion" in 1915, the *Age* declared, "The Chinese players have a big following and a great crowd is expected to be on hand at Olympic Field to cheer and root for them." Under the headline "Lincoln Giants Take Chinese Cues," the *Age* maintained that the 7,000 people who arrived to watch the game comprised the largest crowd of the season in Olympic Field. They saw the Giants down the "Chinese team of the University of Hawaii" rather handily 8–2. However, Apau Kau hit well and the Hawaiians gave the crowd an exhibition of "shadow ball," in which players acrobatically tossed to each other an imaginary ball, winning the crowd's approval.[47]

A derisive *New York Times* also covered the game. The headline reflected the contempt the *Times*' writer displayed for both the Hawaiian and the black athletes: "Chinese Minus Pigtails Lose Game." Because the Hawaiian ballplayers, some of whom possessed no Chinese ancestry anyway, did not wear "pigtails," they "were helpless before the darktown tossers," who were undaunted by the Hawaiians' "funny names." The *Times* perhaps accurately complained that the Hawaiians did not seem to take the game seriously. The visitors engaged in "acrobatic stunts" and performed "handsprings" while the Giants beat them. Moreover, "the men from the Orient jabbered delightedly" when they got two runs, "but the watermelon smile never faded from the dusky Lincoln players."[48]

The next week the Hawaiians came out on top. Apau Kau tossed a shutout against the Giants before another crowd of 7,000. The *Age* enthused, "The Orientals played a flashy brand of ball that kept the 7,000 fans on edge from start to finish." Apparently, the defeat marked the Giants first loss of the summer. However, even Lincoln Giants' fans could go home comforted by the fact that they were "held spellbound" by the "wonderful hitting and fielding of the Chinese team." The Giants, according to the *Baltimore Afro-American,* were not so easily satisfied. They were apparently "furious" at being shut down by the "Chinese University" team and would engage in a "battle for blood" in the rubber game between them and the Travelers. The *Afro-American* predicted an exciting game the following weekend when "Apau the great Chinese pitcher" would hook up with Cyclone Joe Williams. However, sadly, that game was cancelled by rain and the Hawaiians were due to leave the mainland for a stopover in Cuba before returning home.[49]

In May 1916, the Travelers faced the Taylor ABC's. The *Indianapolis Star* expected the Hawaiians to give the ABC's a good battle and promised readers that the "Chinese will also put on an exhibition of shadow ball and juggling before the game." While the Hawaiians lost, the *Chicago Defender* expressed an ethnocentric amazement that the Hawaiians played baseball so well. It declared that "some of the Chinese act like real ballplayers and there is no doubt that they like the game. They were caught on the bases several times by snappy throws, but appeared to know many of the American tricks." Toward the end of the 1916 tour, the Hawaiians competed in a doubleheader against the Taylor ABC's in Indianapolis. The Hawaiian of indigenous ancestry, Luther Kekoa, lost the first game 4–2. In the second game, Apau Kau could do little better as the Travelers lost 5–3. The *Indianapolis Star*, in any event, hailed the "Chinks"' Lai as a fielding star and the base running of "Yim" and "J. Chin."[50]

Representing

In 1912, Honolulu's Chinese Hawaiian community happily supported the Travelers as its bridge to the American mainland. Honolulu's Chinese merchants and business people proved vital in raising $6,000 to send the team to the mainland. And they feted the team to an impressive wharfside reception followed by a banquet on its return to Honolulu in October. Clearly Honolulu's Chinatown was proud of the fact that the Chinese Hawaiian nine achieved a credible record of more victories than defeats on the mainland. A prominent Chinese Hawaiian sports devotee, Kim Tong Ho, served as toastmaster. The players, moreover, were well fed. Honolulu's Chinese cooks "are good baseball fans ... and they intend to offer the boys something which they have been missing during their long absence," the *Pacific Commercial Advertiser* explained. The players sat at "seven round tables," according to the *Star-Bulletin*, "set with all the Chinese delicacies a person can think of."⁵¹

Chinese Hawaiian merchants on both Oahu and Maui celebrated the Travelers' return in 1913. Upon their arrival in Honolulu, the Hawaiian ballplayers were greeted by the Chinese consul, as well as members of the Chung Wah Merchants' Association, which furnished automobiles that transported the ballplayers around Honolulu and to a reception at the Chinese consulate. Within a week, prominent members of Honolulu's Chinese community honored the ballplayers with a large banquet at Sun Yin Wo Hall on the city's Hotel Street. Chuck Hoy, described by the *Honolulu Star-Bulletin* as a community leader, served as toastmaster, while the Chinese consul Chen Ching Ho remarked, with perhaps a bit of an exaggeration, that all of China was proud of the team's accomplishments. He hoped that the team could one day visit China and teach baseball to Chinese eager to learn America's National Pastime. A few days later, the team was in Maui where Chinese merchants of Kahului treated them to a banquet.⁵²

By 1914, Honolulu's Chinese community expressed disenchantment with the Travelers and their manager, Sam Hop, who recruited key Hawaiian ballplayers of non–Chinese ancestry to perform for the supposedly All-Chinese team on the mainland. Just before the team was set to head across the Pacific, Lai Tin and Lang Akana announced they wanted to remain in Honolulu. They maintained that they preferred to hold on to their jobs and Lai Tin added that his parents did not want him to make the trip. Thus Hop was forced to scramble for talent. And he began to bring into the fold Hawaiian players of non–Chinese ancestry such as Luther Kekoa and Chinito Moriyama.⁵³

Claiming they were tired of Hop's "methods," merchants from Honolulu's Chinatown wanted to back what they considered a truly All-Chinese team composed of players entirely of the "Chinese race." This nine would compete locally in the Oahu baseball league and would suit up several players who had formerly played with the Travelers — players such as Lai Tin, "Honolulu's premier third baseman," as well as Lang Akana, and Sing Hung Hoe. According to Hop's Chinese Hawaiian critics, these athletes had apparently grown disillusioned with the manager's "graft."⁵⁴

Li Hong Kong, a Chinatown sports enthusiast, condemned Hop for failing to organize a truly All-Chinese nine. Somewhat inaccurately in the case of Foster Robinson and his brother, Alvin, Li Hong Kong maintained: "Not one half of the men [recruited by Hop] are Chinese. Denny Markham, Foster Robinson, Alvin Robinson, Kekoa and Chinito Moriyama are not sons of the New Republic and Hop knows it and every fan in Honolulu knows." He conceded that when the team first started for the mainland in 1912 it fairly represented Chinese Hawaiians but such was no longer the case. Kong declared that only three or four players on the traveling team actually possessed Chinese ancestry. The rest, he pointed out, were Japanese Hawaiian and part-Hawaiian. Kong believed that Honolulu's Chinese community deserved representation in Oahu baseball circles by a real All-Chinese team just as the Asahis represented the local Japanese community.[55]

W. Tin Chong, president of Honolulu's Chinese Athletic Union, backed Li Hong Kong. Chong called for the formation of a CAU team in the Oahu League. He said that that a CAU team, entirely composed of Chinese Hawaiians, would draw Honolulu fans in general and fans from Honolulu's Chinese community in particular. Chong argued that many Chinese Honolulans had grown into baseball "bugs" who wanted representation from a team that truthfully stood for them and fielded good players such as Lai Tin and Lang Akana. The *Pacific Commercial Advertiser* agreed. It purported that the CAU "represents the sports-loving Chinese of Oahu, and they are loyal in their support of a baseball team, and a representative team as W. Tin Chong proposes putting in the field would be a great drawing card."[56]

Indeed, as the previous chapter points out, a fine CAU nine, led by Lai Tin, was formed while Hop's Travelers still managed to win more than their share of games in 1914. In 1915, Hop remained on the islands as the daily management of the team fell largely to Lai Tin and Apau Kau.

Significantly, the Travelers represented Hawaii as much, if not more, than Hawaiian Chinese. This was widely recognized by non–Chinese Hawaiians as well as some of the players themselves, even those players possessing Chinese ancestry. Honolulu commercial interests, backed by the Honolulu press, claimed that the Travelers generally created excellent publicity for the islands. Initially, the ballplayers were expected to stage Hawaiian-themed theatrical performances after their mainland games — an expectation which apparently went unfulfilled. In 1912, the great Duke Kahanamoku was making American sports fans aware of Hawaii as a nurturer of world class athletes and the Travelers were often associated with the Olympic champion. In July 1912, the *Honolulu Star-Bulletin* claimed that the All-Chinese aided Kahanamoku in dispensing good publicity on the mainland for Hawaii.[57]

Upon their return to Honolulu in 1912, the Travelers were not only applauded by the local Chinese community but by non–Chinese Hawaiians as well. Speaking at the aforementioned banquet honoring the 1912 Travelers, a Mr. Meyer, according to the *Pacific Commercial Advertiser*, declared that "no better promotion work had ever been accomplished" than by the Chinese Hawaiian ballplayers. Meyer was pleased with the Travelers' performances but applauded even more "the good name in the States" the nine had acquired "as a bunch of well-behaved and gentlemanly fellows." Another speaker, W.A. Bowen, informed the audience that the Hawaii Promotions Committee and "several business houses" had collected $125 to buy medals for each of the returning athletes.[58]

When the team arrived home from the even more successful 1913 tour, non–Chinese Hawaiians continued to sing the barnstormers' praises as Hawaiian ambassadors. An editorial in the *Pacific Commercial Advertiser* applauded the promotional work of both the All-Chinese nine as well as the presumably All-Hawaii nine organized by Guy Green. The Hawaiian athletes behaved well, which, according to the *Advertiser*, meant more than victories. Moreover, the Hawaiians teams provided a "splendid advertising medium for Hawaii." The editorial added a hope that the Hawaii Promotions Committee could more systematically fund future tours of the mainland by Hawaiian ball teams, which "advertise the islands and their charms."[59]

At a subsequent banquet, W.R. Farrington, who would later become a territorial governor, supported the contention that the All-Chinese supplied effective advertisement for the islands. However, he urged the Chinese Hawaiian ballplayers to "consider themselves as they are considered, a part of all Hawaii, not any one race community, and work for all Hawaii." Perhaps in response to Farrington, Lai Tin thanked the Chinese community for the banquet and all of Hawaii for its support.[60]

Lai Tin, like other members of the Travelers' squad, acknowledged that their identities transcended ethnic affiliations. Perhaps, Lai Tin and other Travelers were sensitive to the fact that non–Asian Pacific Hawaiians wanted the Travelers to represent them. However, the Travelers were also very aware that despite the identities ascribed to them they were indeed Hawaiian. Before the Travelers headed off on their 1913 tour, readers of the *Pacific Commercial Advertiser* encountered a letter of appreciation written on behalf of the All-Chinese players. The letter writers wished to thank the "people of Hawaii" for their support. It said that while on the mainland, the ballplayers intended "to uphold the name of dear old Hawaii." The letter, signed by Sam Hop and Apau Kau, ended: "Although we are going to be far away from you, we will always remember the good people of Hawaii. As time does not permit, we will simply have to say Aloha Nuui now."[61]

Individual Travelers consistently expressed "aloha" to the folks back home in their letters. Manager Edward Yap wrote toward the end of the 1912 tour that the ballplayers were anxious to see Diamond Head again. They enjoyed themselves on the mainland and would be willing to embark upon another trek across the Pacific, but they also wanted to get back home. Yap declared, "Half a year is a long time to be away from Honolulu."[62]

The 25th Regiment Nine

Few island teams except for the 25th Regiment nine could rival the Travelers. The first game between the Travelers and the 25th took place right before the All-Chinese were scheduled to head on the 1913 jaunt to the mainland. The game ended in controversy as the swift Chinese Hawaiian outfielder, En Sue Pung, laid down a bunt in the ninth inning with the soldiers ahead 2–1. The army pitcher fielded the bunt but overthrew first base, prompting En Sue Pung to move on not only to second but also to try for third. Meanwhile, the overthrow hit the field umpire, an African American soldier named Patterson, who, it seemed, instinctively knocked the ball down rather than get out of the way. A 25th Regiment infielder got ahold of the ball and promptly threw En Sue Pung out at third. The Chinese Hawaiians protested that Patterson had unfairly interfered with the ball and that the 25th had not really won the game. The *Honolulu Star-Bulletin* tried to be impartial. It maintained that however disappointed Sam Hop and his players might be, the 25th Regiment nine had played well and fairly. Still, Patterson's actions, however inadvertent, had blemished the soldiers' victory and the *Star-Bulletin* sadly feared that the All-Chinese would never play the 25th team again.[63]

Indeed, first baseman Albert Akana complained that while on the mainland in 1912, "we were up against raw deals," especially in the smaller towns. He explained that usually small town American ballplayers could not beat the Hawaiians and umpires frequently decided to help out the locals against the "Chinese." However, Akana maintained that the loss against the 25th was "the worse robbery we have been up against." He added that the All-Chinese would not play the 25th again "if they gave us a thousand dollars in cold cash."[64]

Still, Honolulu baseball fans and the city's press backed the idea of a rematch. According to the *Star-Bulletin*, a fever pitch consumed Honolulu baseball fans for another game between the All-Chinese and the 25th before the Travelers embarked for the mainland. Moreover, the *Star-Bulletin* declared that the Chinese Hawaiian ballplayers' dispute was with an umpire and not the opposing ballplayers and manager. If the All-Chinese have "nothing against the players," the daily added, "why should they not play them again." And to hopefully entice the Chinese Hawaiians into another game, the 25th's manager, Lieutenant Sanders, said they could name their own managers. A rematch was arranged. This time the All-Chinese won 7–1. The soldiers' pitchers could not find the plate and Foster Robinson pitched well as Ah Heong. While played mid-week to accommodate the All-Chinese travel schedule, the game apparently drew a remarkably fine crowd.[65]

After returning to Honolulu in the fall of 1915, Lai Tin's Travelers were soon matched up against the 25th in Honolulu. The *Pacific Commercial Advertiser* asserted that there was no love lost between the Travelers and the 25th when it came to baseball. The daily insisted, "These two teams feel for each other as does a couple of strong bull dogs with a bone handy." Early in December, Lai's team beat the error-ridden 25th 6–2. Lang Akana, En Sue Pung, and Kan Yen Chun all helped the Travelers' cause offensively, while Pung, Lai Tin, and Chinito Moriyama aided it defensively. The next weekend, the soldiers got revenge, edging the Hawaiian contingent 4–3, even though Chinito Moriayama hit a homer.[66]

In October 1916 the Travelers, minus Lai Tin, Andy Yamashiro, and Apau Kau, came home to play the 25th, which had gone undefeated in Hawaii for several months, as well as a nine of major leaguers called The All-Americans. The Traveling Chinese, with Hoon Ki pitching, beat the all-black team 5–2, although it should be said that the 25th did not pitch "Bullet" Rogan, because he was perceived as more needed in a game against the All-Americans. At the same time, Vernon Ayau, the Travelers' star shortstop, was not in the lineup. Ayau was at shortstop as the Travelers gave the All-Americans all they could handle. While the All-Americans won 6–3, the *Commercial Advertiser* was impressed with the game put up by the Travelers. Ayau made two great plays, which "were marked real big league stuff without any mistake." A week later, the two teams hooked up in an exciting game that was tied at the end of the regulation nine innings before the major leaguers won. Admittedly, the All-Americans did not have any real stars but they did suit up talented players such as Native American pitcher "Chief" Johnson, who opposed Hoon Ki in a tense pitching duel. The only real blemish on Johnson's performance was Ayau's home run.[67]

Not Even a "Cup of Coffee"

Organized Baseball on the mainland asserted something of an interest in recruiting members of the Hawaiian Travelers barnstorming team. In December 1914, the press reported that "[a] full-blooded Chinese baseball player has been signed by the Chicago club of the American League. He is Lai Tin, captain of the Honolulu Chinese team. Tin is ordered to report to practice in Paso Robles next spring." Readers of the *Washington Post* learned about Lai Tin's signing on December 3. The story maintained, "In the event of Lai Tin fulfilling expectations he will enjoy the unique honor of being the first Celestial to play on a National or American League team." The *Post* called the Hawaiian ballplayer "Capt. Lai Tin of the Honolulu Chinese" and lauded him as "one of the best shortstops in the Far East"—a geographical reference that would have stunned most Hawaiians. The next day, the *Post* asserted that "an invasion from China" threatened "Organize[d] baseball." While Cubans, American Indians, and Italians could claim a place in "America's national game," the *Post* added, "up to the present, no Chinaman or Japanese has shown himself sufficiently proficient to be carried on the roster of a major league team."[68]

In January 1915, the *Oakland Tribune* published a photo of "William Tin Lai." Since the White Sox were to train in California, the photo's caption read: "Chink To Join White Sox Here." Lai Tin was also described as the first "Mongolian" to play major league baseball and a veteran of several teams that had competed "in several parts of the Eastern world," which presumably the Oakland daily did not mean as New York or Boston. In addition to making a geographical hash of Hawaii, the *Tribune* mistakenly identified Lai Tin as a member of the 1914 Travelers. Perhaps correctly, it claimed that Lai Tin's play as a Traveler had "wowed" Eastern observers and his signing, consequently, was no surprise.[69]

While the White Sox invited Lai Tin to the team's Paso Robles training camp in the spring of 1915, the Pacific Coast League's Portland Beavers signed Lang Akana. A fast and powerful outfielder, Akana's venture in Organized Baseball seems to have caused a greater stir than Lai Tin's. Portland sportswriter Roscoe Fawcett praised the home team's recruitment of Akana and the *Los Angeles Times* wondered why one of the city's two PCL franchises had not beaten Portland out for Akana's services. Fawcett claimed that PCL player Johnny Kane had seen Akana in action in Honolulu and thought the Hawaiian was a good outfielder. And acknowledging Akana's ancestry, Fawcett wrote, "No ballplayer blending half portions of poi and chop suey ever before has embellished a professional diamond." Many PCL players, nevertheless, expressed anger over playing with and against Akana. There were at least a few who argued that Akana's skin color was no lighter than that of the controversial African American prizefighter Jack Johnson. And PCL players threatened a strike if Portland chose to suit up Akana. Reluctantly, team owner Walter McCreadie submitted to the threat and Akana never played for Portland.[70]

Reporting on the Akana controversy in the *Sporting News*, Fawcett stated that McCreadie had "exploded a bombshell" when he announced his desire to put the "a half Hawaiian, half Chinese outfielder" in a Portland uniform. Calling Akana "a poi eating prodigy," Fawcett reiterated for *Sporting News* readers the dilemma that forced McCreadie to release "the Chinese horticulturalist." Akana's very short lived career with the Beavers "leaves the Chinese field clear to the Chicago White Sox. The Sox recently signed a full-blooded

Chinese whose mission in life will be to combat Buck Weaver for the job of shortstop."[71]

To its credit, the *Pacific Commercial Advertiser* voiced dismay at Portland's failure to keep its obligation to Akana. It purported that the PCL should let its players go on strike if Akana joined the league. As far as the Honolulu daily was concerned, PCL players were only afraid of losing their jobs to men such as Akana who were less white but more skilled. The *Advertiser* asserted that there was no excuse for allowing Akana to stay in Hawaii— "that the Coast League is simply enforcing an old standby rule not to let Orientals and colored men into the ranks."[72]

While his team trained in Honolulu in the spring of 1917, McCreadie considered giving Akana another shot. But, according to Portland sportswriter Lou Kennedy, Akana did not do well in games against the Beavers. Apparently, "the China boy" was a "sturdy" 181 pounder but also rusty.[73]

As for Lai Tin, he apparently never reported to the White Sox. The *San Francisco Examiner* asserted that Lai Tin did not impress the White Sox sufficiently, although it seems like he never really had the chance. While Lai Tin's racial and ethnic ancestry seems not to have bothered the White Sox openly, there was some grumbling in Honolulu that racial discrimination was the root cause of Lai Tin's failure to play for the White Sox. Another factor was that the manager who invited Lai Tin to Paso Robles was fired before spring training and that, in any event, Lai Tin would have had to compete against more seasoned veterans such as the skillful infielder Buck Weaver.[74]

Mainland professional teams, including major league franchises, apparently sought the services of other Travelers besides Lai Tin and Lang Akana. In May 1913, the *Honolulu Star-Bulletin* published rumors to the effect that the Los Angeles Angels were interested in both Kan Yen Chun and Foster Robinson "alias Aheong." The Honolulu daily was not surprised that a top flight PCL club might be interested in Robinson, but it doubted the Angels really wanted Kan Yen Chun, The *Star-Bulletin* reasoned that while Kan Yen Chun was a good enough catcher, he was physically too small to handle the load of a PCL catcher and was insufficiently talented as a batter. Moreover, readers of the *Williamsport Grit* learned: "Robinson, one of the pitchers of the Chinese baseball team, which has the longest string of victories to its credit on any club invading this country, will be given a rail by a Pacific Coast League club, presumably Los Angeles. Robinson is part Chinese, but he is the Honolulu club's star pitcher, with curves, speed and control." In 1915, the *Honolulu Star-Bulletin* reported that Cincinnati of the National League expressed an interest in signing the Maui-based pitcher. Still, Robinson lingered on Maui, pitching for the Paia nine of the Maui League in 1915.[75]

Vernon Ayau reputedly lured offers from mainland professional teams. Late in 1912, the *Pacific Commercial Advertiser* reported that a professional league in Michigan sought Ayau's services. The *New York World* claimed that the major league Detroit franchise had also wanted to ink Ayau to a contract. Sing Hung Hoe, writing home to the *Star-Bulletin* in 1913, insisted that Ayau had been turning down offers from "minor league managers." Professional teams were also interested in En Sue Pung.[76]

Catcher Kan Yen Chun attracted serious attention from Walter McCreadie, when the Portland Beavers trained in Honolulu in 1917. McCreadie signed "the Chinese catcher" and voiced optimism that he could develop into a PCL star. What had apparently pleased McCreadie the most was Kan Yen's "rifle arm," which picked off a Portland base runner on third after the Chinese Hawaiian catcher had bluffed a throw to second. According to Portland sportswriter Lou Kennedy, Kan Yen was a good hitter, albeit weighing only 130 pounds. Kennedy expected that Kan Yen would not stick with Portland but instead get farmed out for more seasoning in the Pacific Northwest League. In any event, Kan Yen, Vernon Ayau, and their All-Chinese teammates dazzled Kennedy, who confessed that the play of "these Chinese boys" caused one to "sit up and rub one's eyes in amazement."[77]

Kennedy acknowledged that "Celestial athletes" such as Kan Yen and Vernon Ayau were not "full-blooded" Chinese. They possessed, he wrote, Japanese, Native Hawaiian, and Portuguese ancestors. Kennedy cited statistics to prove that interracial marriage was common in Hawaii — that, for example, only half of Hawaii's white males had married white females. He claimed that none of the "Chinese boys" have "American blood." But "Cupid" was cosmopolitan on the islands. Hence both Kan Yen Chun and Ayau possessed indigenous Hawaiian as well as Chinese ancestry.[78]

Unfortunately, McCreadie decided not to give Kan Yen Chun a chance with Portland. The Portland owner declared that while Kan Yen was a "classy" catcher, his hitting was too "light." Thus, he recommended that Spokane employ Kan Yen Chun. However, since the Pacific Northwest League already fielded Chinese Hawaiian Vernon Ayau, the Spokane franchise passed on McCreadie's recommendation. McCreadie, however, considered taking a closer look at Chinito Moriyama, a "Japanese player," for the All-Chinese who was an excellent fielder but not an impressive hitter. McCreadie might have taken that close look, but Moriyama remained on the islands.[79]

Pitcher Apau Kau was as skillful as any of the Travelers. Known on the islands as the only effective Hawaiian spitballer, Apau Kau pitched consistently well for the Travelers and reportedly possessed the kind of ability that might prove inviting to scouts for professional teams. In 1917, he had left the islands for the American East Coast. Living in Philadelphia, he registered for the draft in June. Subsequently, the Hawaiian entered the military during World War I. Several years earlier, it had been rumored he was going to a mainland military academy, "provided," according to the *Commercial Advertiser*, that "he has enough funds." Certainly, the Honolulu daily added, Apau Kau "had enough fighting blood in him." The pitcher never seems to have made it into a military academy. However, in April 1918, the *Washington Post* noted that Apau Kau had left officers training camp for undisclosed reasons and had returned to his regiment, the 315th Infantry. Several months later, Sergeant Apau Kau was killed in action in 1918.[80]

Conclusion

In the spring of 1914, the *Honolulu Star-Bulletin* printed a letter En Sue Pung wrote one of his brothers living in the territory's capital. He talked about his team winning a game in Tucson, Arizona. He mentioned that five hundred Chinese lived in Tucson at the time, all proud of what the Travelers had accomplished. The local Chinese "even opened champagne to celebrate our victory over the haole." To Tucson's Chinese community and En Sue Pung, more than a game had been played earlier that day.[81]

Even if they were not conscious battlers for racial democracy, the Hawaiian Travelers' story ties the various strands that hold this book together. They represent the importance of colonized Hawaii in the development of Asian Pacific American baseball. The support of Honolulu's ethnic Chinese community was essential to the initial success of the Travelers. Nevertheless, the team transcended ethnic boundaries as it included from the very beginning athletes such as Lai Tin and the Akana brothers who possessed indigenous Hawaiian as well as Chinese ancestry. Moreover, within a few years, non–Chinese Hawaiian athletes of indigenous and Japanese descent would fill roster spots.

By crossing the Pacific to play mainland teams generally composed of European American and occasionally African American ballplayers, the Travelers crossed often treacherous racial frontiers. Their skill won respect, albeit sometimes reluctant and tainted by "Yellow Peril" and derogatory racial references. A few of the players, as we will explore more in subsequent chapters, developed into pioneer Asian Pacific American professionals.

It remains hard to gauge how much the Travelers transformed baseball or Asian Pacific American history. Their treks to the mainland received plenty of publicity. Many of their games were reported from coast to coast. Yet despite the Hawaiian ballplayers' ability to compete effectively against several of the mainland's top amateur and semi-professional nines, Asian Pacific

Americans remained subject to a racialization process which denied they could master a physically and mentally tough sport such as baseball as well as whites. Buck Lai and Vernon Ayau remained largely marginalized as racial novelties.

At the same time, the Travelers did not persuade America's leading political and economic institutions to surrender their commitment to the racial exclusion of Asian Pacific Americans. Perhaps Lai Tin and Ayau helped persuade some Americans to be more tender hearted toward people of Chinese ancestry. However, the Chinese Exclusion Law remained the law of the land until 1942. In the 1910s, California and several other states enacted Alien Land Laws that denied Chinese and other Asian Pacific Americans the right to own farmland. Until after World War II, California and several other states retained anti–miscegenation laws that barred Chinese and other Asian Pacific Americans from the right to marry whites.

Still, there remains much to celebrate in the experiences of the Hawaiian Travelers. Hawaii, to be sure, has been no racial paradise. However, out of the sugar fields, docks, and working and lower-middle class neighborhoods, Hawaiians of various racial and ethnic backgrounds have fashioned a local culture — a culture that has encouraged people to transcend racial and ethnic boundaries as they joined trade unions, worshipped, surfed, and played baseball. They might well remember their specific ethnic heritage but they would also continue to remember the deep hurt of being ruled by haoles — a hurt felt by many people of Asian Pacific Islander ancestry during Hawaii's often troubling and inspirational history.

Chapter VI

Asian Pacific American Minor Leaguers

Professional stardom in America's national pastime apparently eluded Americans of Asian Pacific Islander ancestry before 1965. The *Pacific Citizen* lamented in 1947 that the lack of physical size and "not the myth that the *Nisei* can't hit the curve ball" hurt the chances of Japanese Americans in American professional baseball. Nevertheless, before 1965 some ballplayers of Asian Pacific Islander ancestry competed effectively in professional baseball in the United States and Japan. A few starred in the Japanese big leagues. Since 1965, a number of players of Asian Pacific Islander ancestry have excelled in the big leagues. And even those who have not become superstars have given the lie to the stereotype that people of Asian Pacific Islander ancestry cannot joyfully and successfully master a tough, physical team sport such as baseball. This chapter will focus on these American ballplayers of Asian Pacific Islander descent who have played professionally on the American mainland, but for a variety of reasons never made it to either the American or the Japanese big leagues.[1]

Barney Joy

By 1915, the American mainland baseball world had become aware that Hawaiians of Asian Pacific Islander ancestry could play baseball with a skill perhaps surpassed only by American major leaguers. Barney Joy joined the Pacific Coast League's San Francisco Seals in 1907. According to the 1930

U.S. Census manuscripts, Joy's father was born in Nova Scotia and his mother was born in Hawaii. Interestingly, Joy was described in the census as racially a Caucasian-Hawaiian — that is, he possessed both indigenous Hawaiian and European ancestry. Moreover, by 1930 he was employed as a machinist.[2]

Joy was no Walter Johnson, but making it on the Seals' pitching staff was quite an accomplishment given the fact that the Pacific Coast League, in which the Seals competed, was one of the best professional leagues in America outside of the National and American leagues. Joy's Hawaiian background piqued considerable curiosity from the sporting press and baseball fans in general. Late in 1906, the *Washington Post* announced that the Seals had offered contracts to Joy and En Sue Pung, "two Chinese players who were the best men on the Honolulu Athletics team. The offers have been accepted." However, Joy and not En Sue Pung joined the Seals at their 1906 spring training camp. Perhaps En Sue Pung did not wish to leave Hawaii. Perhaps, because En Sue Pung actually possessed Chinese ancestry and San Francisco remained in 1906 and for many years after a hotbed of anti–Asian politics, the Seals withdrew their offer to the dynamic Chinese Hawaiian outfielder. A few months later, the *Post* pointed out in an article headlined, "First Imported Baseball Pitcher," that Joy was a "genuine Hawaiian," which technically meant in 1907 that while he was not born in one of the states, he was still a U.S. citizen and not an "import." Seals manager Danny Long had, according to the article, heard "of the Kanaka's ability from a member of a theatrical group who witnessed the Hawaiian's work in the box down in the islands." On March 29, 1907, readers of the *Fort Wayne Daily News* discovered in the sports' section a headline reading "Frisco Has Novelty In A Kansas Pitcher." While checking over the accompanying article, readers would have also learned that what the headline actually meant was that "Frisco" had a "Kanaka" pitcher. A caption to the photo of Joy in action declared that the Seals "claim the distinction of having the only Kanaka baseball player in the United States." The story revealed that Joy had been playing phenomenal baseball on the islands for three years. He was not only Hawaii's best pitcher, but the islands' best hitter as well. The 200-pound Joy was known, according to the article, as the "Kanaka Korker" and Seal smanager Danny Long "expects him to become the idol of fans." A piece in the *Los Angeles Times* claimed that the "Kanaka ... will undoubtedly be the pitching sensation of the season." Joy's appearance in a Seals' uniform in Visalia for a preseason exhibition game inspired the *San Francisco Examiner* to proclaim the "burly Kanaka" as a "big attraction."[3]

Joy got off to a rough start for the Seals, but by season's end he not only had become a good PCL pitcher but also drew fans who wanted to see the "husky brown skinned lad" perform. In April, the *San Francisco Examiner* questioned Joy's tenacity. In June, Joy finally won his first game "on American soil," as the Seals defeated the Los Angeles Angels 12–2. Soon, the *Los Angeles Times* praised Joy's "drop ball" as the best in the Pacific Coast League. In August 1907, a headline to an account of a Seals game published in the *Reno Evening Gazette* read: "Barney Joy Pitches Usual Game."[4] And the *Sporting Life* conceded Joy's slow start but maintained in August that he was pitching well enough for the Seals that the Hawaiian would get drafted by a major league team. Eventually, Joy wound up winning sixteen of thirty-eight decisions and batting .219 in 128 at-bats.[5]

Indeed, major league teams expressed interest in moving Joy up to the highest rung of Organized Baseball's ladder. The Pittsburgh Pirates sought the Hawaiian, but the National League's Boston franchise landed him. The *Washington Post,* subsequently, published a photo of Joy with text declaring that "Foreigner Creates Stir" when he signed with the Boston Nationals. Significantly, Joy's signing suggested to some in the big leagues that Boston was about to hire a "colored pitcher." One press account asserted that Joy's joining the Boston Nationals would provoke tremendous controversy. Conceding that Organized Baseball had a strong streak of ethnic and racial bigotry, the *Washington Post* declared, "The employment of this negro from Honolulu is like a match in a powder magazine." The Washington, D.C., daily admitted that Joy was racially "Malay" and "not a negro." His skin color, nevertheless, "is as dark as an Ethiopian." Consequently, the *Post* expected that Joy would find it hard to find a roommate while traveling with Boston. The amazed *Post* even wondered how Joy got hotel accommodations while hurling for the Seals. The daily agreed that Joy was a good pitcher but if he could not win over his teammates "his career in the major leagues is likely to be a sad affair." The Boston owner George Dovey responded he was going to give Joy a shot. He insisted that the pitcher was not "colored." Perhaps unintentionally, Dovey misled the public in asserting that Joy was actually Canadian and migrated to the "Sandwich Islands" with his parents. Dovey complained that five major league teams had been after Joy and he believed that jealousy inspired these teams to protest Boston's landing of the left hander. Interestingly, Joy never played a major league inning with Boston or any other major league team. According to the *Pacific Commercial Advertiser*, Joy had actually refused to join the Boston organization. Instead, he remained in Honolulu, where he resided with his wife and four children, while working as a machinist.[6]

Joy expected, however, to return to the ranks of mainland professional ballplayers in 1912. In January 1912, the *Pacific Commercial Advertiser* reported that the southpaw had enrolled in the local YMCA and was fervently getting in shape in preparation for his coming season with Spokane of the Pacific

Northwest League. The *Portland Oregonian* declared that Joy would do well in the Pacific Northwest League. Portland Beaver owner Walter McCreadie was quoted as saying "that the dark-skinned Honolulu side-wheeler" had plenty of talent. Indulging perhaps in racial stereotyping, McCreadie added, "Barney is a little lazy and not much of a fighter, but if the Spokane players back him up he'll show those class B stockers something about pitching." Joy, nevertheless, was not particularly joyful about reporting to Spokane, hoping he could pitch for McCreadie's Portland nine.[7]

In the spring of 1912, Joy failed to report to Spokane, prompting the franchise's owner to declare that the Hawaiian's career in Organized Baseball was over because he had not fulfilled his contractual obligations. Joy replied he would have willingly gone to Spokane but the team's manager had canceled his passage on the SS *Mongolia* to the mainland. The *Pacific Commercial Advertiser* complained that if Joy really wanted to go to Spokane he would have made the necessary arrangements, and that the Hawaiian preferred to play in Portland and hoped that the mix-up in travel plans would allow him to ultimately wind up in Oregon. Subsequently, the Spokane owner admitted that the mix-up was the railroad company's responsibility. Nevertheless, Joy remained suspended from Organized Baseball. Meanwhile, Joy played baseball in Honolulu on Sundays and labored at a Honolulu iron works. Later in 1912, a baseball fan in Honolulu reported to the *Los Angeles Times* that Joy was overweight and out of shape while trying to star in Honolulu baseball. Before Joy pitched a game against the Asahis, the *Commercial Advertiser* was not convinced the former San Francisco Seal would do well. It maintained, "How Barney will stack up against the small but fast Japanese, if he pitches, remains to be seen."[8]

On the mainland reminders of Barney Joy were none too kind. In 1920, the *Sporting News* declared that Joy was "the famous Hawaiian pitcher that Danny Long rescued from a jungle berth and a menu of poi to no avail." Later in the 1920s, Barney Joy was the subject of an unflattering piece published in the *Sporting News*. Raymond Coll, a Honolulu-based journalist, wrote in 1922 that Hawaiian baseball was good but its umpiring was bad. Coll used Joy, who umpired regularly in Honolulu, as an example. Describing Joy as "half-caste and Chinese," Coll maintained that Joy made "calls where they ain't." Joy, according to the very wrong Coll, had but a tryout with the Seals. But the Hawaiian's ego never let anyone forget he wore the uniform of an American professional team, albeit briefly. Coll added that "Kanakas" liked to boast and Joy's PCL experience offered "him an air of authority" that usually overwhelmed opposition to his calls as an umpire. Coll had reportedly criticized Joy's calls against Stanford when the California nine visited Honolulu. And the ex-ballplayer had gone looking for the journalist. It was typical of a "Kanaka " such as Joy, Coll complained, that he could not admit to any mistakes.[9]

Vernon Ayau

In 1917, shortstop Vernon Ayau became the first player in American Organized Baseball acknowledged to possess Chinese ancestry when he joined Seattle of the Pacific Northwest League. As early as 1912, Ayau had attracted interest from the Michigan Central League. Apparently, nothing came of that. After four treks to the mainland with the Travelers, Ayau was signed by Seattle in December 1916. Honolulu's baseball fans and many of Ayau's fellow Hawaiian players were convinced when they heard of Ayau's good fortunes that he would make good in the Pacific Northwest League. His commanding performance against a visiting team of American major leaguers late in 1916 had proven to Hawaiian fans and ballplayers that Ayau could compete professionally on the mainland. Accordingly, readers of the *Connelsville Daily Courier* learned that the "Yellow Peril had invaded professional baseball." Ayau was a "real Mongolian," hailed by Seattle Giants manager William Leard as the greatest ballplayer in the "land of the ukulele." Leard told the press that he thought Ayau was as good a shortstop as any in the East, while word had spread that the Hawaiian conceivably possessed big league potential.[10]

The *Portland Telegraph* was far less certain that Ayau would make good. It noted that, in any event, Great Falls, which had a team in the Pacific Northwest League did not allow "a Chinaman within its limits." Apparently, the ban went back to the late 1800s, at which time a Chinese immigrant reputedly aroused the ire of local militant white workers who decided to chuck the poor fellow into a river. Thus, according to the Portland newspaper, Ayau would not make it and even if he did, "he is certain to meet [opposition] in case he ventures into the forbidden land." Still, the *Honolulu Star-Bulletin* defended Ayau's chances of doing well in the Pacific Northwest League. It praised the shortstop "as a player of good habits [who] should become a popular star with the Seattle team."[11]

Readers of the *Sporting News* learned that Ayau had hit a game winning home run against the Portland Beavers, training in Honolulu early in 1917. Portland sportswriter Lou Kennedy wrote, "If there is no Frank Merriwell for Chinese dime novel enthusiasts to marvel about, we nominate Vernon Ayau." Aside from Ayau's hitting, Kennedy was smitten by Ayau's arm, arguing that only one PCL shortstop had a better one. Kennedy also expressed admiration for Ayau's double play partner, second baseman Chinito

Moriyama—"a Japanese boy ... for the Orientals." Kennedy observed that Moriyama had stopped a hot grounder near second hit by Portland's Babe Pinelli. He then acrobatically flipped the ball to Ayau on second, initiating a stunning double play. Few Portland players, according to Kennedy, had seen anything like it. Kennedy was convinced that Ayau would make good with Seattle if he got the opportunity and did not lose his nerve.[12]

In April 1917, the *Washington Post* called Ayau "the first Chinese ball player to make his debut in organized baseball." Ayau was "a bright looking and English speaking Chinese," who had told the press that there were other Chinese Hawaiians ready to play Organized Baseball on the American mainland. He added that Japanese Hawaiians could also play professionally on the American mainland if they learned to hit as well as they fielded and ran the bases. Readers of the *Fort Wayne News* discovered that the Pacific Northwest press had greeted the "Hawaiian-Chinese" signing as a joke, even though Honolulu sportswriter Riley Allen had assured baseball writers and fans in the Pacific Northwest that Ayau was not just a good ballplayer but "a clean little gentleman." However, "the snappy little shortstop" had changed minds. Observers called Ayau "the fastest thing ever seen on a baseball diamond." An article printed in the *Fort Wayne Sentinel* claimed that managers of the Butte and Great Falls franchises considered boycotting Seattle on account of Ayau. However, they reconsidered as Seattle's owner, William Leard, seemed determined to use the Chinese Hawaiian, described as "a hard hitter and clever infielder and ... certain of making good in organized baseball."[13]

Generally, the Seattle Giants' management and the *Seattle Press-Intelligencer* welcomed Ayau as a potential member of the local minor league team. The daily's Royal Brougham told readers that, indeed, William Leard was not so certain about the wisdom of signing Ayau—that he had investigated Ayau's performance against the Portland Beavers and found that the shortstop hit .305 against the Pacific Coast League club and queried Portland sportswriter Roscoe Fawcett as to the particulars. Convinced that Ayau deserved a tryout, Leard expressed indignation when he heard that Harry Wolverton of the San Francisco Seals had complained that Organized Baseball might as well recruit African American players if it was going to allow a "Chinaman" to play with the Giants. Leard's response, nevertheless, was not exactly a ringing endorsement of racial and ethnic democracy, "Think of it, Ayau is an American-born, half–Chinese, half–Hawaiian, has attended American schools and speaks English almost as well as I do. And Wolverton has on his San Francisco club, Jacinto Calvo, a Cuban who butchers the American lingo."[14]

As the Giants prepared for the coming season, Ayau was handed the starting job at shortstop. The *Post-Intelligencer* identified him as "the only Chinese player in baseball." Ayau was an "uncertainty," but he is highly touted wherever he has performed as a wonder. His friends say he will make good, if given half a chance, and as Leard will give him all the chance in the world to stick, the Chinese phenom ought to be able to handle the job without difficulty." Ayau's progress at shortstop would earn "special attention," the *Post-Intelligencer* conceded. While not explaining why, the daily argued that the "Chinese star" was "handicapped" in his campaign to win the Giants' shortstop job. However, the *Post-Intelligencer* declared that Leard would afford him a fair shot at the job. And after watching him work out, the *Post-Intelligencer* assured readers that "[t]he Chinese player has all the earmarks of a ballplayer, despite his size."[15]

The *Post-Intelligencer* seemed to support Ayau, and so did Seattle's Chinese community. A cartoon appearing in the daily shows a contingent of Chinese Americans cheering in the stands while Ayau works out with the Giants. Royal Brougham enthused that "[l]ittle Vernon Ayau [was] making good at short with a bang." Pointing out the presence of several local Chinese American baseball fans at the Giants workouts, Brougham added that "whenever the little Chinese handles the ball well or pokes out a safe one, their faces are all smiles." Seattle's Chinese consul, moreover, had feted the Hawaiian to a banquet.[16]

As the official season loomed, Ayau seemed to have demonstrated his potential as a minor league shortstop. Hits were not coming easily for the Hawaiian, but his fielding impressed onlookers. For example, in a game against the University of Washington the Hawaiian went hitless. However, the *Post-Intelligencer* reported, "Vernon Ayau, turned another neat play at short. The little Chinese star sprinted far back of second base, scooped a hot roller and tossed the runner out. It was a class bit of work." The "little phenom," as Ayau was described by Brougham, had not gotten used to Seattle's cooler climate. He had, nevertheless, "shown his class in practice games."[17]

Hitting woes continued to dog Ayau as the Pacific Northwest League started. In his first six games, Ayau rapped but four hits out of twenty-three at-bats. Consequently, the *Sporting News* announced in late May that Seattle had released its "Chinese shortstop." Ayau could field, but he could not hit Pacific Northwest pitching, according to "Baseball's Bible." Leard and the team owner both uttered regret that the "speedy little Chinese" had to be released.[18]

Ayau wound up back in the Pacific Northwest League before the circuit collapsed in mid-summer. League leader Tacoma picked him up. And his comeback, according to a *Sporting News* correspondent, was a success. The Tacoma club let go of a white player to make room for Ayau and made the Hawaiian a regular. Subsequently, Ayau was mentioned in an article published in the *Fort Wayne News*. This piece purported that "Chinese ballplayers are breaking into the minor leagues and taking away jobs from regular Americans." Buck Lai and Fred Markham were identified as professionals playing for pay in Upland, Pennsylvania. This was probably more of a semi-professional affiliation than a professional one. The article also discussed Andy "Yim," who was truly playing professional ball in Gettysburg, Pennsylvania. As for Ayau, he was described as a professional in Spokane. By this time, the Pacific Northwest League had collapsed. Thus, Ayau was probably competing as a semi-professional.[19]

Meanwhile, Ayau registered for the draft in Portland, Oregon, in May 1917. The draft card describes him as racially a Mongolian and occupationally a clerk. Ayau left the Pacific Northwest for the East Coast. In 1918, a box score appearing in the *Philadelphia Inquirer* shows an Ayau playing for a team representing the Chester Shipbuilding Company in Philadelphia. A. Mark, the name that Fred Markham played under as Ayau's Hawaiian Travelers teammate, also appeared in the same lineup. At about the same time, Ayau, Mark, and "Yim" appeared in the Brooklyn Bushwicks lineup as the famed semi-pro team took on an African American nine, the Philadelphia Royal Giants. In 1942, Ayau registered for the World War II draft. According to his draft card, the forty-eight-year-old lived in Penns Grove, New Jersey, and worked as a wholesale confectioner. In 1976, the eighty-two-year-old Ayau died in Penns Grove.[20]

Andy Yamashiro

When he played for the Hawaiian Travelers, Japanese Hawaiian Mayayoshi "Andy" Yamashiro was known as Yim in order to abet the fiction that the team after 1913 remained largely or totally Chinese Hawaiian. While most of the Travelers returned to Hawaii in the fall of 1916, Yamashiro stayed behind on the East Coast, seemingly at Traveler teammate Buck Lai's behest. In Philadelphia, he attended Temple Prep School in order to study dentistry and played right guard in football. Indeed, his exploits in a game against La Salle gained national attention. He told the press he enjoyed football, but "[b]aseball, though, I think is better. You can use your hands in baseball but not in football." Yamashiro, moreover, was "longing for the baseball season to grasp a trusty willow and bat the old sphere." When baseball season did begin in 1917, Yamashiro competed for the low level Blue Ridge professional league team in Gettysburg, Pennsylvania. In the process, he joined Vernon Ayau in pioneering Organized Baseball as an Asian Pacific American ballplayer.[21]

Before the Blue Ridge season began, the *Gettysburg Times* informed readers that "Yim, a member of the Chinese University team, which toured this country the past seasons is expected in Gettysburg daily." The Japanese Hawaiian did well from the start. While hitting was not normally one of his strengths, Yamashiro proved fairly effective as a batter in the Blue Ridge League. More conspicuous still was his speed and base running guile. In one of his first games, "Mr. Andy Yim" led Gettysburg to victory by playing a strong center field and hitting a home run and a double. As "the Chinese University youth" quickly circled the bases when he slugged a deep fly over an outfielder's head, one opponent was heard saying to a teammate, "Just watch that Chink go." A few days later, Yamashiro made a great catch in center field to save the game in the ninth for Gettysburg. The *Gettysburg Times* called his fielding gem a "wonder play" and noted that ten minutes later, "the popular fielder" was in his room strumming a ukulele, which "he can play ... almost as well as he can play base ball." The next day, "the popular little Hawaiian" scored his team's winning run on a great slide. An opposing player expected that the Hawaiian's run of clutch plays was about over, claiming "Yim's about done now, for a week or two at least."[22]

Gettysburg baseball fans were getting so used to Yamashiro's fine play that when "Yim" was picked off at first, the *Gettysburg Times* proclaimed astonishment. On May 23, the *Times* notified its "exchanges" that "Yim" had never seen China and could not speak a word of Chinese. Instead, it noted that Yamashiro was a "native of Hawaii." Whether the *Times* or anyone in Gettysburg knew he was a *Nisei* is unknown. In any event, a highlight of 1917 for Yamashiro most likely occurred when he won fifty dollars by hitting a drive that smacked the Bull Durham sign in Hagerstown.[23]

Yamashiro, however, apparently encountered racial abuse from Blue Ridge League fans. The *Gettysburg Times* enthusiastically seconded a Frederick, Maryland, daily which denounced such abuse. The *Frederick Post* described Yamashiro as a "little fellow" who acted like a gentleman and should be treated as such. Baseball fans in Hanover, Maryland, were particularly insulting to the "little Chinaman," according to the *Post*.[24]

Several years later, Frank Culley, a veteran sportswriter who had covered East Coast baseball, recalled Gettysburg's "Chinese" ballplayer: "Sure there was plenty of talk about him. How fast he was, how he could run the bases, and throw. He was a left hander and that is as far as he went." Culley also remembered that when "Yim" heard the Gettysburg nine was going on its first road trip of the 1917 season he packed as if he was journeying across America, inspiring ridicule from his teammates. He also riled teammates when he made two errors in his first game against Martinsburg. Cully said that while "Yim" never made the major league he made "big league copy." Still, Yamashiro hit a solid .291 for the Pennsylvania franchise. Moreover, the *Sporting News* praised "Yim" as one of several "clean-minded" players on the Gettysburg team, which finished third place in the Blue Ridge League. However, he did wind up next to last in fielding percentage, handling without errors only .848 of the balls hit to him.[25]

The next year, Yamashiro joined Buck Lai on the Eastern League's Bridgeport nine. The *Bridgeport Telegram* introduced "Yim" as a fast outfielder who batted left and threw right. He came from Hawaii but was living at the time in Philadelphia. Both Lai and Yamashiro got off to auspicious starts. Asserting that the "Chinese are leading players," the *Telegram* maintained that the "Chinamen" were essential to the Bridgeport Americans' early success. Readers learned, "The men with the almond eyes and the yellow skin are very near the entire works for Bridgeport team in 1918." According to the *Telegram*, Yamashiro, "the other Chinaman," was a competent hitter and, of course, a speedy base runner. However, in reference to the Chinese laundry stereotype, the *Telegram* maintained that "Yim" was not as fast as Lai—"his fellow wielder of the iron."[26]

As the season progressed, Yamashiro continued to earn praise from the *Telegram*. On a hot day in late May, the Bridgeport Americans played Waterbury. The *Telegram* insisted that neither of "the Chinese players" minded the warm weather. Along with the fellow selling pop drinks, Lai and Yamashiro "bathed in the heat with pleasure." More than Lai, "Yim" conformed to the stereotype of "Oriental stoicism." The *Telegram* claimed that "unlike Lai, the Chinese third baseman, Yim is of the stolid type." Yamashiro had his bad days. For example, he committed a key error that helped New London beat Bridgeport in an extra inning game.[27]

Still thought of as "Chink Yim," the Hawaiian reported to Bridgeport again in 1919. Described by the *Telegram* as "formerly of Hawaii," Yamashiro claimed he was ready to have a good season for Bridgeport. However, he did not play for Bridgeport in 1919, but wound up taking part in nineteen games for Hartford of the Eastern League, batting a respectable .253. He also played for a semi-professional team in Philadelphia called Logan Square. According to a 1919 *Gettysburg Times* report, Yamashiro scored the winning run in an exhibition game against the Philadelphia Phillies in August. In January 1920, the same newspaper referred to his "clever base running."[28]

Yamashiro eventually returned to Honolulu, where he remained active in local baseball affairs and helped his father run a hotel in 1930. Yamashiro also got involved in Democratic Party politics. In 1932, Yamashiro arrived in San Francisco as "a Japanese American to a National Democratic Convention" in Chicago. Yamashiro informed the press that all six Hawaiian delegates were pledged to vote for Franklin D. Roosevelt, but he could not predict what would happen if FDR's bid for the party nomination stalled. Yamashiro added that the Hawaiian delegates all supported the repeal of the Eighteenth (Prohibition) amendment.²⁹

Buck Lai

In 1918, Buck Lai Tin, who by that time was frequently referred to as Billy or Bill Lai, as well as Lai Tin, got another chance to play major league baseball. The Chinese Hawaiian had fallen in love with a European American woman named Isabel Reynolds, with whom he eventually married and settled on the East Coast. In June 1917, Lai registered for the draft in Philadelphia as William Tin Lai. According to the information provided on the draft card, Lai lived on Arch Street in Philadelphia and worked as a clerk for the Pennsylvania Railroad Company. Interestingly and inaccurately, he is described as a naturalized citizen of the U.S. Lai was still single but possessed a mother who was apparently dependent upon his income. Racially, Lai was depicted as a Mongolian, tall, medium built, with black hair and brown eyes.³⁰

A national wire report published in the summer of 1917 declared in a headline: "Chinese Player Helps In Recruiting." According to this account, "William T. Lai" played third base for the Brooklyn Bushwicks, a well-publicized semi-professional team run by the controversial Nat Strong. Lai still lived in Philadelphia but commuted to Brooklyn to play baseball on Sundays. The twenty-two-year-old YMCA resident worked in a West Philadelphia Car Shop office for the Pennsylvania Railroad. Lai had been assigned to help recruit for the Philadelphia-based 9th Regiment of Engineers, destined for France.³¹

As for baseball, Lai had competed in 1917 for Upland in the Delaware County League as well as for the Bushwicks. His performance for Upland was described as a "sensation," as Lai led the apparently semi-professional circuit in base stealing. Consequently, the infielder was invited by the Philadelphia Phillies to the team's spring training camp in St. Petersburg. In the spring of 1917, the Phillies, like many major league teams, were willing to show a little more open-mindedness about prospects, given the widespread fear that World War I would drain talented ballplayers from big league and minor league rosters.³²

Lai demonstrated promise with the Phillies. In mid–March, the Hawaiian joined a contingent of Phillies that departed New York City by steamship for spring training in St. Petersburg. The *Philadelphia Inquirer* described him as "third baseman Lai, a Chinese who played with Upland, PA, last year."

An *Inquirer* sportswriter going by the name of "Jim Nasium" asserted that "in picking 'Billy' Lai, the Chinese third baseman from Honolulu, the Phillies have added a cracker jack ukulele tinkler." In his first exhibition game wearing a Phillies uniform, Lai started at third, batted second in the lineup, and rapped two hits out of five at-bats against a military team. The Phillies' manager, Pat Moran, also tried Lai out at shortstop. "Jim Nasium" reported that "Bill Lai, the Chinese player" showed speed but seemed shaky on grounders. Accordingly, the sportswriter predicted the Hawaiian probably would not play regularly for the National League club.[33]

Lai started in three exhibition games at third against the Boston Braves in Miami. Statistically, he was not impressive. In those three games, he got but two hits in eleven at-bats and made a disappointing two errors. The swift Lai did manage to steal a base for the Phillies. Nevertheless, the *Inquirer* insisted that Lai demonstrated big league potential. Joe Vila, a nationally syndicated sports columnist, declared that "Lai Tin, a Chinaman," was one of the young recruits that could make a major league roster in 1918. Indeed, despite committing an error in a Philly intersquad game, Lai traveled north with the rest of the team. And the *Sporting News* announced that "Lai Tin" made the Phillies' official opening day roster.[34]

Still, Lai did not make baseball history by playing officially with the Phillies. The May 23, 1918, edition of the *Sporting News* proclaimed that the franchise had released "Bill Tin Lai, the Chinese infielder" to Bridgeport of the Eastern League, a relatively high level minor league circuit. Lai got off to a good start for the Connecticut nine. Before the season began, a Bridgeport sportswriter speculated that "Willie Lai Chinese infielder will be used at third" until he played himself out of the lineup. Lai had aided his own cause by doing well in an exhibition game against a team of submarine sailors. The *Bridgeport Telegram* announced, "Billy Lai, the new Chinese infielder, was the attraction of the afternoon. He showed up well both in the field and at bat and looks like a really good man." Lai later helped the Bridgeport Eagles defeat an all–African American nine called the Philadelphia Red Caps in an exhibition game. According to the *Telegram*, "Lai, the Chinese addition," sparked the team by smacking two hits and demonstrating speed on the base paths. When Lai ran from first to third on a grounder, the *Telegram* enthused, "the Chinaman scampered around from first to third showing that he was to be considered a fast base runner." What was more, "the chink displayed plenty of pepper and he didn't talk in Hong Kong either." The *Telegram* concluded, "If he can field he can help the locals."[35]

In an article introducing the team to Bridgeport readers, the *Telegram* described Lai as a right handed hitter and thrower, who wielded a fair bat but fielded well. It added that Lai came from Hawaii rather than China and was presently living in New York. By this time, moreover, Andy Yamashiro had joined the Bridgeport club. After the season officially began, therefore, the "Chinese players for locals" looked good in a game on May 26 against Springfield. The *Telegram* declared, "Bill Lai, the Chinese thirdbaseman and Andy Yim, the Oriental rightfielder for the locals were the leading lights." Lai batted three for three, including a double, and stole two bases. Yim hit a triple in two bats. While on third, Yim's manager called for the suicide squeeze bunt. The *Telegram* observed that because of Yim's speed, the Hawaiian was almost at home by the time the catcher was able to capture the bunted ball.[36]

Early in the season, the *Telegram* reported that Lai was not a steady fielder, but capable of spectacular fielding plays. His strongest suit was as a hitter, base runner, and "quick thinker." The daily pointed out, "So far catchers have been practically powerless to intercept the Chink." The *Telegram* reveled in "the Celestial third sacker's" all around skills and feats such as the time against Waterbury Lai and player manager Paul Krichell pulled off a double steal. Lai's hustle and enthusiasm stirred admiration. The *Telegram* announced he was "the prize pepper box" of the Eastern League. Defying the stereotype of "Oriental stoicism," Lai was "always chattering and moving in some direction." Because "the Chinese players of the locals, Bill Lai at third and Andy Yim in right, had another field day each," Bridgeport defeated Providence early in June. Yim slugged a homer for Bridgeport, while Lai went three for four, hitting double and a triple.[37]

As the 1918 season continued, Lai and Yim proved invaluable to the Bridgeport nine and provoked interesting and often complimentary press commentary. In mid–June, the *Telegram* reported that while the team headed to Hartford, "Andy Yim, the Chinese right fielder" took out his ukulele and serenaded the players. Lai apparently sang along. The two still entertained teammates once they were ensconced in their Hartford hotel. When player-manager Paul Krichell resigned in late June, the *Telegram* praised the future New York Yankee scout for signing Lai and Yim, who not only helped the team but were "the only two Chinese playing in professional baseball." However, perhaps putting a damper on at least Lai's early weeks in American Organized Baseball was that his "grip" was apparently stolen from the Bridgeport clubhouse in June. The robbery was reportedly not personal as the thieves had as well broken into the team's ticket office in the hopes of finding loose cash lying about.[38]

Since Lai and Yim were working out so well, Bridgeport announced in June 1918 that it was going to sign another "Chinese" pitcher, surnamed See. As it turned out, See was given a chance to pitch for Bridgeport. However, he did not do well and, in any event, he apparently did not possess any Chinese ancestry after all.[39]

William Tin, or Buck Lai, was one of the stars of the Hawaiian Travelers. An adept third baseman and dynamic base runner, he played four years of minor league ball for the Bridgeport Americans, several years for the famous Brooklyn Bushwicks, and got tryouts from the Philadelphia Phillies and New York Giants. In the mid– and late 1930s, he led a team of barnstorming Hawaiians throughout the mainland. (Courtesy of Library of Congress, Prints and Photographs Division.)

The *Bridgeport Telegram* noted Andy Yim's big game against New Haven in July 1918. It also breathed a sigh of relief that Lai might not have to go into the army or leave the team for defense work. Sportswriter T.F. Magner called the game "Andy Yim Day" as the outfielder led his nine to victory with two triples. Magner also described Yim as "the slant-eyed ukulele stretcher." Magner reported as well that "Billy Lai" was notified by his Philadelphia draft board that he would not have to report as had been feared. Magner wrote that the Americans could ill-afford to lose Lai as he was "easily the best third sacker in the league."[40]

A correspondent to the *Sporting News* also noted "Billy Lai's" tussle with the Philadelphia draft board. "The Chinese third baseman" had heard from the draft board that he had to quit baseball and find war-related work. The correspondent mistakenly maintained that Lai had been in the U.S. for only four years. Now married, Lai said he was willing to comply with the draft board's demand. However, he reputedly wondered what a "Chinaman could do to help win the war." The *Sporting News* claimed Lai was a stenographer by occupation.[41]

Because of the war, the Eastern League, like many minor leagues, stopped short of a complete season. Before the Bridgeport players dispersed, they took on the Pittsburgh Pirates in an exhibition game. The Americans surprised their local fans by edging the Pirates 2–1 in extra innings. Yim and Lai both helped key the Eastern Leaguers' victory. Pirates manager Hugh Bezdek claimed to be impressed by "Billy Lai, the Celestial shortstop." Bezdek could "see no reason why" Lai could not make it into the big leagues. Bezdek said Lai was fast — faster than most big leaguers and too fast for the Eastern League. Subsequently, Lai fulfilled his commitment to wartime America by heading to a shipyard at Chester, Pennsylvania.[42]

After showing he could compete effectively in the Eastern League, Lai was back in Bridgeport in 1919 and for two more years, as well. The *Telegram* voiced relief when Lai signed his 1919 contract with the local minor league club. Apparently, some worried that "Bill Lai, the best Chinese ballplayer in the Eastern League last season, and one of the star third basemen of the circuit" would not return to Bridgeport. Lai's ethnic identity moved the *Telegram* to tediously quip in May 1919. "Bill Lai," it maintained was "the celebrated Hawaiian-Chinese (or, do you say it, Chinese-Hawaiian?)." The Bridgeport management must have trusted Lai's baseball IQ in that when he got hurt in mid-summer, the team dispatched him on a trip to Philadelphia to scout young prospects.[43]

By the end of the 1919 season, Lai played 107 games for the Connecticut nine, all but six at third base. His manager, Ray Grimes, had tried him out at shortstop earlier in the season but the experiment had stirred criticism from those who believed that the "Chinese athlete" made a better third baseman than a shortstop. He hit .260, eight doubles, five triples, and no home runs, while tying for second in the league in stolen bases with thirty. The next year, the Chinese Hawaiian played 118 games for Bridgeport. He managed a .265 batting average, eleven doubles, four triples, and one home run. Lai stole twenty-seven bases for the Americans.[44]

Lai must have had something of a rough season in 1920 in comparison to 1919. In June, injuries forced manager Ed Walsh to switch the man the *Telegram* called an "Oriental" to shortstop in one game. The *Telegram* reported that "the change was anything but of benefit to his play." The usually "reliable" Lai committed an important throwing error, allowing the opposition to beat Bridgeport. In August, the *Telegram* reported that manager Walsh had been trying to drive "Bill Lai" out of the league, but had changed his mind about the Chinese Hawaiian and the daily observed with an undercurrent of relief that Lai was playing the "brilliant ball that caused the fans to sing so loudly his praises a year ago." To be fair, Walsh's animosity toward Lai may not have been racial as he had managed to alienate many of his ballplayers for a wide variety of reasons. Perhaps, however, the experience may have soured Lai on continuing his Eastern League career. In February 1921, the *Sporting News* announced that even though Gene McCann had replaced Walsh as manager, "Buck Lai, the Chinese second baseman, has decided to quit baseball," because he had a "good position in Philadelphia." Moreover, Lai had just become a father and believed he should "stay home and watch the little Celestial grow." In any event, Lai was back in Bridgeport in 1921. And he still came up with big plays and hits for the Eastern League nine, including a key rap down the third base line that sparked a victory over Springfield in May. Moreover, after playing several disappointing games in the outfield, Lai was returned to third base, where he performed an unassisted double play late in the 1921 season. According to the *Sporting News,* however, Lai voluntarily left Bridgeport after the 1921 season.[45]

Lai, meanwhile, had indeed settled in the Northeast, with his wife and growing family. In 1920, he worked as a recreation leader in Philadelphia and remained employed by the Pennsylvania Railroad Company. Lai also competed in semi-professional ball with teams such as the Camden Giants and the Brooklyn Bushwicks. As for the latter, a *Sporting News* writer claimed in 1953 that they "became a national legend." For years, Brooklyn baseball fans would often sadly quip that the Bushwicks were better than the Dodgers and often the former club outdrew the Dodgers. Run by Max Rosner and Nat Strong, the Bushwicks played out of Dexter Park and fielded several top players such as not only Buck Lai but also famed major leaguers Dazzy Vance and Lefty Gomez. The Bushwicks, moreover, faced talented opposition from East Coast Negro League teams.[46]

In 1927, the Bushwicks took on a barnstorming team headed by Babe Ruth. A crowd of 20,000 packed into Dexter Park to see the Bustin Babes beat the Bushwicks 3–2. Making Ruth's team even stronger was the presence of Yankees teammate Lou Gehrig, who happened to score a key run after Lai committed an error at third. In any event, Lai batted second for the Bushwicks and managed a hit in three at-bats.[47]

In 1928, the New York Giants gave the Hawaiian a tryout. In January, a press report declared that Lai was the "first of his kind" to have a shot at major league baseball. Another press release claimed that if Lai made the Giants, he would be the first "Hawaiian … [to] cavort about the infield of a major league club." Indeed, readers of the *Gettysburg Times* learned on January 14, 1928, of confusion as to whether Lai was "Chinese" or "Hawaiian." A *Los Angeles Times* pundit observed, "Buck Lai, signed by the Giants, is the first Chinese player in major league baseball. Now give us a Chinese golf pro and we'd rate China among world powers." In announcing Lai's signing, the *New York Times* insisted that the Giants must have "exhausted all the resources of these United States, [and] went out yesterday and signed a Chinese infielder." Forgetting that Lai was an American citizen and resident of the American East Coast for ten years, the *Times* conceded that Lai was at least a versatile infielder and could perhaps help the Giants in a utility role.[48]

Lai, unfortunately, did not stick with the New York franchise. According to one press account, "Lai, the Chinese infielder" was the first player cut by the Giants and dispatched to a minor league team in Little Rock, Arkansas, for "for more experience." Over thirty-two years old and playing competitive baseball against professionals and semi-professionals since 1912, it is not clear how much more experience Lai actually needed. More to the point, he apparently had trouble with major league hitting, and the Giants' manager, the famed John McGraw, entertained doubts about his slender physique and thought he already had a good third baseman. Thus, McGraw shipped Lai to the minor leagues, inspiring the *New York Times* Richard Vidmer to remark, "Buck Lai, the Chinaman, who never had a Chinaman's chance, had been sent to Little Rock." Moreover, a headline to a brief wire story proclaimed, "No More Chink" after McGraw cut Lai. But Lai was not about to let McGraw send him to Little Rock. Refusing to leave the Giants' camp, Lai told the press that he would rather "go in the laundry business" than take his baseball skills to Arkansas.[49]

However, the whole situation seems to have arisen without much rancor. Red Reeder, a former West Point athlete and coach who was in the Giants camp in 1928, recalled that McGraw allowed the great, but tempestuous, Ty Cobb to work out with the Giants. After the Giants were done with their spring training day by 5 P.M., Cobb would take the field with a few Giants players — Lefty O'Doul, the young Mel Ott, Reeder, and Buck Lai, even though the Hawaiian was supposed to be in Little Rock. Apparently, Cobb's well-known and vicious racism did not extend to Buck Lai and the usually tough McGraw was willing to put up with Lai's insubordination.[50]

Eventually, Lai was sent to Jersey City. Seemingly not bitter, Lai, according to biographer and descendant Keoni Everington, claimed he learned a great deal about baseball from the colorful McGraw. Meanwhile, Frank Donnelly, secretary of the Jersey City franchise in the talented International League, announced to the press that the "Chinese infielder" had been acquired from the New York Giants. Donnelly stated that Jersey City would carry Lai as an extra infielder. Lai performed well in a pre-season exhibition game against New Haven of the Eastern League. According to a press account of the game, "Buck Lai, the Chinese player ... filled in cleverly at shortstop" while rapping out key hits. After the formal International League season started, Lai could be found in the Jersey City lineup at shortstop against Newark and other International League opponents. However, according to the *Sporting News,* Lai was returned to the New York Giants in May, where he seems not to have played officially for McGraw's club.[51]

With his major league prospects behind him, Lai abandoned Organized Baseball or was abandoned by it. He continued to play regularly for the Bushwicks, as well as a team called the State Hospital Grays, which played out of Middletown, New York. In October 1928, the Bushwicks took on another Ruth-Gehrig barnstorming contingent. An impressive crowd of 22,000 crammed into Dexter Park to watch the Bushwicks come out on top 10–8. Lai batted one for five, with a double. In 1930, he participated in what the *New York Times* described as New York City's first night game when the Bushwicks lost to Springfield of Long Island 3–0 at Dexter Park. Leading off, Lai got no hits that night. But the Bushwicks insisted that the experiment worked out well and they would continue to play under the lights. The next year, the Bushwicks beat a nine from Japan's Hosei University 5–3. Lai earned one hit out of four at-bats. However, many of the 10,000 fans at Dexter Park erupted into a near riot when the umpire made a crucial call against the visitors. A smaller crowd of 2500 watched Lai and the Bushwicks beat the New York Athletic Club 6–1. The Chinese Hawaiian batted two for four. In 1932, 20,000 fans crowded Dexter Park to see the New York Giants defeat the Bushwicks under the lights. Lai managed two hits in five at-bats. In 1933, Lai led off and handled third base for the State Hospital Grays in a game against the Black Yankees. A year later, the Black Yankees beat the

Bushwicks 6–0. A good crowd of 15,000 attended the game, largely drawn by the fact that Dizzy Dean and his brother, Paul, competed for the Bushwicks that afternoon, while another St. Louis Cardinals great, Joe Medwick, cavorted in left field. Lai batted one for three and stole a base.[52]

In the mid–1930s, Lai returned to Hawaii to form a traveling team that journeyed throughout North America, playing semi-pro and African American professional nines. To honor a Hawaiian prodigal son, a Chinese Hawaiian youth league was named after Lai. According to one press report, Lai had dreamed for nineteen years of returning to his home and putting together a traveling squad that would be "greater than the one he came over originally with." Another declared that Lai believed that a Hawaiian team would inject needed spirit into American baseball. Sponsored by the territorial government, as well as Honolulu's chamber of commerce, Buck Lai's Hawaiian All-Stars consisted largely of players of Asian Pacific Islander ancestry and some were good enough to attract interest from mainland professional franchises. Despite being over forty, Lai not only managed the team but played third base as well.[53]

In Honolulu, the press seemingly supported Lai's efforts to duplicate the feats of the Travelers twenty years earlier by assembling a talented barnstorming Hawaiian team. The *Honolulu Advertiser*'s Red McQueen encouraged Honolulu's business community to back Lai's team. Honolulu's business people needed to know, the sportswriter declared, that Lai would promote Honolulu and "Hawaii, U.S.A." on the American mainland. Another *Advertiser* sportswriter, Andrew Mitsukado, praised Lai as a "[s]hrewd and a good judge of ball players." In 1936, Don Watson, a *Honolulu Star-Bulletin* columnist, applauded Lai's 1935 trek across North America: "Last year's trip was very successful as far as getting publicity for the islands is concerned, although we would not go so far as to give the baseball tour as the reason for Honolulu hotels being crowded this tourist season." Watson conceded that the trip did not make much money but it did not lose much either. Moreover, Lai's Hawaiian All-Stars made a good showing and apparently Lai received invitations for 1936 from many of the cities his team visited in 1935.[54]

The Honolulu press expressed some misgiving about Lai's venture. Before inaugurating his team's first trek to the mainland, Lai's squad was "humiliated" by a team headed by Earl Vida, according to Mitsukado. The fact that Vida's aggregation won 13–4 was, indeed, not a comforting sign. Lai's team departed in April 1935, carrying a fine group of Hawaiian athletes that included John Kerr, Al Nalua, Francis Goo, Wallace Arakawa, Richard Yamada, Hans Pung, and Shipp Lo. Earl Vida would join the team later. In any event, some baseball followers in Honolulu wondered if Lai had put together the strongest team possible.[55]

In 1935, the *Chicago Daily Tribune* called Lai's aggregation the "Chinese

All-Star team." It predicted that "Oriental baseball fans in Chicago will stage a celebration tomorrow" when the "all-star Chinese team from Honolulu" went up against the Mills semi-pro nine in a doubleheader. The *Tribune* expected the Chinese vice-consul to throw out the first ball while other members of Chicago's Chinese consulate would also attend. The *Tribune* praised Lai's team as so good that when it opposed Babe Ruth and the American League All-Stars, the Bambino advised Lai to take the Hawaiian nine to the American mainland. Indeed, the *Tribune* claimed that Lai had assembled a team with players that were "famous in their homeland."[56]

Talented Negro League teams, as well as other semi-pro nines, gave Lai's contingent more than it could handle. In June 1935, the New York Cubans trounced the Hawaiians 12–1 at New York City's Dyckman Oval. The *Chicago Defender*, nevertheless, called the losers, "Buck Lai's strong Hawaiians." In Middletown, New York, the Black Yankees beat pitcher Eddie Tam 4–1. In Syracuse, the Hawaiians stayed busy by playing a nine called the Detroit Clowns at the city's Municipal Stadium. The *Syracuse Herald* promoted Lai's nine as "composed of Chinese, Japanese, and Hawaiians from Honolulu." The Hawaiians were scheduled to pitch John Kerr in the second half of a twin bill against the Clowns. They were also going to play a doubleheader against an African American nine, the Syracuse Black Chiefs, who competed in the Central New York Semi-Professional League.[57]

Playing in more bucolic places like Helena, Montana, Lai's Hawaiian All-Stars were promoted in the local press as the "great Oriental Traveling squad" and, with a little hyperbole, hailed as "the greatest attraction to ever invade the United States." To woo Helena's baseball fans into taking in the game between Lai's team and a local semi-pro squad, the *Helena Independent*'s press release claimed that the visiting nine was "composed of the best players of the Hawaiian Islands and made up of Chinese, Japanese, and Hawaiians." Blending baseball commentary and racial "science," the press release asserted that the "Chinese and Japanese" would "supply the fielding and running thrills expected of them by baseball fans," because "Chinese and Japanese players [were] noted for their deceptive speed and agility." Since they were of "short stature" the Chinese and Japanese players were not supposed to wield powerful bats but they apparently hit well for Lai. Still, "Buck has added six foot Hawaiians to give team some homer power."[58]

After beating the East Helena nine, the *Helena Independent* declared that "the little brown boys" played "a snappy and interesting game." Insisting upon the foreignness of the Hawaiian ballplayers the *Independent* added, "Buck Lai's boys were all they were advertised to be and possibly more. They were snappy, active little fellows and their actions show they thoroughly understand this American game of baseball and could play it pretty well."[59]

In mid-summer Lai's contingent reportedly got hot. The Hawaiians won fifteen games in a row until they came to Olean, New York. There a club called App Driscoll's Nationals ended the streak before 1500 at Bradley Stadium. After leaving upstate New York, Lai's contingent returned to Chicago for a second and extended stay. In May, the team was in the Windy City. At that time, the *Chicago Daily Tribune* announced a game between the "All-Star Chinese-Hawaiians" and the Duffy Floral nine at Shewbridge Field. In late August, the "Chinese-Hawaiian All Stars" were still in Chicago. Taking on the Spencer Coal semi-pro nine on August 30, the Hawaiians lost both ends of a doubleheader before 2500 at Spencer Field. A few days later, Lai's team lost to the African American Chicago American Giants 6–5 in South Bend, Indiana.[60]

The 1937 edition of Buck Lai's Hawaiian All-Stars included Kay Kahuha, "Hula" Hopii, Al Wong, Teo Tanaka, Sam Su Choe, Wekiki Abele, Al Nalula, and Lai, described in one promotional piece as "probably the best athlete to come out of the Pacific Islands." Buck Lai, Jr., also competed for the Hawaiian All-Stars. Moreover, Jackie Mitchell, a then well known female professional, traveled at least a bit with the Hawaiians, as did a young European American male pitcher, Ross Hoff. Curiously, the team performed in hula skirts during the early innings of their games.[61]

Back in Chicago in 1937, "Buck Lai's Hawaiians," the *Chicago Daily Tribune* reported, split a doubleheader with the Mills nine. Lai's losing battery in the first game was a pitcher named Hanahana and a catcher named Kundi. In the second game, Al Nalua pitched the Hawaiians to a victory. A few months later, Buck Lai's team was scheduled to oppose the East Chicago Giants in Hammond, Indiana. Readers of the *Hammond Times* learned that Lai ran the best team ever to come out of the Hawaiian Islands and that the Chinese Hawaiian ballplayer was a former major leaguer. Looking half his age, Lai was reportedly faster than anyone on his team except his son, Buck Lai, Jr. The *Hammond Times* also asserted that the Hawaiians actually preferred playing in grass skirts to regulation uniforms. Women in attendance, according to the piece, might be inspired to wear similar attire. A few days later, the Spencer Coal nine took a doubleheader in Chicago from the "Hawaiian All-Stars." Kahuku and Abbele composed Lai's battery in the first game, while William Whaley, who possessed a Hawaiian mother and a haole father, pitched and Abbele caught the second game. Apparently, according to the *Tribune,* Lai's team featured a hurler named Sammy SoSan, who was reputedly one of the best pitchers in the "Orient."[62]

Small town American newspapers represented Lai's team in an exotic light. In Oklahoma, the *Ada Evening News* published a photo of Lai and two other Hawaiian ballplayers wearing hula skirts. The caption read, "They're ballplayers — and hula dancers." The accompanying article declared that the Lai's ballplayers were more comfortable in hula skirts than in baseball uniforms. The *Evening News* conceded one problem — fans would have trouble pronouncing the names of the Hawaiian All-Stars. In rural Ohio, the *Newark Advocate and American Tribune* promoted an upcoming game between Lai's nine and the Richmer Oil semi-pro contingent late in June 1937. The Newark newspaper declared: "Lai's team has achieved quite a record appearing against the country's leading professional and semi-pro clubs.... All are native Hawaiians and many, like Lai himself, are of Chinese ancestry. Their type of play reflects the Hawaiian trait of speed afoot, cleverness and a sense of showmanship to make up a colorful and interesting baseball attraction." Furthermore, Lai's Hawaiian ballplayers had entertained record crowds wherever they went. And because they played most of their games at night, Lai's squad transported lighting equipment as did other barnstorming teams such as the famed House of David nine.[63]

Later in the summer, Lai's team was in Mansfield, Ohio. The team was greeted with the usual publicity, although the *Mansfield News Journal* claimed incorrectly that Lai was the "only Chinese ever to play organized baseball." One thousand watched the Hawaiians lose to the Mansfield Red Sox 12–3. However, the game was distinguished by the appearance of Jackie Mitchell, who hurled an inning for the Hawaiians.[64]

Several talented Hawaiian ballplayers suited up for Lai aside from the versatile John Kerr, who played for Lai's team in 1935, and others already mentioned. A future institution in Japanese Hawaiian baseball, Lawrence Kunihisa, covered second base. Kunihisa was called in a *Helena Independent* story, the "little giant of Hawaiian baseball" and "base running champion of the islands." Others who played at one time or another with Lai's Hawaiian All-Stars were pitcher Manual Kahuku, and catcher Kenichi Enomoto, described in a press blurb as "the smartest catcher produced in a decade in Hawaii."[65]

Lai continued to receive some press attention even after his long playing career ended in the late 1930s. When the Washington Senators signed a Chinese Cuban named Manuel Hidalgo in 1945, Lai's life in baseball got a bit of newspaper exposure. Some believed that Hidalgo was the first ballplayer of Chinese ancestry to get a shot at the big leagues. However, an Associated Press report published in the *Reno Evening Gazette* declared that the "Giants [f]ielded the [f]irst Chinaman" and that "Chinese utility infielder Buck Lai" wore a New York Giants uniform twenty years earlier. The *Sporting News* noted inaccurately that Buck Lai played a few games with the New York Giants. In the 1950s, Lai ran a semi-professional outfit in Camden, New Jersey. In 1956, a sportswriter for the *Berkshire Eagle* spotted Lai at the World

Series. He reminded readers that Lai was the "Chinese-American third baseman whose fielding exploits thrilled Eastern League fans." Lai looked considerably younger than his admitted age of fifty and told sportswriter Roger O'Gara that he worked for a ship-building concern in Camden and was a part-time scout for the Dodgers. Lai died twenty years later in New Jersey.[66]

Trolling the Minors

Players of Asian Pacific Islander descent suited up for the famed All-Nations team, a professional nine playing out of Kansas City that boasted a multi-racial, multi-ethnic roster and barnstormed mainly in the Midwest in the 1910s. In 1916, I. Tashiro, a University of Chicago student, took the diamond for the All-Nations nine as a pitcher, infielder and outfielder. By 1920, the All-Nations team had morphed into the Kansas City Monarchs, a team that for years stood out as an all-African American nine. However, in 1920, Frank Blukoi, described as a Filipino second baseman, competed for the Monarchs after a previous stint with the All-Nations nine.[67]

Late in the 1932 season, a Japanese Hawaiian ballplayer, living and working in California's Central Valley, was signed by the Sacramento Solons of the PCL. Perhaps desperate for publicity and fans, the Solons hired Kenso Nushida, a clever southpaw who had pitched for Japanese American community teams in California since the early 1920s, as well as worked in the area as an agricultural laborer and a store clerk. Nushida, according to catcher Paul Vinci, was up to the challenge. Vinci told the press that the Hawaiian "is one of the smartest pitchers he has ever seen." Nushida was not overpowering but "had good control of curve balls." Pitching in Stockton, "poor little" Nushida won his first game after hurling five innings against the Los Angeles Angels.[68]

Nevertheless, Nushida's presence in the Pacific Coast League provoked the expected stereotypical depictions. For example, the *Los Angeles Times'* Harry Williams wrote that Solons owner Cy Moreing "had a warehouse up in Sacramento said to contain 2000 tons of rice. Nushida, who is not much bigger than a mouse, can burrow into the rice next winter and live happily until spring." After Hollywood beat the Solons, Williams reported, "Nushida, the Tom Thumb of the diamond," was the starter. When Nushida's Solons showed up at Los Angeles' Wrigley Field to play the Los Angeles Angels, Williams declared, "There was a distinct saffron sheen reflected by the crowd and the lights, perhaps of the crowd of 7000 being Japanese out to see their country man do his stuff." Moreover, "a pretty little Japanese sheba dolled up in a gay kimono" presented Nushida with three large bouquets of chrysanthemums.[69]

Most likely inspired by Sacramento, the Oakland Oaks signed Lee Gum Hong. Nearly six feet tall, Lee Gum Hong was known as a power pitcher in Bay Area semi-professional circles after hurling for Oakland High School. While there, he had struck out thirteen batters in one game. Among the teams he pitched for was Oakland's Wa Sung nine, which the *Oakland Tribune* asserted had one of the biggest followings of any "bushball team in the East Bay." Interestingly, Lee Gum Hong pitched under the name of Al Bowen. Twenty-one years old and an employee of Berkeley's International House, Lee Gum Hong was, according to the *Oakland Tribune*, "the first Chinese pitcher to be given a contract in organized baseball." Subsequently, Hong hoped, he told the press, that his signing would open future doors to Organized Baseball for other Chinese American ballplayers. Indeed, according to the *Tribune's* Eddie Murphy, "there was much rejoicing in many quarters of Oakland and San Francisco's Chinatowns."[70]

The announcement that Hong and Nushida would take the mound against one another in Oakland excited Bay Area Chinese and Japanese American communities. The international backdrop to the game was that Japan and China were engaged in military conflict over Manchuria and many Americans of Japanese and Chinese ancestries could scarcely ignore what was happening across the Pacific and often openly sided with either the Japanese or Chinese government. Nushida and Hong's PCL employers and the Bay Area sporting press were not above exploiting the bloody conflict ensuing in Asia. The *Oakland Tribune's* Murphy wrote about "Japan vs. Chinese in a pitching duel at the Oakland Coast League Park." According to Murphy, local Japanese and Chinese Americans were expected to show up and demonstrate their partisanship as spectators to "the first Oriental duel in organized ball." The Wa Sungs, Murphy asserted, had sold one hundred tickets to the game. Lee Gum Hong, meanwhile, got in on the act. Before he took the slab against Nushida, Hong presumably declared, "This is a battle of nations. I represent China. Nushida represents Japan. And China shall win."[71]

About 3000 fans arrived to witness Hong and Nushida hook up for the "Oriental pitching war." Murphy wrote, "Supporters of the Oaks pitcher used up a good supply of fireworks in letting the slender moundsman know that they approved of his work." The Wa Sung Club presented Hong with a floral horseshoe, while Japanese Americans from Alameda did the same for Nushida. "The Chinaman," according to Murphy, pitched better than expected. Yet neither Nushida nor Hong were good PCL pitchers in 1932. However, it would seem that they pitched well enough to earn at least a few more pitching appearances in the PCL in 1933. Yet neither Nushida nor Hong pitched in Organized Baseball again. In 1983, the eighty-two-year-old Nushida died in Honolulu.[72]

A few years later, the Sacramento Solons signed another player with a Japanese Hawaiian background. From his island home, Fumito "Jimmy" Horio headed to California where he played semi-professional ball for, among other nines, the Los Angeles Nippons. In 1934, Horio was in Sioux City, Iowa, playing Class D minor league ball. In Iowa, Horio put up decent numbers — a .282 batting average in 148 games and garnered a bit of national press attention. Early in the season a *Sporting News* correspondent asserted that Horio had become "a real yellow threat for Sioux City" as a hitter and fielder. Readers of the *Charleston Gazette* learned in August that the twenty-one-year-old "son of Nippon" was hitting well for Sioux City despite batting only .250 at the time. Horio's power defied preconceptions as he smacked a 425 foot home run into a stiff wind.[73]

Horio then joined the newly formed Yonimuri Giants, Japan's first professional team. In the spring of 1935, the Yonimuri Giants journeyed to the American mainland. Arriving with his teammates in the U.S. on the *Chichibu Maru* from Yokohama, Horio was described in the ship's manifest as an American citizen born in Maui. His father was a resident of Japan, while a sister lived in Los Angeles. The professional ballplayer was five feet eleven and apparently "dark complexioned." While on the American mainland, the Giants opposed professional teams such as the Solons in a series of games. The Solons liked what they saw in Horio, offering him a contract to join the PCL club when the Giants ended their American tour in June. Horio was used as a pitch hitter in his first game as a Solon and did not get a hit. The Japanese Hawaiian subsequently suited up as a Solon as a reserve outfielder, but Horio did not rejoin the Solons in 1936.[74]

Two very talented Hawaiian athletes flirted briefly with Organized Baseball. Even though he had no professional experience, John Kerr, one of Hawaii's most prominent baseball players of the 1930s, was signed by the Philadelphia Phillies in November 1935. The Phillies expected to use Kerr as a pitcher. However, the Hawaiian Chinese instead showed up at the San Francisco Seals spring training camp in the spring of 1936. While hailed as a rookie with great promise, Kerr did not make the Seals' roster. Far better known as a football player, Hawaiian Herman Wedemeyer still managed to play minor league baseball on the mainland after World War II. Possessing indigenous Hawaiian and Chinese ancestry, Wedemeyer stood out as a baseball player in high school and then St. Mary's College of Moraga during and after the war. He was so good that the famed sportswriter Grantland Rice insisted he could make it in the major leagues.[75]

Early in 1950, Wedemeyer tried to make a career change from a tenuous life in pro football to Pacific Coast League baseball. He reportedly hoped to hook up with the Oakland Oaks, but that PCL team decided it was not interested despite Wedemeyer's popularity in the East Bay. Subsequently, Wedemeyer tried out for the San Francisco Seals along with the Japanese Hawaiian Wally Yonamine. Indeed, the *San Francisco Chronicle* noted, "Wedemeyer and Yonamine ... reported wearing aloha shirts looking cool and confident as they began the job of making the varsity." Moreover, according to the *Chronicle,* Wedemeyer claimed he wanted to play for the Seals all along and not the Oaks. Like Yonamine, Wedemeyer was not deemed ready for the PCL. The *San Francisco News* not only recognized that Wedemeyer preferred professional baseball to professional football but that the Hawaiian was not going to be playing PCL baseball any time soon. Thus, the daily wondered if Wedemeyer would accept a pay cut to compete for a Class C minor league club. Seal manager Lefty O'Doul admired Wedemeyer's athleticism, but declared he was ill-prepared for PCL pitching. When the Seals decided to send Wedemeyer down the minor league ladder, the one time football great did not know if he wanted to head to Yakima, Washington. However, Wedemeyer agreed to play for the Yakima franchise and initially showed some ability by hitting a homer and a single in an exhibition game against a San Francisco Police Department nine.[76]

Yakima turned out to be a temporary stop for Wedemeyer. By June 1950, he had journeyed from Yakima to Salt Lake City, where he briefly rejoined Yonamine. Then he moved on to Modesto of the California League. When that did not work out, he headed south to Porterville of the Sunset League. Eventually giving up on professional baseball, Wedemeyer decided to take one more crack at professional football, showing up at the San Francisco 49ers training camp for a failed attempt to make that team's roster.[77]

Before, during, and after the onset of World War II, other Asian Pacific American ballplayers got at least a taste of professional baseball on the American mainland. In 1933, Clarence Kumalae, "a high school product who is of Hawaiian extraction," showed up at the Los Angeles Angels' spring training camp. The only southpaw at the Angels' camp, Kumalae displayed potential but apparently not enough to stick with the PCL squad. At the same time, Hawaiian Ted Nobriega was in camp with the major league St. Louis Cardinals. The *Sporting News* announced that the National League team brought "a genuine Hawaiian ukulele" to spring training. Claiming correctly that Nobriega's father was Portuguese and his mother Native Hawaiian, the *Sporting News* forgot about John B. Williams in maintaining that Nobriega "may gain the distinction of being the first man from Uncle Sam's island possession in the Pacific to break into the highest baseball society." A three sport athlete at the University of Hawaii, the twenty-two-year-old pitcher was a son of a public school principal. The Cardinals eventually sent Nobriega to Houston, which in turn dispatched him down the minor league ladder to

Springfield, Illinois, where the Hawaiian reportedly became a big sensation with the radio stations along the Missouri Valley. The *Sporting News* announced that Nobriega "twangs a mean ukulele and sings like Rudy Vallee." According to the *Honolulu Advertiser*, Nobriega's chances of sticking it out in Organized Baseball were curtailed by a hurt arm. Nevertheless, the Hawaiian maintained he enjoyed his stint in the American minor leagues.[78]

George Ho began a minor league sojourn during World War II. In June 1942, the *Sporting News* reported that the Class B Trenton Packers had signed the "Chinese outfielder" after he had previously tried out for Hartford of the Eastern League. Ho's stay with Trenton was brief as the "Baseball Bible" announced in July that he was playing for a Class C Virginia League team. The *Sporting News* provided a little information about Ho at this time. It declared that the twenty-two-year-old ballplayer was born in Canton but brought to the U.S. as a five year old. Ho attended and played ball at St. John's University in New York City. His performance lured the Boston Braves into signing him to a contract and shipping Ho to Hartford. Ho, however, apparently signed with Staunton of the Virginia League as a free agent.[79]

In a matter of days, the nomadic Ho was inked by the Chattanooga Lookouts of the Southern Association. The *Sporting News* pointed out that the "Chinese outfielder" joined a team that reportedly possessed an international flavor because it already suited up four Latinos. Lookouts fans apparently were looking forward to seeing Ho in action and greeted the Canton native warmly in his first pre-game practice. Upon suiting up with the Lookouts, *Sporting News* readers learned a little more about Ho, who, reputedly, studied law at St. Johns. Before heading to the pros, Ho had batted .380 in a New York semi-professional league. And he continued to hit for Hartford, getting three hits in three at-bats. Still, the Braves organization wanted to send him down to lower level classification and Ho successfully sought his release. Ho, subsequently, went hitless in one at-bat in his Chattanooga debut. On August 11, the Lookouts released the peripatetic ballplayer.[80]

After World War II, Ho rejoined the Lookouts. According to *Sporting News* correspondent Allan Morris, Ho had served during the war in the U.S. Intelligence Corps. Owned by the colorful Joe Engel, the Lookouts hoped that the "Chinese infielder" would help them remain competitive in the Southern Association. Engel, Morris wrote, believed that with Ho he "has a better than Chinaman's chance to win the Southern playoff series." Once again, Ho failed to stick with the Lookouts. In 1948, the Sacramento Solons gave George Ho a tryout, but the "Chinese outfielder" could not make the PCL team.[81]

A few other Asian Pacific Americans got chances to play Organized

Baseball after World War II. They included California Leaguers Hank Matsubu, Jiro Nakamura, Fibber Hirayama, and George Fujioka. Matsubu and Nakamura became the first all–*Nisei* battery with the Modesto Braves. Catcher Matsubu had previously starred for the College of Idaho nine, while Jiro Nakamura pitched effectively for San Mateo Junior College as well as for the semi-pro El Cortez nine, which played out of the East Bay. Hirayama suited up for the Stockton Ports before heading to the Japanese major leagues. Fujioka also joined the Tijuana entry in the Sunset League, after starring on the powerful *Nisei* Fresno All-Star squad. At the same time, Bill Shundo played for the Arizona-Texas League and Hawaiian Percy Ching competed in the New Mexico–Texas League.[82]

Described in the *Sporting News* as the son of a Filipino mother, Tampa, Florida natives Buck and Rudy Tanner became minor leaguers in the 1940s. Buck Tanner, who pitched three no-hitters in the lower minor league levels was the more famous of the two brothers. Signed by the Montreal Royals in 1944, Buck Tanner jumped to the Mexican League — a move which got him expelled from North American Organized Baseball in 1946. Tanner, however, was reinstated in 1949 and in the spring of 1950, pitched his third no-hitter while wearing the uniform of the Florida International League's Fort Lauderdale franchise. Apparently, Tanner's no-hitter, impressively accomplished over eleven innings, was the first such pitching feat to be televised. Rudy, at the same time, roamed the outfield in the same league for St. Petersburg.[83]

In 1956, the Brooklyn Dodgers "astonished [the] baseball world" by signing Bill Nishita. In late May, Bob Cole wrote in the *Sporting News* that Nishita was the "most prominent" of four Hawaiians trying to make it in Organized Baseball. Cole called Nishita a "24 year old pitcher of Japanese extraction." Describing Nishita as a "small Hawaiian," Cole mentioned that Nishita had won thirty games for Santa Rosa Junior College before heading to Cal. After a year at Cal, Nishita toured Japan with the Rural Red Sox. The Tokyo Giants liked what they saw and signed the Hawaiian to a two-year contract. However, Nishita was drafted by the U.S. military, but wound up back home in Hawaii where he pitched two years for Fort Shafter. In October 1954, a team called the Eddie Lopat All-Stars came to Hawaii. Featuring some fine American major league players, this squad faced Nishita's pitching at Honolulu Stadium. "Billy the Kid" did a good job, but his defense reportedly let him down. Indeed, Dodgers star Duke Snider remembered Nishita's skill in getting American major leaguers out. But after leaving the U.S. military, Nishita returned to Japan's major leagues. Cole wrote, however, that the Hawaiian "had his heart set on the [American] major leagues."[84]

The *Sporting News* announced Nishita's signing in an article headlined,

"Japanese-Ancestry Hurler Gets Trial at Dodger Camp" and claimed the Kohala-born pitcher could make the Brooklyn club if he lived up to advance notice. The *New York Times* announced Nishita's arrival at the Dodgers' Vero Beach camp with a photo of the Hawaiian with Dodgers manger Walter Alston. The *Times*' correspondent, Roscoe McGowan, insisted that Dodgers fans might be yelling "banzai" in cheering on the new hurler. Nishita, McGowan maintained, "speaks good English with an accent." Described in a UPI story as a "Hawaiian-born pitcher of Japanese ancestry," Nishita eventually joined the Dodgers' top minor league team—the Montreal Royals—after pitching ten innings of one run ball in exhibition game appearances for the Dodgers. According to the UPI account, Nishita had never pitched in Organized Baseball. While technically true, he was no novice—having pitched for a top-flight college baseball program in Cal, as well as the Japanese major leagues. Nishita had paid his own way to the Dodgers' Vero Beach training camp and impressed the franchise's decision makers with his determination and ability.[85]

In late April 1956, Nishita notched his first win in the International League as he beat the Havana Sugar Canes. Earlier, Nishita had made his pitching debut for Montreal in a losing effort against Columbus. In July, Nishita earned his first shutout, an eight hitter against Buffalo. Still, Nishita was optioned to Fort Worth of the Texas League after winning four and losing five and achieving a 4.97 ERA for the Royals. Nishita, subsequently, returned to the Japanese major leagues. Bill Nishita died in Honolulu in 2003 at the age of 72.[86]

Jack Ladro was another Hawaiian mentioned by Bob Cole. When the New York Yankees toured the Hawaiian Islands in 1955, Ladro's center field play pleased them as he competed for a Fort Shafter nine. A Honokoa native, Ladro eventually showed his talents on the mainland when he played for the Rural Red Sox in the Global World Series held in Milwaukee. The Yankees signed Ladro and sent him initially to Denver, one of the Yankees' highest minor league teams. Then, he was moved down the minor league ladder to Quincy of the Three I League.[87]

George Fujishige was the third Hawaiian of Asian Pacific Islander ancestry to attract Organized Baseball in America in 1956. Fujishige had been signed by the Nankai Hawks of the Japanese major league after the Hawks had toured the islands. A native of Waipahu, Fujishige played six years with the Rural Red Sox. He was an adequate third baseman and outfielder along with being a good catcher. Like Ladro and Nishita, Fujishige starred for his military team. However, Fujishige played for Hickham. Interestingly, Cole does not mention whether Fujishige was on any Organized Baseball roster in 1956 Like his Santa Rosa Junior College teammate, Fujishige had better luck getting into Japan's major leagues than America's. In 1963, George Fujishige signed with the Hawaii Islanders of the PCL.[88]

Crispin Mancao and Jerry Ako were Hawaiians who pitched professionally in two different regions of the world. In 1961, the Hawaiian Islanders made their debut in the Pacific Coast League. Crispin Mancao was one of the locals recruited to help the Islanders win games and attract local fans. Mancao, who was then forty-seven, recalled in 2000 that the Islanders called him at work: "I thought it was a joke. My boss said go ahead. Next thing I know, I'm in Seattle on a road trip." Mancao, according to a *Sporting News* report, did a "credible job" in his PCL debut against Spokane. The "control pitcher" hurled two innings, while giving up no runs and two hits. Nearly twenty years later, Jerry Ako, described in the *Sporting News* as a Native Hawaiian, pitched for Holyoke of the Eastern League. The St. Louis weekly claimed that "Holyoke enjoyed a Hawaiian-Japanese victory" as Ako went eight innings before Kuni Ogawa of Japan relieved him. In 1982, Ako pitched in the Mexican League for Aguascalientes.[89]

Conclusion

There are different ways one could look at the historical experiences of ballplayers such as Buck Lai. On the one hand, mainland professional baseball in the twentieth century was inclusive enough to give Lai a chance to make money doing something he obviously loved very much. And clearly evidence of overt racial discrimination hindering the baseball career of Lai, Yamashiro, Nushida, Hong, Horio, and Nishita is not extensive.

Nevertheless, one wonders how many lesser but white players Lai saw promoted upward from the Eastern League toward the higher rungs of the minor leagues and even into regular major league lineups. The fact that Lai was a .260 hitter in the Eastern League should prevent unwarranted speculation that the Chinese Hawaiian, if white, was bound for major league stardom. But athletic, fast, and smart infielders were not so numerous in Organized Baseball that Lai, if white, could not have made it earlier into the International League as a regular third baseman or even in the big leagues as perhaps a utility infielder. Moreover, given Vernon Ayau's outstanding ability to field as a shortstop and that shortstops were not then expected to bat well, would it have been so hard to imagine he would have been given more of a chance by Seattle to show his stuff in 1917 if he had been white? Admittedly, Kenso Nushida and Lee Gum Hong did not remind anyone of Lefty Grove or Dizzy Dean. It seems, however, that they pitched adequately enough to get another shot at PCL ball in 1933. Sadly, it is not at all clear that even those Asian Pacific Americans who made it into the big leagues in either America or Japan totally escaped racism's traveling eye.

Chapter VII

Asian Pacific American Big Leaguers in the United States and Japan

Perhaps occasionally racism's traveling eye was looking the other way, but there have been American players of Asian Pacific American ancestry who have made it into big league ball in the United States. However, until recent years, Japan's major leagues proved more receptive, especially to Japanese American ballplayers. Few American big leaguers of Asian Pacific Islander ancestry could be called stars in the United States until the last twenty years or so. Today, Johnny Damon, possessing Thai ancestry, stands out as one of MLB's most charismatic figures and can conceivably bat, field, and run his way into the American baseball Hall of Fame. However, Damon stands on the shoulders of very talented Asian Pacific American ballplayers such as Henry Oana, Bobby Balcena, Wally Yonamine, Milt Wilcox, Tony Solaita, and Mike Lum.

Barney Joy was not the only American of Asian Pacific American ancestry to attract the major leagues in the early 1900s. In the spring of 1908, the national press reported that Frank Chance, manager of the powerful Chicago Cubs, was interested in signing a "Chinese ballplayer" from Hawaii. Readers of the *Atlanta Constitution* learned that "if a Mongolian goes south with the famous Chicago 'Cubs' he will certainly add zest to the training period." After visiting Hawaii, Chance wrote home that "the most remarkable baseball player in Hawaii is a Chinese boy named En Sue, who plays third for St. Louis College." Chance suggested that other big league teams had tried to lure En Sue Pung to the mainland but had failed. Chance hoped that an invitation from the powerful Cubs would do the trick. Chance praised En Sue Pung's speed and hitting ability, adding that the future Travelers standout's command of baseball was not all that surprising given Hawaii's love of the game: "The small boy, be he Chinese, Japanese or Hawaiian, or the result of a mixture of several of these races, takes to baseball as naturally as does the American small boy, whose forebears have played the game since it started."[1]

John Williams

As it turned out, En Sue Pung remained unmoved by the possibility of playing major league ball in Chicago or anywhere else for that matter. Johnny Williams was, accordingly, the first Hawaiian and the first person of indigenous Hawaiian ancestry to compete in major league baseball. In 1911, Williams pitched his first PCL game for Sacramento against Vernon. Subsequently, Sacramento shipped him to a club in Victoria, British Columbia, for more seasoning, but Williams rejoined the PCL team before the baseball year ended. The *Pacific Commercial Advertiser* expressed pride in Williams' achievements in 1911 and told readers during the off-season that the Honolulan, enticed by Sacramento's generous salary offer, was determined to make good in the PCL when he returned to California in the spring of 1912.[2]

When Willliams showed up for Sacramento's 1912 spring training camp, the *Sacramento Bee* noted "Dusky Williams" had gotten better. Keeping Williams in 1912 was a good idea for Sacramento as he accumulated more wins than any other PCL pitcher that season. Not only did Williams pitch well for Sacramento, but he proved a good draw for fans wishing to see a real live Hawaiian in action. Moreover, he attracted major league interest. In June 1912, the *Pacific Commercial Advertiser* published a report that Connie Mack's Philadelphia Athletics would land the Hawaiian pitcher.[3]

Williams remained with Sacramento in 1913, after all. Sacramento seemed glad to have him and Honolulu remained proud of Williams' accomplishments in the PCL. In California's capital city, Williams was hailed as the "dusky warrior from across the sea." The *Honolulu Star-Bulletin* asserted that Williams made big news in Sacramento — "bigger than the Webb anti–alien land law," which would deny farm ownership in California to Asian immigrants. One Sacramento baseball fan even bothered to take pen to paper in order to write a poem to Williams — a poem which included the not terribly memorable words: "If you've any other friend in Hula-hula land/Who can twirl (boy or girl)/If he's there we'll pay his fare, But here to you our hand." However, late in the 1913 season, it seemed all but certain that Sacramento would sell Williams to a major league team rather than wait for one to draft the Hawaiian, which would have meant less money for the PCL franchise. The *Los Angeles Times* claimed that as many as ten major league clubs had sought Williams' services earlier in 1913. However, enthusiasm had dimmed because Williams' performance briefly and slightly declined. Sacramento's manager, Harry Wolverton, seemed willing to part with Williams but the *Times* maintained that the former major leaguer was an honest man who would not want to sell Williams unless the pitcher truly returned to his earlier winning form. Still, Williams put together a 17 and 7 record in 1913 and major league teams could not disguise their intrigue.[4]

In 1914, Williams finally put on a major league uniform after the Detroit Tigers signed him. When he wintered in Honolulu before the 1914 season, Williams evoked both pride and a little consternation. Upon returning home with his California bride, Williams told adoring locals of his signing with the Tigers, adding, "They tell me Hugh Jennings is a fine fellow to work for and I will certainly give him the best that is in me." Local fans and the sporting press looked forward to a New Year's game between the Travelers and a picked nine of the best ballplayers in Honolulu. Many hoped to see what Williams could do against the best team on the islands. However, the Travelers prevailed in a 4–2 game. Williams apparently showed his talents, but, according to the *Honolulu Star-Bulletin's* Lawrence Reddington, disappointed fans with his behavior. Williams treated fans and the umpire with contempt, displaying "sneering indifference to fair play." Williams, Reddington wrote, "slobbered the ball with various concoctions taken from his pockets and pulled other bushy stuff that delayed the game. If he doesn't pitch another game here this winter the crowd won't be much disappointed." To be fair, the *Pacific Commercial Advertiser* greeted Williams' New Year's performance more generously, although it noted that Williams loafed occasionally during the game and tried to get away with putting coal tar on the balls he pitched.[5]

When Williams arrived at the Detroit Tigers training camp, he piqued a great deal of curiosity. He also stirred some controversy back home in Hawaii as he complained to a Detroit sportswriter about the prevalence of players of Chinese and Japanese ancestry in island baseball, as well as in Hawaii's labor market. At the same time, Williams defended his indigenous Hawaiian heritage. He told the press that he was tired of hearing how he had descended from cannibals, while declaring that mainlanders misapplied the term "Kanaka." "We are Hawaiian," he said, "and nothing else." Williams, however, pitched his way to a short, forgettable career with the Tigers—short perhaps because Ty Cobb did not like to share the Tigers with a person of non–white ancestry. Just as likely, if not more so, he did not perform well for the Tigers. In May 1914, *Star-Bulletin* readers learned that Williams had been knocked out in the first inning and that "it is easy to see that the Honolulan is in wrong as a starter." Williams, it appeared, showed major league speed but not major league control. Yet while Williams proved unsuccessful as a major leaguer, his presence on the Tigers' roster made an impact, according to the *Fort Wayne News*. With Williams' help, Tiger manager Hughie Jennings reportedly did base coaching in the Hawaiian language in order to fool the opposition.[6]

The end of his brief major league career marked the beginning of the end for Williams' professional career. Later in 1914, Williams was back in the PCL, pitching for the San Francisco Missions. His first two games for the Missions proved disastrous as the Venice Tigers used him for batting practice. The *Los Angeles Times* speculated that Williams' problem was that he had a hard time acclimating to San Francisco after moving about the globe from Honolulu to Sacramento to Detroit and back to the American West Coast. In 1915, he could not catch on with the PCL's Salt Lake City nine. Yet he, subsequently, wound up with the PCL's Los Angeles Angels. Williams still could win a game or two. The *Times* contended that the Hawaiian was just "too shrewd" for Oakland in a 5–1 victory. Over a year later, Williams got into the *Sporting News* for pleading with Walter McCreadie to make a deal for him so that he would not have to report to the St. Joseph, Missouri, franchise of the Western League. St. Joseph was apparently Williams' last minor league stop before giving up professional baseball on the mainland.[7]

After leaving the professional ranks, Williams remained active in Hawaiian baseball. In the 1920s, Williams played for the nominally European American contingent, the Wanderers. In 1930, Williams told a U.S. census taker he was racially a Caucasian-Hawaiian. A machinist in 1930, Williams' father, according to the census, was born in England and his mother was Hawaiian.[8]

Early in 1934, nationally respected sportswriter Dan Daniels correctly remembered Williams as the first Hawaiian to make it to the American big leagues. He said that Williams' mother was indeed "Polynesian" while his father was English. Williams did not "make the grade" as a big leaguer. Still, the Hawaiian possessed all the "tricks of a Native Kanaka," including the dubious ability of curling his toes around a suitcase handle and tossing the suitcase across the room with impressive velocity. Indeed, according to a piece published in the *Honolulu Star-Bulletin* in 1914, Ty Cobb himself requested that Williams fling the "Georgia Peach's" travel bag by foot and was pleased with the results.[9]

Henry Oana

Henry Oana became the second Hawaiian to make it onto an American major league roster. Born and raised in Oahu's rural Waipahu, Oana's father was a Native Hawaiian railroad station agent in 1920, while his mother was Portuguese. A talented, all-around athlete, he was known as "Nutsky" while attending St. Louis College in Honolulu. As an adult, Oana dedicated himself to the nightlife — a dedication that perhaps cost him a more secure professional career. Nevertheless, he played many years professionally from one coast of the mainland to the other and into the south and southwest.[10]

According to a *Sporting News* writer in 1942, Oana was on a Hawaiian team that barnstormed Japan in the late 1920s. Ty Cobb saw him and suggested he give mainland baseball a try. Apparently not always as mean-spirited as the reputation he acquired, Cobb, who lived in the San Francisco Bay Area for many years, arranged for the San Francisco Seals to give Oana a tryout. On November 16, 1928, the manifest of the SS *Wilhelmina* shows an eighteen-year-old Oana disembarking in San Francisco.[11]

By 1929, Oana began to gain notice not only as a talented ballplayer but also as a Hawaiian. A press account of his early minor league career was headlined, "Good Looks, Too." The youthful and handsome Oana was called inaccurately, "Hawaii's first gift to professional baseball." The Seals, however, dispatched him to the Arizona State League for more seasoning. During the 1929 season, the *Sporting News* reported that "Henry Oana, the Hawaiian prince ... is hitting the ball hard."[12]

In 1931, Oana fought for a regular job with the San Francisco Seals. San Francisco sportswriter Ed Hughes thought he had a good chance to make the team, noting that Oana "is a good fielder, he is fast and he has a strong throwing arm." Oana won a regular job with the Seals and put up imposing numbers in 1931, slugging twenty-three home runs, hitting .345, and helping the San Franciscans win the PCL championship. A bout with the law in San Francisco almost and perhaps should have cut Oana's career short, however. A Bay Area woman accused Oana and two other ballplayers of assaulting her, although a wire report in the *Los Angeles Times* identified a San Francisco attorney as the only other person charged. Fortunately for Oana, he was cleared. Suspecting that Oana loved chasing women and downing alcohol a little too enthusiastically, the Seals decided to send the Hawaiian up to Portland. Spencer Abbott, manager of the Beavers at the time, speculated that Oana's departure from the Seals moved the franchise to seek to replace the Hawaiian with a young Joe DiMaggio.[13]

In any event, Abbott could not have been more pleased with Oana. He remembered in 1946 that the Hawaiian strayed only once "from the straight and narrow." More to the point, Oana drove in 163 runs, a striking number even in the PCL — a league that was notoriously tough on pitchers' ERAs in the early 1930s. Oana's 1933 performance prompted the Philadelphia Phillies to add him to the roster in 1934. However, the Phillies, according to the *Sporting News* gave Oana a "quick Aloha." On the occasion of Oana's memorable move up to Organized Baseball's highest rung, the *Lima News* published a wire photo of Oana, captioned, "The rookie is Prince Oana ... an outfielder in whose veins course the blood of Hawaiian royalty." Readers were told that that the Phillies had acquired Oana from the Portland Beavers for two players and cash.[14]

When it appeared as though Oana would make the big leagues in 1934, Dan Daniel wrote an article about the Hawaiian in the *Sporting News*. Accompanying the article was a cartoon showing Oana, along with drawings of Cuban Dolph Luque, as well as Native Americans Chief Bender and Chief Myers. The cartoon's subject was baseball's reputation as a melting pot. The cartoon included a panel that showed a respectful depiction of Kenso Nushida and reminded readers that he pitched for Sacramento. A not so respectful depiction of Buck Lai was displayed in another panel. It exhibited "Lai Tin" missing a ground ball at third base and supposedly swearing in Chinese. Buck Lai was called "a Chinaman who failed to make the grade with the Giants."[15]

Daniel pointed out that despite the prevalent publicity surrounding the Phillies' rookie, Henry Oana would not be the first Hawaiian major leaguer. That distinction, Daniel well knew, belonged to Johnny Williams. Noting Oana's mixed racial and ethnic identity, Daniel wrote, "He is quite dark in complexion and has the ideal build for an outfielder. He is swift and like most Hawaiians graceful." However, Daniel told a different story about how Oana headed to the San Francisco Seals. Not mentioning Cobb's role, Daniel claimed that Oana was scouted by Charley Graham, the Seals' part-owner. While vacationing in Hawaii, Graham spotted Oana playing baseball barefooted, which, according to Daniel, was what "kanakas" liked to do. Upon signing the Hawaiian, Graham decided to market Oana as a "full-blooded" Hawaiian prince. Graham thought if Hawaiian swimming great Duke Kahanamoku could be a duke, Oana could be a prince. However, Daniel wrote, major league scouts worried that if Oana was truly a "full-blooded" Hawaiian, his presence on an American major league roster would provoke racial prejudice.[16]

Daniel reported that Graham was reluctant to rid himself of Oana, even if major league franchises wanted the Hawaiian. However, Oana's "playboy" ways and falloff in production apparently convinced Graham to sell the outfielder to Portland. In the Pacific Northwest, Oana straightened out and regained his playing form. Daniels, consequently, predicted that Oana's success as a major leaguer would depend upon his ability to deal with the pressures of major league life. That is, Oana needed to lead a life of sobriety and sexual abstinence — like Babe Ruth.[17]

The Phillies got off to a bad start in 1934. The manager hoped that by giving Oana a shot at left field, the team's fortunes would improve. Oana did not prove to be the curing elixir the Phillies hoped for and they relegated him to the minor leagues. Spencer Abbott, who managed the Atlanta Crackers at the time, thought Oana would be a good fit for the team. He recalled that the Crackers needed a right handed slugger who could hit the ball into the "Negro bleachers" and develop into "a hero for our colored citizens." Atlanta decided to merchandise Oana along the same lines as Graham — as "Hawaiian royalty." Abbott insisted it was not much of a deception since Oana "comes from the best stock in the islands."[18]

After departing the Phillies, Oana bounced around the minor leagues. Oana even considered becoming a professional wrestler, although, according to the *Sporting News*, he finished off the 1934 season well with Atlanta as his 100 RBIs ranked second in the league. Oana told the press in the fall of 1934 that he was going to "stay in this country" rather than return to Hawaii. He thought he could do well as a professional wrestler because he had learned much from "Japanese grapplers" on the islands and wanted to apply that knowledge in mainland rings. Perhaps fortunately for Oana, a career in professional wrestling eluded him.[19]

According to *Sporting News* writer Zeke Handler, Oana's propensity for "extracurricular" activities proved a major problem for his professional baseball career. To Spencer Abbott, Oana was "a big lovable guy" who never grew up. After Atlanta, Oana moved to Syracuse of the International League, where, according to sportswriter Bill Reddy, he did well. Oana "played gracefully, colorfully, and besides that hit .300" for the team that eventually won the International League championship. From Syracuse, Oana headed to Baltimore of the same league. In 1936, Oana found himself in the middle of a horrible slump while playing for Baltimore, although once his manager persuaded him to use a lighter bat, the Hawaiian started to hit better. However, during a playoff series between Baltimore and Buffalo, Oana got into a "red hot scrap" with Buffalo's Tony Kaufman. Umpires and cooler heads had to separate the "Oriole's Hawaiian prince" and the Buffalo pitcher. While still on the Baltimore roster in the spring of 1937, the *Sporting News* observed that Oana's Hawaiian background helped make the Triple A franchise a multinational aggregation. Later in 1937, Oana was shipped back to Atlanta and then further down the minor league hierarchy to Little Rock. Even then he could not stick and found himself playing semi-pro baseball in North Carolina. In 1938, Oana failed to make the Milwaukee Brewers of the International League because of his slumping bat. Nevertheless, he caught on with the Jackson franchise of the Southeastern League. In Jackson, Oana began hitting again. Early in the season, he hit homers in three consecutive games, while batting .352 in the first sixteen games. Oana finished the season with thirty-nine home runs, 127 runs batted in, and a nice .323 batting average. According to Zeke Handler, the management of Fort Worth of the Texas League really wanted Oana because of the "pop in his bat." Thus, early in 1940, Fort Worth announced it had purchased the only "full-blooded" Hawaiian in organized baseball. Once the 1940 season started, the *Sporting News* asserted that the "big Hawaiian outfielder ... ha[d] captured the fancy of Fort Worth fans." Meanwhile, Oana, pronounced "O-wah-nuh," according to Zeke Handler, had married Patricia Hall of Atlanta.[20]

In the early 1940s, Oana transformed himself from an erratic hitter to a consistently effective pitcher for Fort Worth. In 1940, Oana was still trying to make it as an everyday player. The "giant outfielder" did manage to stall Dizzy Dean's comeback bid as a Tulsa pitcher with a homer and a double. Yet hitting woes plagued him. Aided by his manager, the usually cranky and uninspiring Rogers Hornsby, Oana in 1942 became a full-time pitcher and "the sensation of the Texas League," according to Don Watson of the *Honolulu Star-Bulletin*. Pop Boone, a syndicated NEA sportswriter, contended that Oana's career as an everyday player was coming to a halt. Hornsby would let the "pure-bred Hawaiian" pitch batting practice and saw that Fort Worth batters were having a hard time with him. Initially, Oana was tried in relief, but after two sparking performances as a reliever, Hornsby inserted him into Fort Worth's starting rotation. From there on, Oana's professional career rose and fell on his ability to get batters out, which in the Texas League he proved able to do. "Doting fans," Boone observed, affectionately called Oana "Hankus Pankus."[21]

Sportswriter Zeke Handler maintained that the "good natured, husky" Oana pitched a no-hitter for Fort Worth, although the game occurred on the back end of a doubleheader and hence lasted only seven innings. Finding success on the mound, Oana told the press he always wanted to be a pitcher and, as such, became a big draw for Fort Worth, where, in 1942, he put together a very nice 16–5 record.[22]

After the 1942 season, Fort Worth sold the Hawaiian to Milwaukee of the American Association partly because the Texas League expected to go out of business due to economic pressures exerted by World War II, while Milwaukee expected that Oana was ineligible for the military draft. Subsequently convinced that Oana would become 1-A in draft status and that Fort

Worth had tricked them, the Brewers returned the Hawaiian to the Texas League franchise and sought their money back. The commission in charge of Organized Baseball ordered Fort Worth to refund Milwaukee and declared Oana a free agent.[23]

The Detroit Tigers learned that Fort Worth was right after all. Oana's 3A draft status meant he was not likely to join the military. Oana joined the American League club instead. His momentary return to the major leagues was not triumphant but was hardly a failure. The highlight of Oana's 1943 season perhaps occurred when the Tigers took on the New York Yankees in an early July doubleheader. In the second game, the Tigers fell behind the Yankees. Oana was brought in as a relief pitcher. He not only pitched two shutout innings that kept a lid on the Bronx Bombers, but he hit a three run home run which put the Tigers within hailing distance of the New Yorkers. In the ninth inning, Detroit came back to win the game. Valuable as a pinch hitter, Oana hit .343 for the Tigers in 1943. Commissioner Landis believed that the Milwaukee Brewers had been cheated of Oana's services, although it is not clear as to who exactly was to blame. Landis, in any event, returned Oana to the Brewers.[24]

Oana's baseball career became anything but stable at this time. Instead of wearing a Milwaukee uniform in 1944, he pitched for Buffalo of the International League. On Memorial Day of 1945, Oana tossed a one-hit shutout into the ninth, only to give up a couple of hits in a run in the last frame. In 1945, the Tigers once again signed him. Tigers teammate Virgil Trucks remembered for writer Richard Goldstein, "I talked with Hank. I got to know him real well and he definitely was a prince. But you know not like being a queen or king or something like that. He wasn't that type of prince. He was just, you'd say, a minor league prince."[25]

In 1946, Oana was back the minors, but he received national attention for putting together a string of victories that some expected would raise him over the forty wins mark, impressive in any professional league. He did not make it to forty victories, but the man often referred to as the "Prince" because a press agent claimed he possessed royal Hawaiian ancestry, still won plenty of games. Indeed, the "handsome Hawaiian" won twenty-four games for the Dallas Rebels and was the Texas League's Pitcher of the Year. The former outfielder also batted .307 and slugged seven home runs. Consequently, grateful fans in Dallas built Oana a home for free in recognition of his outstanding 1946 season.[26]

Oana remained in Texas. From 1948 to 1950, he pitched for and managed Austin of the Big State League. In 1951, Texarkana of the Big State League named Oana a player-manager. In August of the same year, the *Sporting News* reported that a "severe allergy" had kept Oana out of uniform for several weeks. Consequently, Texarkana fired Oana. According to Bill Reddy,

Oana's baseball career was damaged by cataracts. Oana confided in Reddy that Paul Richards, who then managed the Chicago White Sox, offered him a coaching job with the Southside club. However, Oana had to turn him down because of his failing eyesight. The Hawaiian died in Austin in 1976.[27]

Bobby Balcena

Bobby Balcena was the first Filipino American to play major league baseball. However, it took him several years of fine minor league performances to reach the big leagues and when he got there, he did not stay long. Born in San Pedro, California, in 1928, a U.S. census taker found him as a toddler in 1930 living in Inglewood with his mother, two sisters, a brother, a brother-in-law, and one cousin. Both of Balcena's parents were Filipinos. At the time of the census, his auto salesman brother-in-law was apparently the family's major breadwinner.[28]

Filipino American Bobby Balcena played several years in the minor leagues for teams such as the Seattle Rainiers of the Pacific Coast League. In 1957, Balcena got a brief cup of coffee with the Cincinnati Redlegs. (Courtesy of Bill Hickam.)

While standing about five feet six, Balcena possessed plenty of pop in his bat and plenty of speed. In high school, he starred in both baseball and football. After serving three years in the military, Balcena signed with the St. Louis Browns of the American League and began his professional career with Mexicali of the Sunset League. Playing for Mexicali in the late 1940s, Balcena was called a "swift little centerfielder." He also achieved success, winning the league batting crown with a .369 average, as well as all-star honors. Toward the end of the 1949 season, the Mexicali ball club and fans staged

While with the Seattle Rainiers, Bobby Balcena became a favorite of the city's large Filipino American community. Here he is sitting, first on the left, in the front row of a 1956 team picture (author's collection).

a night to honor Balcena. The "Filipino outfielder" received seventy dollars, a watch and diamond ring among other gifts. The honor was deserved as Balcena rapped sixteen home runs and drove in 132 runs in 123 games. In 1950, Balcena moved up the minor league ladder to Wichita. And the next season he was promoted to San Antonio of the Texas League.[29]

Texas proved just as welcoming for Balcena as it had been for Oana. While trying to hang on with San Antonio in the spring of 1951, Balcena hit a home run against the New York Yankees in an exhibition game. Moreover, "the diminutive Filipino outfielder," as he was called by a *Sporting News* correspondent, slugged two home runs in a game against Houston. One of the home runs was a grand slam.[30]

Once the 1951 Texas League season began, Balcena got off to a good start with San Antonio. After thirty-four games, he batted .320 and received national publicity for acrobatically snaring a line drive against Oklahoma City when the bases were filled. At mid-season, Balcena was named to the Texas League all-star game. In July, *Syracuse Herald-Journal* readers learned that "little Bobby Balcena" was considered a part of the St. Louis Browns' future. While with San Antonio, Balcena "has been hitting consistently and winning daily plaudits with his speed on the base paths and his rifle-like throws from the outfield." In September, Balcena slugged a game winning two run homer against Beaumount. The clutch home run not only assured San Antonio of a second place finish but also earned Balcena fifty dollars, collected by San Antonio fans. At the end of the season, he batted .272, hit 26 doubles, 6 triples, and 9 home runs. He might have done better, according to the *Sporting News*' Dick Peebles, had he not fractured a finger.[31]

The next season, Balcena climbed toward the top of the minor league hierarchy by heading northward to Toronto of the International League. There, he batted .322 until he was "mysteriously" sent back to San Antonio. A discouraged Balcena also had to deal with the death of a sister and returned to San Antonio after her funeral with perhaps his heart not totally in baseball. His statistics, accordingly, suffered. He batted .252, hit seventeen doubles and seven triples. But he did manage to pound thirteen home runs. Indeed, late in the season, Balcena hit two ninth inning home runs in a row to beat Tulsa and Oklahoma City respectively. In any event, Balcena was voted as San Antonio's most popular player in 1952 by members of the Fraternal Order of Eagles. The Southern Californian received a rod, reel, and fishing tackle box as a result.[32]

In the spring of 1953, Balcena was in camp with the St. Louis Browns. But he wound up again in San Antonio, for which he put together a nationally reported fifteen game hitting streak early in the season. A *Sporting News* piece in June 1953, called the California native the "little Filipino flyhawk." It told readers that after a very poor start, Balcena got hot and took off on the hitting streak. Correspondent Dick Peebles praised Balcena as "Mr. Center field" in the Texas League and pointed out that "Little Bobby" was "the hustlingnest player in the league." Balcena, moreover, told the press that he was set to "go for broke" and win a job in 1954 with the Baltimore Orioles — the franchise into which the St. Louis Browns had morphed. The "stocky, spry outfielder" finished the 1953 season with twenty home runs and a .270 batting average.[33]

After the 1953 season, Balcena's contract was bought by the Baltimore Orioles and it looked like he had a good chance to play in the big leagues. During the Orioles' spring training, Balcena managed to hit a home run against the Chicago Cubs in Yuma, Arizona. Unfortunately, Baltimore sent Balcena down to Toronto of the International League. Toronto then optioned Balcena to Kansas City, where he batted .261 and hit seven home runs. Kansas City then returned Balcena to San Antonio.[34]

In late 1954, Balcena was drafted from San Antonio by the Seattle Rainiers of the Pacific Coast League. A few weeks later, he was signed by the Rainiers and thus began perhap his most productive minor league years. That spring training season of 1955 the *Seattle Post-Intelligencer*'s Paul Rossi notified Rainier fans that the "Filipino Flyer" was a "slugging outfielder," making a strong bid for the PCL team's lineup. Just before the 1955 season officially began, it was expected that Balcena would battle Carmen Mauro for time in the center field position. Emmett Watson of the *Post-Intelligencer* pointed out that Balcena got a better jump on the ball but that Mauro was good, too. Rainiers manager Fred Hutchinson, Watson predicted, would probably alternate Mauro against right-handed pitchers and the right-hand hitting Balcena against lefties. A few days later, the *Post-Intelligencer* informed readers that Balcena was a "little mite with good power."[35]

Devoting a column to Balcena, Watson wrote that Seattle fans would find that the Southern Californian was "a somewhat darker edition of Jo-Jo White"—a former Rainier who tutored Balcena back in San Antonio. "The little Filipino," according to Watson, "has a face like a Pekinese and the speed of a startled greyhound." Watson asserted that Balcena was not an outstanding hitter but possessed surprising power. Watson predicted that Balcena would become the Rainiers' most popular player since Jim Rivera, a dynamic Puerto Rican American ballplayer who roamed the outfield a few years earlier for Seattle. One reason why, Watson maintained, was that Balcena clearly enjoyed the game.[36]

After the 1955 season began, Balcena showed his worth to the PCL team. Balcena flourished in his first start for the Rainiers against the Oakland Oaks. He batted three for five, and, according to the *Post-Intelligencer*'s Paul Rossi, was the team's hitting star. Veteran sports columnist Royal Brougham predicted that Seattle's Filipino American community would embrace Balcena. He warned readers before Seattle's home opener, "Shrill-voiced Filipino fans are noisiest of all sports followers and if you hear an earpiercing whoop at your elbow at the ball park, it will be a dark-skinned rooter cheering for Bob Balcena, the boy with the bolo punch at the plate who is leading the hitters." As expected, Balcena seemed to make a hit, but not just with Filipino American fans. He excited the entire home crowd by batting two for five in the home opener.[37]

A few days later, Balcena starred in a tense, extra-inning victory for the Rainiers in Seattle. Consequently, Brougham declared, "Bobby Balcena was nominated for mayor of Seattle's Filipino colony in the sixth inning of yesterday's spinetingler after his home run tied the score." Filipino fans cheered loudly again when Balcena's single knotted the score again in the fourteenth inning. Brougham observed that the Filipino rooters were led by Florenca Della, who was a barber in a Filipino community shop "where Filipino fans gather every day to talk about their newest idol." Among Balcena's Filipino fans was Max Calos, known, according to Brougham as "Pee Wee." An elevator operator, Calos could not quiet his admiration for Balcena: "First Filipino boy ever to make professional league team.... See all our people out to game? All come to see Balcena play. Lots of good baseball men in Manila. Maybe Hutch better send scout to Philippines, sign couple more Balcena."[38]

Balcena put together a solid 1955 season for the Rainiers. Even though the team's power hitters were failing in the clutch in mid–season, Emmet Watson declared "Balcena, who can hide behind a milk bottle," was doing their job. In 150 games, Balcena batted a fine .291, knocked in sixty runs, and hit seven home runs. While heading home to San Pedro, California, after the 1955 season, Balcena expressed a desire to stay with the Rainiers. A UPI article claimed that "Seattle's hustling little outfielder" even preferred remaining in Seattle over getting drafted by a major league team. Balcena said he liked Seattle's fans. And the Rainiers' management obviously liked Balcena, who not only hit well but played "outstanding" outfield. Indeed, Dewey Soriano, the Rainiers' general manager, praised Balcena as the best defensive outfielder in the PCL. The Rainiers convinced him to sign a "draft waiver" clause in his contract — a clause which would prevent a major league team from drafting Balcena.[39]

Balcena's 1956 season proved memorable. In two games against Portland in May, Balcena reached base nine times out of ten at-bats. The outfielder rapped six singles and a double, took a walk, and reached base by way of an error. Balcena was named the starting outfielder for the North in the PCL all-star game. Called "the scrappy San Pedro Filipino" by Frank Finch of the *Los Angeles Times*, Balcena led the PCL in doubles, with thirty-eight. Bobby Bragan, who managed the Pittsburgh Pirates, was interested in acquiring Balcena, "the Rainiers' Filipino outfielder." Nothing came of this but the Cincinnati Redlegs did bring Balcena and teammate Art Schult up late in the season to hopefully help the team win a National League pennant that eventually was copped by the Brooklyn Dodgers. Readers of the *Coschocton Tribune* learned: "Balcena [is] believed to be the first Filipino to reach the major leagues."[40]

Balcena made his major league debut pinch hitting against the Brooklyn Dodgers' tough Sal Maglie. Unfortunately, he struck out. Sportswriter Oscar Ruhl noted that Balcena's manager, Birdie Tebbetts, tried to console the "glum faced" California native. Tebbetts explained that he had struck out in his first at-bat in the big leagues and stuck around as a major leaguer for sixteen years. Balcena subsequently managed a ground out against another strong National League pitcher, Sam Jones.[41]

Despite playing little for the Reds, Balcena was given a shot at making the Cincinnati ball club for the 1957 season. After the 1956 season, Reds general manager Gabe Paul claimed that Balcena and Schult had the best chance of any of the prospects to make the Reds' opening day roster in 1957, while the Rainiers' new manager, Lefty O'Doul, expressed regret that Balcena would no longer roam Seattle's center field. Moreover, Balcena played in the Venezuela League during the winter and raised some eyebrows. Clay Bryant, who managed Balcena in Venezuela, believed he could make the Reds as a fill-in outfielder. The *Sporting News*, indeed, predicted Balcena would be watched closely in the Reds' camp, although it noted that he would also be the shortest player on the Reds' spring training roster. Nevertheless, Balcena was among the first cuts made from the Reds' roster in the spring.[42]

Balcena returned to Seattle and Lefty O' Doul, where he continued to play well, although he cracked an ankle early in the season. The PCL's correspondent to the *Sporting News* praised Balcena as the "brilliant little Filipino." San Francisco sportswriter Jack McDonald hailed the Southern Californian as one of the best centerfielders in the PCL. According to famed sportswriter Shirley Povich, the Washington Senators were interested in signing Balcena. Scout Charlie Dressen and owner Calvin Griffith both headed to the Pacific Coast to check on Balcena. Apparently, they found out that Balcena could field but had trouble hitting, despite the fact that he was batting .300 at the time. Balcena finished the 1957 season with a .286 batting average in 130 games. He hit six home runs, knocked in forty-nine RBIs, and stole eight bases.[43]

In 1958, "little Bobby Balcena" moved on to the Buffalo Bisons of the International League and batted in his usual lead off spot. When he hit a game winning homer against Richmond, 6,000 Buffalo fans gave him a standing ovation. In mid–summer of 1958, an AP wire story reported, "Bobby Balcena, little centerfielder playing for the Buffalo Bisons, is the hottest hitter in the International League ... batting .453 in 16 games he has played since 'recall' from Seattle in early July."[44]

In 1960, Balcena returned to the PCL, playing for Vancouver. In June of 1960, Balcena was hitting .325 for the Canadian club. Later in the year, Balcena rejoined Buffalo only to go on an impressive hitting streak of nineteen games. In 1961 Balcena came back to Vancouver, but was batting well below .300 when the Canadian franchise sold his contract to the Hawaiian Islanders. In its first year of business in Honolulu, the PCL team wanted a Filipino American to attract the numerous Filipino Hawaiian fans. In 1962, Balcena was released first by the Islanders in July and then by Vancouver in August. At the end of a distinguished and long minor league career, Balcena disappeared from the ranks of Organized Baseball players to work as a longshoreman in Seattle. He remembered for the *Los Angeles Times* in 1983 that he had no regrets; that perhaps his size worked against him spending more time in a big league uniform. Balcena died seven years later in front of a television set in Los Angeles at the age of sixty-four. Reportedly, it took two days before anyone knew he had died. Yet he remained well remembered by his San Pedro friends and old time Filipino American baseball fans. Well remembered, in fact, by a niece, Jodie Legaspi, who became a star shortstop for UCLA's softball team. To honor "Uncle Robert," she wore the same uniform number 12 he did while a Red.[45]

Hawaiian Big Leaguers

In the 1970s, American Major League baseball proved somewhat receptive to Hawaiian Japanese hurler Ryan Kurosaki. Signed by the St. Louis Cardinals out of the University of Nebraska in the early 1970s, Kurosaki initially pitched for the Cards' minor league team in Little Rock, where he did well. In 1975, he made his major league debut, thus becoming the first Japanese American to make it to the American big leagues. Kurosaki pitched in seven games for the Cards, figuring in no decisions and achieving no saves. His ERA of 7.62 did not show a lot of promise. In any event, that was it for Kurosaki's major league career. He later returned to Little Rock where he became a firefighter.[46]

Mike Lum developed into one of the most durable Hawaiian major leaguers. Possessing Japanese ancestry, he was the adopted son of Mun Luke and Winnifred Lum, Mike Lum played for an assortment of major league teams. He was the first Hawaiian to play in the postseason and then the first to play in the World Series. Perhaps understandably identified as a "Chinese-Hawaiian," Lum's best season came in 1973 when he slugged sixteen home runs and drove in eighty-two runs. Lum played major league ball for a bit in Japan once his playing days were over in the United States. After a long playing career, Lum remained in baseball as scout for the Chicago White Sox and was rumored to succeed an ailing Les Murakami as head baseball coach of University of Hawaii in 2000. Lum declared little interest in the job.[47]

Japanese Hawaiian Lenn Sakata played eleven years in the major leagues, most notably with the Baltimore Orioles. Sakata went to Gonzaga in Spokane, Washington. From there, he sought a career in American professional baseball. And while he was never a star, he clearly put together an enviable career. The Milwaukee Brewers signed Sakata after making him their first draft choice in 1975. However, it was as an Oriole that Sakata became the first *Nikkei* to compete in the American World Series. Probably, 1982 was Sakata's best season in the MLB. He appeared in 136 games, batted 343 times, and averaged .259, while hitting six home runs, driving in thirty-one, and stealing seven bases. After nine seasons with the Orioles, Sakata played one more for the New York Yankees and another for the Oakland Athletics. After his major league playing career ended in the late 1980s, Sakata tried a year in the short-lived Senior Professional Baseball League with the San Bernadino Pride. He

Lenn Sakata was a utility player for years with the Baltimore Orioles. The Japanese Hawaiian transformed that experience into a fine coaching and managing career. Most recently, Sakata has been managing the San Francisco Giants' minor league franchise in San Jose. (Courtesy of San Jose Giants; photograph by Barry Colla.)

then went on to coach and manage professional teams in Japan and the United States. He coached for the Oakland Athletics and the California Angels and managed minor league ball in the Chiba Lotte Marines organization in Japan as well as more recently in the San Francisco Giants organization.[48]

Sakata recalled for an *Asian Week* reporter in 2000 moments in Organized Baseball that were more bitter than sweet. Sakata maintained that his lack of size and the smallness of many Asian Pacific American ballplayers often hurt them in the eyes of big league scouts, despite the fact that several Hall of Fame ballplayers such as Joe Morgan, Phil Rizzuto, and Pee Wee Reese were not strapping six footers. The five-foot nine-inch Sakata said, "I used to hear a lot of cracks about my size.... Because I was small, people thought I was weak. So at times, I think I tried to overcompensate by trying to hit home runs." Sakata added that he heard "ethnic slurs" while in the big leagues, "especially in eastern cities like Cleveland and Detroit." Still, Sakata maintained, "There are always going to be mean bastards out there. Baseball provides a great learning experience in human relations. People come from all over the world and live together with one common link: the love of baseball."[49]

Despite Sakata's minor league coaching experiences, it might seem that he has been on the outside looking in when it comes to MLB coaching, let alone managing jobs. Yet in 2000, Sakata told Ethen Lieser of *Asian Week* that managing at the big league level was not a major goal. A big league managing job had "too many strings" attached to it; too much "crap." Sakata apparently preferred working and continues to prefer working with the kind of young prospects fielded by the San Jose Giants.[50]

While he never played major league baseball, Wendell Keolohapauloi Kim was the first Korean American to don a major league uniform when he became a coach for the San Francisco Giants. Born in poverty in Honolulu, Kim is the son of a prominent Korean Hawaiian boxer, Phil Kim. Eventually, he was brought to the mainland where he grew up in a tough Los Angeles neighborhood. After his minor league playing career ended, Kim remained in the Giants organization, pushing up the ladder to become manager of the Triple A Phoenix Firebirds. There, Kim managed talented young prospects such as Will Clark. Kim subsequently made the big leagues as the Giants third base coach. After leaving the Giants, Kim served as third base coach for the Boston Red Sox and the Chicago Cubs.[51]

In the late 1990s, Benny Agbayani, identified as a Hawaiian of Filipino Samoan ancestry, began to cause a stir in the New York Mets organization. In 1993, Agbayani was drafted in the thirtieth round out of Hawaii Pacific University. In the late 1990s, Agbayani made his way up to the New York Mets' roster.[52]

Filipino American journalist Emil Guillermo paid tribute to Agbayani by pointing out that "Hawaiian born Benny is not your typical Asian in America playing baseball by pitching a ball 90 miles an hour every 5th day." Rather, Agbayani was an outfielder, an everyday hitter who could, indeed, hit the ball often and hard. In describing Agbayani, Guillermo maintained he was "built low to the ground, with the width of an island sunset. And a heart to match. The guy has no quit."[53]

Agbayani told reporter Anthony Hayes in 2000 that adjusting to professional baseball on the mainland was not always easy. He lamented that no one on his teams possessed a similar background, while teammates and fans often thought he was either Latino or African American. The lonely Agbayani missed Hawaii, where people greeted him with a "hug" rather than a "handshake" and where a feeling of "ohana" thrived.[54]

Agbayani's career with the Mets was relatively short but eventful. When the Mets opened the National League season in Tokyo in 2000, Agbayani became the first major leaguer of the twenty-first century to slug a grand slam. For his feat, the Hawaiian won a Kabuto, a shogun helmet, as the game's Most Valuable Player. Agbayani's bat often proved invaluable to the Mets, especially in 2000—the year they most recently got into the World Series. However, the Mets' released Agbayani, who wound up toiling in the minor leagues. Indeed, the American major leagues seem to have given up on Agbayani, who in 2003 played for the minor league Omaha Royals. In eighty-eight games, he hit sixteen homers, but his batting average was a mediocre .237.[55]

Benny Agbayani's career on the American mainland may be over as of 2004. However, he continues to play professionally in Japan for the Chiba Lotte Marines, managed by his former New York Mets field boss, Bobby Valentine. Agbayani's rookie year in Japan proved a success. Toward season's end, he had well over a .300 batting average, socked thirty-five home runs, and knocked in 100 RBIs. In 2005, Agbayani helped lead the Marines to the championship of major league baseball in Japan.[56]

Other Hawaiian ballplayers of Asian Pacific American ancestry are worth noting. Native Hawaiian John Matias and his brother Bob were high school stars in Honolulu for Farrrington in the early 1960s. Both signed contracts with the Baltimore Orioles. In 1970, John made it into the big leagues, playing seventy-eight games for the Chicago White Sox. He then moved on to places like Mexico where he competed in minor league ball for several years. In 1980, he finished his professional career with the Hawaii Islanders. He remained in baseball, however, coaching in Hawaii at Pearl City and Damien High Schools. Possessing indigenous Hawaiian ancestry, Doug Capilla was a right handed pitcher who suited up for a number of major league teams from 1976 to 1981. In 1978, he and Mike Lum became the first pair of Hawaiians to play on the same team. Capilla's best season was in 1978 when he won seven and lost eight as a starter for the Reds. In the late 1970s and early 1980s, Fred Kuhaulua pitched eight games in the major leagues. A one time Hawaiian Islander, Kuhaulua returned to the islands to coach high school ball at Waianae. In the 1980s, Joey De Sa, Johnny Matias' nephew, played major league ball for St. Louis Cardinals in 1980 and then the Chicago White Sox in 1985. Sadly, De Sa died in a car accident while playing winter ball in Puerto Rico in 1985. Samoan Hawaiian Mike Fetters pitched for Iolani High School before heading east for Pepperdine. Fetters signed with the California Angels after being drafted in the first round. Fetters put together a career as a fine reliever for several major league teams. Onan Masaoka proved less successful than Fetters in carving out a permanent niche on some major league team. In 1995, the Los Angeles Dodgers drafted him third out of Waialea High School. Eventually, he pitched his way up the Dodgers organization into the big leagues in the 1990s. Hurling two seasons for the Dodgers in 1999 and 2000, Masaoka achieved a not too shabby 4.02 ERA in eighty-three games. Middle infielder Keith Lu'uloa became the first Hawaiian major leaguer from Molokai'i in 2000. Wearing an Anaheim Angels uniform, Lu'uloa got only eighteen at-bats. But he managed six hits and a nice .333 batting average.[57]

Jerome Williams emerged as a potential pitching standout for the San Francisco Giants in the early 2000s. Williams' father is an African American career soldier and his late mother possessed indigenous Hawaiian ancestry. Williams was drafted out of Waipahu High School in 1999. His baseball coach, Jerome Takenaka, promised the school would retire Williams' number if he made it to the American big leagues. Indeed, in Williams' 2003 year, the rookie pitcher put up solid numbers and his sophomore year, while not spectacular and limited by injury, proved he still possessed the potential to be a solid major league starter. Nevertheless, arm problems plagued Williams' ability to get batters out at the onset of the 2005 season. The Giants, consequently, traded him to the Chicago Cubs who subsequently shuffled Williams off to the Oakland Athletics.[58]

Not Just Hawaiians

Several other Americans of Asian Pacific Islander ancestry have made an impact on professional baseball in the United States. The tragic case of Tony Solaita deserves mention. Born in Nuuuli in America Samoa, Solaita competed for a number of major league teams in the 1970s. As a youth, he played cricket in American Samoa before his family moved to Hawaii. There, Little League acquainted the eight year old Solaita with baseball. His father, Tulafona, had joined the U.S. marines and was shipped to Oceanside, California, and then to the San Francisco Bay Area. In San Francisco, Tulafona also served as a preacher for an all–Samoan American congregation. Meanwhile, Solaita's older brother, Tulafona Jr., had become something of a prospect, receiving an invitation to try out for the San Francisco Giants' organization. Preferring his Samoan name of Tolia to Tony, Solaita starred in football as well as baseball at Daily City's Jefferson High School. There, former baseball great and New York Yankees scout Dolph Camili saw him. Impressed, Camili had to convince the Solaita family that the Yankees were a better fit for Tolia than the San Francisco Giants.[59]

As it turned out, Solaita started his professional career as a New York Yankees minor league prospect in 1965. The next year, his .324 batting average for Ft. Lauderdale led the Gulf Coast League. In 1967, Solaita began to develop some pop in his bat as he slugged fourteen home runs. He showed much more power in 1968, hitting over fifty homers for the Yankees' Carolina League affiliate, as well as earning a late season call up to the parent club. Solaita's accomplishments in 1968 won him the Topps' Minor League Player of the Year Award.[60]

Arriving in the Bronx palace known as Yankee Stadium, Solaita's reputation as a slugger conjured up dreams of another Ruth, Gehrig, or Mantle wearing the famed pinstripes. The rookie even won a home run hitting contest that featured notable American League power hitters such as Rocky Colavito, Ken Harrelson, Reggie Smith, Carl Yastremski, as well as the aging Mantle. Solaita got into official major league action, replacing Mantle in a game against Detroit. He struck out in his only at-bat. Meanwhile, an AP photo showed Solaita swinging a bat in a Yankees uniform. The caption read, "Hot Tune from South Pacific," in reference to the popular Rodgers and Hammerstein musical.[61]

Solaita had also pleased the Yankees with his home run power during one spring training season in the late 1960s. However, Solaita lingered for a couple of years more with Syracuse of the International League. In 1970, Solaita put up solid numbers for Syracuse, hitting .308, with nineteen home runs and eighty-seven RBIs. Ray Buck told *Sporting News* readers that Solaita was "a refreshingly unselfish personality," because he wanted to use his future earnings in the big leagues to help finance the construction of a church for his father.[62]

Solaita languished in the Yankees organization. Fortunately, he was traded to the Pittsburgh Pirates and more fortunately to the Kansas City Royals, where he got some serious playing time. While he generally served as a backup to John Mayberry, Solaita showed power by hitting sixteen home runs in only 231 at-bats in 1975. On September 7 of that year, Solaita became the first player to hit three home runs at Anaheim Stadium — all slugged deep over the center field fence. The next year, Solaita joined the Angels. The Angels organization, in turn, staged a "Samoan Salute to Tony Solaita," with pregame entertainment by "Polynesian" dancers and musicians. Offered two tickets for the price of one, thousands of Samoans who lived in Southern California showed up. Sadly, however, Solaita's hitting production began to fall off. Baltimore Orioles lefthander Mike Flannigan quipped about pitching to "Tony Obsolete-a."[63]

In 1980, Solaita signed a contract with Japan's Nippon Ham Fighters. Sportswriter Stan Isle reported that at the time, Solaita "prospered as the only car wash owner in Samoa." Isle maintained that Solaita's brother was a member of the Samoan legislature and had helped out by writing a law that mandated government cars receive regular car washes. Solaita, for awhile, thrived in Japan. As a designated hitter, Solaita averaged thirty-nine home runs and ninety-three RBIs in the four 130-game seasons he played in Japan. On September 28, 1980, he became the second Japanese major leaguer to hit four straight home runs. Only the great Sadaharu Oh had previously accomplished the feat. In 1981, Solaita slugged a league-leading forty-four home runs, while tying for the lead in RBIs with 108. Cultural conflict seemingly made life for Solaita increasingly difficult in Japan. And while the San Francisco Giants expressed some interest in the Samoan, Solaita decided to retire from professional baseball in the mid–1980s.[64]

Solaita, subsequently, devoted a great deal of energy in developing and maintaining baseball's popularity in American Samoa. In 1987, he led a team of Samoan Little Leaguers to Taiwan and teams of older youngsters to Hawaii in 1988 and Los Angeles in 1989. In February 1990, Solaita was murdered near his hometown of Tafuna. Solaita at this time was working in the athletic division of American Samoa's education department. Solaita's brother Ben was also involved in baseball. He served as president of the American Samoa Baseball Association, as well as coach of the national team, and president of the Olympic team. According to Ben Solaita, Tolia left a memorable legacy to baseball loving Samoans. Ben Solaita stated that significantly thanks to his brother, "The public here loves the sport.... Businesses love the sport and love to donate. The parents get involved. People here have confidence that the ones running the program are looking out for their kids and their betterment. We're careful about the coaches — we get guys who are calm, don't cuss at the players. The Pee Wee games, they play at night time, and the place is packed!"[65]

In the 1980s, Attlee Hammaker was a frequently effective southpaw for the San Francisco Giants. Born in Carmel, California, Hammaker's mother was Japanese and his father was a white career military man. A source of pride to Bay Area *Nikkei*, Hammaker was named to the National League All-Star team in the mid-1980s, but his career appears to have been shortened by arm problems and the reputation, whether deserved or not, of not being able to come through in the clutch. Hammaker's best season was probably in 1983 when he won the ERA title with a 2.25. A year earlier, Hammaker achieved his most victories in winning twelve. Aside from pitching most of his twelve major league seasons with the Giants, Hammaker also hurled for the Kansas City Royals, San Diego Padres, and the Chicago White Sox.

The son of a Hawaiian of indigenous ancestry, Milt Wilcox had some good years pitching for the Cincinnati Reds and the Detroit Tigers. The Reds drafted the Hawaiian born Wilcox out of Crooked Creek High School in Oklahoma. In 1970, the twenty-year-old Wilcox helped the Reds beat the Pittsburgh Pirates in a National League Championship Series gain. Years later, he achieved a 17–8 record in 1984 when the Tigers won the 1984 World Series.[66]

The Hawaiian born Ron Darling was probably the most successful of late twentieth century American major leaguers who possessed Asian Pacific Islander ancestry. A son of a Chinese Hawaiian mother, Darling moved as a youth to the mainland and first attracted national attention as a pitching star on the Yale University baseball team. There have not been many Yale students who went on to big league stardom. Early in his Mets career, Tom Boswell of the *Washington Post* described the pitcher as a "swarthy Hawaiian-Chinese intellectual from Yale." In 1986 the *New York Times*' George Vescey wrote that Darling "is a walking display of the polyglot beauty of

Ron Darling, possessing Chinese Hawaiian ancestry, developed into a fine major league pitcher for the New York Mets and Oakland Athletics in the 1980s and early 1990s. Here he is wearing a Texas League uniform, hurling his way up the professional ladder. (Courtesy of the Texas League.)

Hawaii: the looks of his French father and Chinese mother make him strikingly handsome." Darling was no superstar, but he pitched several years with the New York Mets in the 1980s and had some fine seasons. He was especially known as a superb athlete who could field his position as well as pitch.[67]

In the 1990s, Don Wakamatsu and Jim Vo Parque appeared in official major league games. The Oregon born Wakamatsu achieved a short career in the MLB. In 1991, he got into eighteen games for the Chicago White Sox for whom he batted .226. After leaving the playing field, Wakamatsu became a coach, serving eventually as manager Buck Showalter's chief assistant for the Texas Rangers. In 2006, he was considered as a prospect. Californian Jim Vo Parque had his moments with the White Sox. The left hander pitched five seasons for the Windy City team. In 2000, he looked like he was on the way to a solid major league career, putting together a thirteen and six record. However, injuries forced him out of the major leagues after 2003.

In the 1990s and 2000s, Danny Graves ranked high among mainlanders of Asian Pacific Islander ancestry to make a mark on the American big league. A son of a Vietnamese-born mother and an American army sergeant, Graves became an excellent relief pitcher for the Cincinnati Reds. Graves was drafted originally by another Ohio team, the Cleveland Indians, and actually made his major league pitching debut for the Indians in 1996. By 2000, Graves had moved on to the Reds. Appropriately responding to fellow reliever John Rocker's derogatory remarks regarding a wide variety of immigrant groups, Graves told the *Cincinnati Post* that he was "cheesed off."[68]

A son of a Thai mother and a European American father, Johnny Damon became one of the best lead off men in major league baseball in the early 2000s. With the Boston Red Sox, Damon was integral in helping the franchise get its first World Series victory in decades. (Courtesy of David Marasco.)

Johnny Damon, whose mother is Thai, became one of baseball's best leadoff men with the Kansas City Royals and Oakland Athletics. But it was as a member of the famed Boston

Red Sox World Series champion team of 2004 that Damon gained his greatest fame. Deciding to wear his hair down to his shoulders and a beard, Damon's play inspired Red Sox fans to bring signs to Fenway reading "Johnny Saves" and wear T-shirts adorned with Damon's picture and the question, "What would Johnny Do?" In 2006, Damon braved the scorn of Red Sox fans by relocating to the hated New York Yankees but also to a great deal more money. Unlike some of the Yankees' high priced free agents, Damon seemed to be worth Steinbrenner's money.[69]

Dave Roberts was Johnny Damon's teammate on the 2004 World Series champions. Born in Japan, the fast outfielder has a Japanese mother. Roberts carved out a reputation as a base stealer first for the Dodgers and then as a late season pickup for the Red Sox. His speed helped give the latter just a little more impetus toward the 2004 World Series championship. Hitting leadoff, Roberts became an important regular in the San Diego Padres' outfield in 2005.[70]

The Japanese Big Leagues

The Japanese major leagues offered sometimes reluctant opportunities for Japanese Americans to play professional baseball and play it well. Three notable Hawaiian *Nisei*, Yoshio Tanaka, Ted Kameda and Henry Wakabayashi, starred in the Japanese major leagues before World War II. The Oahu-born Wakabayahsi emerged as one of Japan's best pitchers. Just out of Honolulu's McKinley High School, Wakabayashi accompanied a team of Japanese Americans headed for Japan in 1928. The youthful Hawaiian remained to go to Hosei University, pitching the university nine to two league championships. After graduation, Wakabayashi joined the Hainshin Tigers, winning MVP awards in 1944 and 1947. Throughout his major league Japanese career, Wakabayahsi won 243 games and lost 141, while achieving a very imposing 1.99 ERA. Wakabayahsi, subsequently, managed the Mainichi Orions, which suited up Honolulu *Nisei* Isao Odachi in the early 1950s. In 1964, Wakabayashi was selected for Japan's Baseball Hall of Fame. The next year, the native of Wahiawa died in Japan at the age of fifty-seven. Two mainland Japanese Americans, George Matsura and Sammy Takahashi, also played professionally in pre–World War II Japan.[71]

After World War II, the Japanese professional leagues recruited a number of *Nisei* players from Hawaii and the mainland. Hawaiian Wally Yonamine is perhaps the most notable. Yonamine, whose real first name is Kaname, is the son of a Hawaiian born mother of Japanese ancestry and a Japanese immigrant father. In 1930, the family lived in Maui's Olowalu Village. His father

Several Nisei ballplayers competed in the Japanese major leagues after World War II. The Tokyo Giants fielded perhaps the best, Wally Yonamine, as well as several others such as Jyun Hirota, Dick Kashiwaeda, and Bill Nishita. Here the four are pictured together. From left to right: Yonamine, Hirota, Kashiwaeda, and Nishita. (Courtesy of Rob Fitts and Wally Yonamine.)

worked as a sugar plantation laborer. Like many of Hawaii's best athletes, Yonamine was superbly versatile. Football, however, may have been his best sport. And after a brief pro football career with the San Francisco 49ers, Yonamine decided to concentrate on baseball, in part, he told author Arthur Suehiro, because he could make more money in America's national pastime. To be sure, he was undoubtedly a good baseball player. Fresno State's George Abo remembered Yonamine as "a great athlete, big and fast for a *Nisei*.... He could have been a good major-league player."[72]

While playing baseball in Hawaii and winning the AJA League's batting crown two years in a row, Yonamine caught the eye of Japanese major league organizations such as the Tokyo Giants. Yonamine also attracted interest from Lefty O'Doul, the famed manager of the San Francisco Seals. O'Doul claimed late in 1949 he would sign Yonamine if the Hawaiian gave up football for good. According to Japanese American journalist Larry Tajiri, the Giants offered Yonamine the "virtual certainty of stardom" and a $2800 annual salary if he would head east for the 1950 campaign. Instead, Yonamine decided to give American minor league baseball a chance.[73]

Yonamine did well at the Seals' camp. The *Pacific Citizen* noted that the "Hawaiian flychaser" showed he could play pro ball on the mainland. A plethora of good outfielders on the Seals' roster meant it was doubtful that Yonamine could stick with the San Francisco club. However, "the *Nisei* is determined to make good in the big jump from semi-pro ball to the Coast League's Class AAA." He did not make the team but impressed O'Doul, who told the press that Yonamine had "a perfect swing and great power." Eventually, the Seals signed the Hawaiian and O'Doul sought to reassign Yonamine to the class B Yakima franchise, which had a working agreement with the Seals. While Yakima was higher on the organizational ladder, Yonamine preferred going to the class C Salt Lake City Bees franchise. In Salt Lake City Yonamine had friends, including notable Hawaiian athletes such as Jimmy Miyasato and Herbert Sumida, both of whom went to college in Utah's largest city. The Seals complied with Yonamine's wish and moved him to Salt Lake City.[74]

Yonamine flourished in his one season of American mainland minor league baseball. While training with the Salt Lake Bees in Palo Alto, California, Yonamine's hitting led his team to an exhibition game victory over the San Jose Red Sox of the California League. Salt Lake City's team owner, Bert Dunne, and manager, Earl Bolyard, praised Yonamine's hustle, speed, and timely hitting. Dunne hoped that Yonamine could climb up Organized Baseball's ladder and do nothing less than help America win the Cold War. According to Larry Tajiri, Dunne believed "that Wally Yonamine may prove to be an American 'secret weapon' in the ideological tug-of-war for Japan: 'The sight of Wally Yonamine playing for the Seals in a tour of Japan will prove to the Japanese people that racial democracy works in the United States.'" The *Salt Lake City Tribune* claimed that Yonamine achieved "a sensational debut in organize baseball." Indeed, he hit .335 for Salt Lake City, while rapping three home runs and stealing twenty-three bases. Yonamine's batting skills prompted one former Brooklyn Dodgers pitcher to claim in 1953 that the best hitter he ever saw was "Y-A-N-A-M-I-N-I, maybe. He's a Jap." After the 1951 season, several class B teams including two in Texas sought the Japanese Hawaiian's services.[75]

In April 1951, the *Honolulu Advertiser* announced that Yonamine had become the Tokyo Giants' first "bonus baby." The Giants paid Yonamine a million yen or a 3,000 dollar bonus to sign and then 300 dollars or 100,000 yen a month to play for the best known Japanese baseball franchise. In addition, the Giants agreed to pay for Yonamine's round trip fare to Japan and back to Hawaii, as well as the Hawaiian's living expenses. Working as a firefighter at Pearl Harbor, Yonamine had just finished playing simultaneously for the Honolulu AJA nine and the Moiliili contingent which competed in the Hawaii Baseball Congress tournament and was just beginning a stint with the Wanderers of the HBL when the announcement that he was headed westward was made. A longtime Japanese American baseball supporter in Hawaii, Sam Uyehara, served as the Giants' front man in the Yonamine negotiations. By heading to Japan, Yonamine turned down a chance to play for the Salem, Oregon, franchise.[76]

It is not entirely clear as to why Yonamine departed American baseball for good, although he has never claimed racial prejudice played a role. In 1953, he told the press that he feared stagnating in the American minor leagues. He said, "I figured my parents are Japanese. Why not give it a try." In 1967, he informed the press that Lefty O'Doul convinced him that his injured left arm made it tough to make it into the American big leagues. Yonamine also claimed, "If I stay in the States, the best I can do is play Triple A ball, you're not going to make money. You gotta play in the majors to make money." In more recent years, Yonamine explained to oral historian Robert Fitts that O'Doul said he could have made the Seals eventually, but would be better off in Japan.[77]

Making it in the Japanese big leagues was not going to be easy for the Hawaiian. The noted American historian of Japanese baseball, Robert Whiting, points out that anti–American feelings ran high in post–World War II Japan. And despite his ancestry, Yonamine was widely considered an American and, at heart, a *gaishin* or white American, at that. However, Whiting maintains, "Opening the doors to American players, however, was a categorical imperative if Japanese was to improve the level of her game, and someone had to be the guinea pig." Thus, with perhaps some exaggeration, Whiting calls Yonamine an "Oriental Jackie Robinson."[78]

On top of the fact that the Japanese government compelled Yonamine to wait a month to gain official clearance before joining the Giants, Yonamine had to win over reticent Japanese fans and teammates. Among other epithets, Yonamine heard spectators yell, "Yankee Go Home." Yonamine declared, "The Japanese didn't like me because I was a *Nisei* and because they thought I was a dirty player." Indeed, his aggressive play apparently stirred fans to hurl rocks at him and even three gangsters to attack him. Fortunately, the *Nisei* was protected by teammates. And his manager and assistant manager encouraged Yonamine to play aggressively. His assistant manger told him, "As a rule, we don't like *nisei*. But you didn't grumble. You're a good *nisei*."[79]

Yonamine's sparkling play made believers out of many of his doubters, and the fact that he was willing to do everything they did, won over skeptical teammates. Yonamine claimed that from the beginning he was confident he could do well in the Japanese major leagues. He maintained, "I think ... I can just about lead this league in doubles and triples for as long as I play. They throw sidearm from the outfield. It's like they are begging me to take an extra base and I do. The pitching? These managers have their guys throwing in the bullpen every day. By the time their turn in the rotation comes along, it's like they are coming off four straight days as a starting pitcher."[80]

Yonamine put up excellent numbers and helped the Giants win pennants. In 1954, Yonamine won a league batting championship with a sparkling .361 average. In 1957, Yonamine had such a good year that Oscar Fraley, an American sports columnist, speculated that he "could run for emperor and nobody would sell his chances short." Even when his peak playing years were over Yonamine could unselfishly aid the Giants. Teammate Sadaharu Oh recalled Yonamine's generosity when the great Japanese slugger was breaking into the Giants' lineup and the Hawaiian's playing career was winding down.[81]

However, Yonamine's nativity continued to spark controversy even after he retired from his many years of playing, coaching, and managing in the Japanese major leagues. In the early 1990s, Yonamine was elected to the Japanese Baseball Hall of Fame, but only after getting rejected in the first year he was eligible for the honor. Many were convinced that had Yonamine been a Japanese national, he would not have had to wait a year.[82]

Yonamine stood out as a cultural bridge between Japanese and American baseball. When the Tokyo Giants joined the San Francisco Seals in spring training in 1953, the *Sporting News* went to the "English-speaking" Yonamine for insights on how much the Giants were getting out of the experience. Yonamine informed the *Sporting News* correspondent Jack McDonald that the Tokyo Giants were the best team in Japan, but not ready to face the New York Yankees and probably not up to the PCL's caliber. Still, Yonamine felt that Japanese major league baseball had improved partly because Japanese hitters were realizing that trying to slug home runs "is not our specialty." Moreover, Yonamine asserted that his team had learned a great deal from the Seals, especially in developing more aggressiveness on the base paths. Yonamine's Tokyo Giants, meanwhile, played mainland professional and semi-professional nines in the spring of 1953. In Santa Maria, California, the Giants used rookie pitchers and lost to the local Santa Maria Indians. Nevertheless, Yonamine hit a triple for the losers.[83]

Occasionally, the American mainland press noted Yonamine's accomplishments in Japan. In an article on an American *Nisei* conference held in

Tokyo in 1957, the *New York Times*' Robert Trumball pointed out that "*Nisei* Wally Yonamine of Hawaii" had won Most Valuable Player honors in Japanese major league baseball. A few days later, the *Times* published an Associated Press article focused on the hoopla attending the Japanese World Series. The article's author observed that Yonamine was essential to the Giants' efforts at winning the Japanese World Series, as was another Hawaiian *Nisei*, Andy Miyamoto. Both hit key homers in the third game, giving the Giants hope of a Japanese major league championship. In 1960, Lee Kavetski acclaimed Yonamine as "Mr. Baseball Ambassador" in the *Sporting News*. Kavetski said that the "34 year old Hawaiian *Nisei*" was more important than any other player in breaking down the barriers between the United States and Japan and helped clear the path for more Americans to play major league ball in Japan.[84]

Yonamine remained a fixture in Japanese major league baseball after his playing days ended. Ignoring Wakabayashi, the mainland press called him the first American to manage in the Japanese big leagues when he took over the Chunichi Dragons in the 1970s. In the spring of 1975, the Dragons trained with the National League's Pittsburgh Pirates. Sportswriter Will Grimsley asserted that Yonamine's team failed at picking up the unsanitary and ultimately dangerous tobacco chewing habits of the American big leaguers. Yonamine, described by Grimsley as a "pleasant, professional type with horn-rimmed glasses," said his players tried bubble gum instead but did not like it either. In 1987, Yonamine was a coach for the Nippon Ham Fighters when the team trained in America. Yonamine informed the press that he enjoyed his stay in the United States but worried that the players he coached would pick up bad habits from American major leaguers. "In Japan," he commented, "they don't want guys standing around. We stress a lot of training." In the mid–1990s, Yonamine took a turn as a scout for the Tokyo Giants, signing prominent major leaguer Dan Gladden. Yonamine was also quoted as remarking that Japanese major leaguers were generally fifteen years behind American major leaguers.[85]

An affectionate bond continued to exist between Yonamine and Hawaii. After Yonamine won a league batting title in Japan in 1957, he was honored by the Honolulu Senior AJA baseball league at a Japanese restaurant in Honolulu. A turn-away crowd of 275 attended the event along with Honolulu's civic leaders, the Japanese consul-general, sportswriter Red McQueen, and Masa Koike, president of the AJA baseball league. In 1998, Hawaii's governor, Ben Cayetano, appointed Yonamine as a special advisor to the governor's office on sports promotion. One of his duties was to prevail upon Japanese major league teams to train in Hawaii, then experiencing economic duress. Cayetano declared, "Yonamine is best suited for this assignment because he knows Japanese baseball better than anyone in Hawaii." On a salary of a dollar an hour, Yonamine responded, "I just want to do something good for Hawaii, so I am delighted that the Governor has asked me to promote Hawaii as a sports center." That same year, the Japanese government honored Yonamine with the Order of the Sacred Treasure "for his many accomplishments of the baseball diamond and society in general." Yonamine responded to the honor by mentioning his service to Hawaii: "I want to bring as much attention and positive publicity to Hawaii as I can. The economy is not good there right now, as you know. Tourism is down, especially from the Japanese."[86]

In 1958, Fibber Hirayama was the subject of an eloquent Mark Harris piece in *Sports Illustrated*. Harris did not shrink from the ugly business that was the internment of Japanese Americans during World War II. Hirayama and his family, according to Harris, were exiled to the Postan camp in Arizona. Like many other young people in the camps, Hirayama found an outlet in sports — in particular baseball. Harris told readers that after leaving the camp Hirayama was the only "Oriental" at Fresno's Exeter High School. At Exeter, Hirayama "discovered that it was also the nature of Americans to admire athletic skill. Devoting himself with all earnestness and all joy to games, he proceeded toward redemption, and on the playing fields of America, as afterward in Japan, he soon won not only acceptance but distinction." From high school, Hirayama went on to excel in both baseball and football at Fresno State. After leaving Fresno State, Hirayama tried his hand at mainland professional baseball. He may not have been good enough to play American major league ball, but the Hiroshima Carp thought Hirayama was good enough to play for them.[87]

Upon arrival in Hiroshima, Harris wrote, Hirayama quickly ingratiated himself with the locals. He was greeted by 10,000 fans and tried to tell them in Japanese, "I am Satoshi Hirayama. I will do my best." Actually, Hirayama said, "I am Satoshi Hirayama and a splendid fellow." However, Hirayama showed fans he was a "gracefully aggressive right fielder" for the Hiroshima Carp. Hirayama's hustle and egalitarianism helped re-shape the character of the Carp. Reminiscent of W.E.B. Du Bois' notion of double consciousness, Harris maintained, "In the person of Fibber Hirayama, whose ancestry is Japanese, whose techniques are American and who contains in fine balance within himself his double heritage, the humiliated but emerging city of Hiroshima glimpses the ideal fusion of West with East." Meanwhile, Japanese Americans did not forget about Hirayama. In 1955, the *Nichi Bei Times* named him *Nisei* of the year. Hirayama, subsequently, took up the career of an educator in central California. He became a high school principal, while also scouting for the Hiroshima Carp.[88]

Jyun Hirota was another prominent Hawaiian *Nikkei* who played

Japanese major league baseball after World War II. In 1950, the *Pacific Citizen* reported that "Jyun Hirota, probably the top *Nisei* catcher in Hawaii and former University of Hawaii star," had signed to play in Japan with the Tokyo Flyers. Born on Oahu's Ewa Beach, Hirota decided to remain in Hawaii. According to Brandon Masuoka of the *Honolulu Advertiser*, Wally Yonamine recommended Hirota to the Tokyo Giants. Consequently, Hirota joined the Giants in 1952, playing with them through the 1956 season. While on a Japanese All-Star team facing the New York Giants in the early 1950s, Hirota encountered Ronald Takaki's notion that no matter where they were born or what they have done, Asian Pacific Americans have been widely considered by non–Asian Pacific Americans as "Strangers From A Different Shore." That is, Giants manager Leo Durocher simply yelled at his base runners to steal, convinced that the opposing catcher did not understand English. Unsurprisingly, Hirota consistently gunned down would-be Giants base stealers. The Hawaiian catcher finished his Japanese major league career with a .260 lifetime batting average and four appearances in the Japanese World Series. Hirota was not done with Japanese professional baseball. After coaching baseball for the Asahis and the University of Hawaii for several years, Hirota returned to Japan to manage a farm team for the Kinetsu Braves. In 1970, his team won its first pennant in twenty-three years. Subsequently, Hirota came back to Hawaii, where he worked at Aloha Stadium as an events manager and scout for Kinetsu. Wally Yonamine remembered Hirota as a tough competitor who helped clear the path for Hawaiian *Nikkei* such as Andy Miyamoto and Dick Kashiwada. Hirota died in Honolulu in 2003 at the age of eighty-one.[89]

Other Japanese Americans have played in the Japanese major leaguers. Dick Kashiwada handled third base solidly for the Tokyo Giants in the early and mid–1950s. Brought up on a Kauai plantation, Kashiwada could hit as well, batting over .300 in 1953 and 1955 as a part-timer for the Giants. In 1955, the *New York Times* reported that in a game between the New York Yankees and a Japanese All-Star contingent the latter scored only two runs — both by *Nisei*. Fibber Hirayama scored one run, while Dick Kashiwada scored the other. After graduating from Cal, Bill Nishita joined the Tokyo Giants. When the Tokyo Giants visited California in the spring of 1953, Nishita was scheduled to start against the Oakland Oaks of the PCL. However, sportswriter Jack McDonald wrote, the "American citizen and graduate of the University of California" was served with a draft notice just before he was to pitch and would not return to Tokyo. Nishita subsequently pitched for the Mainichi Orions. Harvey Zenimura, the son of Fresno's godfather of Japanese American baseball, suited up for the Hiroshima Carp, as did his brother Howard. Joe DiMaggio, who went to Japan to help give pre–season coaching tips to Carp players in 1954, was impressed with Zenimura's hitting ability and claimed that the

Nisei showed "real promise." Andy Miyamoto played with Yonamine on the Tokyo Giants. A former Rural Red Sox star, Miyamoto displayed his potential by smacking a home run off of Brooklyn Dodgers ace Carl Erskine when the Eddie Lopat All-Stars visited the islands. George Fujishige competed for the Nankai Hawks, as did Carlton Hanta. And Stan Hashimoto and Eddie Takei suited up for the Mainichi Orions.[90]

Notably, Japanese journalist Sotaro Suzuki acknowledged Wally Yonamine's role in clearing the way for *Nisei* to play Japanese professional ball. Writing for the *Sporting News* in the early 1960s, Suzuki declared, ""Wally's smooth, lefthanded hitting, his smart base-running, and his clever fielding enchanted Japanese fans." Yonamine's achievements also led to what Suzuki called "the *Nisei* rush"—the signing of several Japanese Americans to Japanese big league contracts. However, Suzuki termed "the *Nisei* rush" a failure as no Japanese American matched Yonamine's contributions, while compelling a regulation mandating that Japanese big league teams could retain only three foreigners on their rosters.[91]

Conclusion

The experiences explored in this chapter in addition to achievements forged by non–American ballplayers such as Hideo Nomo, Ichiro Suzuki, and Hideki Matsui should eliminate talk of inherent, racial barriers to Asian Pacific American seeking to excel in the highest levels of professional baseball. More important, these experiences reveal real pioneers of baseball racial and ethnic frontiers. Bobby Balcena, for example, was the first Filipino American to play major league baseball. To be sure, he did not play much major league baseball. But for nearly a decade he persevered in minor leagues all over the nation to sip a cup of coffee for the Cincinnati Redlegs in 1956. Wally Yonamine, although possessing Japanese ancestry, braved a great deal of animosity in order to carve out a distinguished career in the Japanese major leagues. An American baseball fan of Asian Pacific American ancestry might regret the fact that as yet no American of Asian Pacific ancestry has become a superstar in the MLB. But there is much in the careers of Balcena, Yonamine, and now Johnny Damon in which not only Asian Pacific Americans but all Americans should express pride. Moreover, as this is being written, American rookies of Asian Pacific Islander ancestry are showing up in major league uniforms. In 2006, Travis Ishikawa showed promise for the San Francisco Giants in a brief tour of duty with the Bay Area club, while Shane Komine did the same as a pitcher for the cross-bay Oakland Athletics.

Afterword

Clearly, baseball has meant a great deal to Americans of Asian Pacific Islander ancestry. For over one hundred years, they have played baseball well and supported it enthusiastically. Through baseball, Americans of Asian Pacific Islander ancestry have been able to maintain a sense of community under often harsh circumstances. Through baseball, they have been able to cross perilous cultural borderlands to compete with and against people of varied racial and ethnic backgrounds. Through baseball, they have won honors, gained at least a measure of fame, and, in the case of Johnny Damon, procure an indecent amount of money — especially now that the dynamic center fielder has moved on to the New York Yankees for the 2006 season. Most important, Americans of Asian Pacific Islander ancestry have through baseball enjoyed themselves both as participants and spectators.

However, this is not a success story in the conventional American sense. Baseball, America's national pastime, has only sporadically rewarded Asian Pacific Islander Americans for their enduring love of the sport. The Hawaiian Travelers were frequently greeted with respect as they cut a swath through mainland college and semi-pro nines in the early 1910s. Yet the praise often generously lavished upon young men such as Buck Lai Tin, Vernon Ayau, and Lang Akana was colored by the widespread astonishment that they could play baseball so well — that underneath it all "Orientals" were not supposed to master a tough, "manly," and competitive game such as baseball. Moreover, their appearances in mainland towns and cities prompted numerous publications to dredge up the "Yellow Peril" stereotype, rendering the Hawaiians somehow threatening to white America's domination of a racialized hierarchy. Yet while none of them has gained a place in Cooperstown's Baseball

Hall of Fame, the Hawaiian Travelers won ballgames and perhaps temporarily transcended racial and ethnic stereotypes. They succeeded in asserting a sense of agency when the American political-legal system denied Asian Pacific Americans much of a place in the civic community.

In recent years more American athletes of Asian Pacific Islander ancestry have gained access to college, minor league, and now major league baseball. In 2006, Travis Ishikawa made the jump from playing for Lenn Sakata's Single A San Jose Giants to the San Francisco Giants. Will he be a star? Probably not, because so few prospects of any ethnic background become MLB stars. But, in a manner of speaking, Ishikawa has already changed the face of baseball.

Will there be others to join Ishikawa, Johnny Damon, and Kim Ng on their journeys? Ron Darling told Anthony Hayes back in 2000 that major league scouts might have to surrender their preconceptions of what makes a good MLB prospect. Scouts, Darling claimed, generally are enamored by raw athletic talent and size. "But," he added, "just because [a prospect]'s big and strong doesn't mean he knows how to pitch, or has finesse and good control." That "Asian kid," who might lack the size that makes scouts drool, may know how to pitch — throw strikes and perform "with heart." Darling hoped that the influx of Asian talent in the MLB might inspire a greater open mindedness toward Americans of Asian Pacific Islander ancestry, as well as inspire Asian Pacific American athletes to take a career in baseball seriously.[1]

Around the same time, Kim Ng argued that the greatest obstacles facing her advancement as a major league baseball executive revolved around gender more than race or ethnicity. She was optimistic that as more Asians and Asian Pacific Americans make big league rosters more Asians and Asian Pacific Americans would find coaching, managing, and front office jobs. To a significant extent, she believed, it was up to Asian Pacific Americans to make the effort. However, since 2000, we have seen more players of Asian Pacific American ancestry on big league rosters and as yet the number of coaches, managers, and front office people has not correspondingly risen.[2]

Likewise, Americans of Asian Pacific Islander ancestries have earned the right to claim partial ownership of baseball. After all, young people such as Buck Lai, Nancy Ito, and Kim Ng have carried their love of the sport throughout America. Perhaps white males in the United States originated baseball. But baseball ultimately has belonged to no particular social group or nation. This is why assimilation remains an inadequate means of understanding the relationship between baseball and Americans of Asian Pacific Islander ancestry. For example, Asian Indian Americans journey to neighborhood parks close to where I live. There, they play both cricket and baseball. What are we to make of this except that baseball has contested simplistic and static attempts to categorize millions of complex, dynamic people?

Chapter Notes

Introduction

1. Joel S. Franks, *Hawaiian Sports in the Twentieth Century* (Lewiston, NY: Edwin Mellen Press, 2002).

2. Kerry Yo Nakagawa, *Through a Diamond: 100 Years of Japanese American Baseball* (San Francisco: Rudi, 2001); Gail M. Nomura, "Beyond the Playing Field: The Significance of Pre–World War II Japanese American Baseball in the Yakima Valley," in *Bearing Dreams, Shaping Visions: Asian Pacific American Perspectives*, edited by Linda A. Revilla, Gail M. Nomura, Shawn Wong, and Shirley Hune (Pullman, WA: Washington State University Press, 1993); Jay Feldman, "Baseball Behind Barbed Wire," *The National Pastime: A Review of Baseball History*, no. 12; Sam Regalado, "Sport and Community in California's Japanese American 'Yamato Colony' 1930–1945," *Journal of Sport History* 19 (Summer 1992); Ralph M. Pearce, *From Asahi to Zebras: Japanese American Baseball in San Jose, California* (San Jose, CA: Japanese American Museum of San Jose, 2005).

3. There is a growing literature of Asian Pacific American historical scholarship. A few places to start include Ronald Takaki, *Strangers from a Different Shore: A History of Asian Americans* (Boston: Little, Brown, 1989); Sucheng Chan, *Asian Americans: An Interpretive History* (New York: Twayne, 1991).

4. Samuel Regalado, "Sport and Community"; Gail M. Nomura, "Beyond the Playing Field"; Susan G. Zieff, "From Badminton to the Bolero: Sport and Recreation in San Francisco's Chinatown," Journal *of Sport History* 27 (Spring 2000).

5. While the late Harold Seymour is typically cited as the sole author of *Baseball: The People's Game* (New York: Oxford University Press, 1990), his wife, Dorothy Seymour, is widely credited as at the very least the book's co-author.

6. Ian Haney Lopez, *White By Law: The Legal Construction of Race* (New York: New York University Press, 1998).

7. Renato Rosaldo and William V. Flores, "Ideology, Conflict, and Evolving Latino Communities: Cultural Citizenship in San Jose, California," in *Latino Cultural Citizenship: Claiming Identity, Space, and Rights*, edited by William V. Flores, and Rina Benmayor (Boston: Beacon Press, 1997), 57; Michael Omi and Howard Winant, *Racial Formation in the United States: From the 1960s to the 1990s*. 2nd ed. (London and New York: Routledge, 1994), 55–56; Gary Y. Okihiro, *Margins and Mainstreams: Asians in American History and Culture* (Seattle: University of Washington Press, 1994); Gloria Anzaldua, *Borderlands/La Frontera: The New Mestiza* (San Francisco: Spinsters/Aunt Lute, 1987).

8. Richard White, *The Middle Ground: Indians, Empires, and Republics in the Great*

Lakes Region, 1650–1815 (New York: Cambridge University Press, 1991); Peter Levine, *Ellis Island to Ebbets Field: Sport and the American Jewish Experience* (New York: Oxford University Press, 1992), 25.

9. Elaine Kim, "Preface," *Charlie Chan Is Dead: An Anthology of Contemporary Asian American Fiction*, edited by Jessica Hagedorn (New York: Penguin Books, 1993).

Chapter 1

1. Richard Drinnon, *Facing West: The Metaphysics of Indian Hating and Empire Building* (New York: Chicken Books, 1991), 300–301; Gerald R. Gems, *The Athletic Crusade: Sport and American Cultural Imperialism* (Lincoln: University of Nebraska Press, 2006).
2. *Sporting News*, 27 April 1901; *Washington Post*, 24 December 1909.
3. *Sporting Life*, 24 February 1912.
4. *Sporting Life*, 10 August 1912.
5. S.W. Pope, *Patriotic Games: Sporting Traditions in the American Imagination, 1876–1926* (New York: Oxford University Press, 1997), 75.
6. *Spalding's Official Base Ball Guide, Thirty-Seventh Year 1913*, edited by John B. Foster (American Sports Publishing Company), 9; *Current Opinion*, November 1913.
7. *Washington Post*, 21 April 1913.
8. *Daily Commonwealth*, 10 May 1913; *Los Angeles Times*, 28 May 1913; *Honolulu Star-Bulletin*, 7 May 1913.
9. *Nevada State Journal*, 8 June 1913.
10. *Coshocton Tribune*, 2 July 1913.
11. *San Francisco Chronicle*, 15 June 1913.
12. *Ibid.*, 23 June 1913; *Coshocton Tribune*, 23 August 1913.
13. *Honolulu Star-Bulletin*, 26 September 1913, 29 September 1913; Joseph Reaves, *Taking in a Game: A History of Baseball in Asia* (Lincoln: University of Nebraska Press, 2002), 102.
14. Reaves, *Taking*, 102.
15. *Honolulu Star-Bulletin*, 24 June 1915.
16. *Washington Post*, 22 August 1915.
17. *Honolulu Star-Bulletin*, 5 June 1915; *Pacific Commercial Advertiser*, 14 November 1915.
18. *Baseball Monthly*, April 1916.
19. *The Playground*, April 1917.
20. Reaves, *Taking*, 102; Janice A. Beren, "Physical Education and Sport in the Philippines," *Sport in Asia and Africa: A Comparative Handbook*, edited by Eric A. Wagner (Westport, CT: Greenwood Press, 1989), 152.
21. *Sporting News*, 6 January 1921.
22. *Ibid.*
23. *Ibid.*
24. *Ibid.*, 9 August 1922.
25. *Ibid.*, 7 April 1932; Reaves, *Taking*, 103.
26. *Sporting News*, 13 December 1934.
27. *Washington Post*, 22 August 1915.
28. Albert G. Spalding, *America's National Game* (Lincoln and London: University of Nebraska Press, 1992), 256–257; quoted in Jules Tygiel, *Past Time: Baseball as History* (New York: Oxford University Press, 2000), 10.
29. Thomas Kaulukukui, "The Development of Competitive Athletics in the Schools of Hawaii" (master's thesis, University of Hawaii, 1941), 18; *Hawaiian Gazette*, 2 April 1895; 12 April 1895; 14 May 1895.
30. *Hawaiian Gazette*, 21 May 1895, 8 September 1896, 7 March 1899 1, 23 May 1899.
31. *Ibid.*, 7 May 1895; 9 July 1897; 31 August 1897; 7 March 1899; 20 June 1899.
32. *Ibid.*, 20 April 1895, 14 August 1896, 22 September 1896.
33. Jeffrey Wilson, "Chinese History, Even in Baseball, Stretches Back Far in Time," *International Baseball Rundown* (August 1996), p. 17; "Dr. Khai Fai Li," www.hml.org, accessed 31 March 2003; Nakagawa, *Through a Diamond*, 4–5.
34. *Hawaiian Gazette*, 4 August 1903.
35. *Washington Post*, 3 November 1904.
36. *Ibid.*, 2 December 1906.
37. *Ibid.*, 24 December 1908.
38. *Decatur Review*, 19 September 1910.
39. *Ibid.*, 22 September 1910.
40. *Los Angeles Times*, 5 July 1912.
41. *Pacific Commercial Advertiser*, 8 June 1912.
42. *Honolulu Star-Bulletin*, 20 March 1913.
43. *Ibid.*, 18 March 1913.
44. *Sporting News*, 24 December 1914, p. 5
45. *Pacific Commercial Advertiser*, 2 March 1915; *Honolulu Star Bulletin*, 14 July 1914.
46. *Honolulu Star-Bulletin*, 20 August 1915.
47. *Sporting News*, 15 March 1917, 29 April 1917.

48. William Peet, "Baseball in Hawaii," *Sporting News*, 6 February 1926.
49. *Decatur Review*, 3 January 1931.
50. *Williamsport Grit*, 17 January 1932.
51. Bob Considine, "On the Line," *Washington Post*, 20 January 1941.
52. Joel S. Franks, *Hawaiian Sports*, chapters 2–4.
53. *Honolulu Star-Bulletin*, 3 January 1949; *Chicago Daily Tribune*, 24 January 1949.
54. *Honolulu Star-Bulletin*, 26 May 1913.
55. *Ibid.*, 28 May 1913, 30 May 1913, 31 May 1913; Jeffrey Powers-Beck, *The American Indian Integration of Baseball* (Lincoln: University of Nebraska Press, 2004), 190–191.
56. *Honolulu Star-Bulletin*, 23 June 1913.
57. *Ibid.*, 27 June 1913, 16 July 1913, 2 September 1913.
58. Franks, *Hawaiian Sports*, chapter 4.
59. *Official Baseball Annual 1956, Rules, Teams, Photos* (Wichita, KS: National Baseball Congress, 1956), 14–15.
60. *Honolulu Star-Bulletin*, 11 January 1913; Lewis R. Freeman, "Baseball at Pago-Pago," *Los Angeles Times*, 10 August 1913.
61. C.L.R. James, *Beyond a Boundary* (New York: Pantheon Books, 1983).
62. *Ibid.*; Antonio Gramsci, *Selections from the Prison Notebooks*, Q. Hoare and G. Smith, eds. (New York: International Press, 1971).
63. James, *Beyond*; Raymond Williams, *Marxism and Literature* (New York and London: Oxford University Press, 1977); Stuart Hall, "Gramsci's Relevance for the Study of Race and Ethnicity," *Journal of Communication Inquiry* 10 (Summer 1986).
64. James, *Beyond*; Renato Rosaldo, *Culture and Truth: The Remaking of Social Analysis* (Boston: Beacon Press, 1989); Lisa Lowe, *Immigrant Acts: On Asian American Cultural Politics* (Durham and London: Duke University Press, 1996).

Chapter 2

1. *Pacific Commercial Advertiser*, 9 April 1912; *Honolulu Star-Bulletin*, 10 May 1915.
2. *Pacific Commercial Advertiser*, 13 November 1911, 4 March 1912; *Honolulu Star-Bulletin*, 6 September 1915, 23 September 1915, 3 December 1949.
3. Loui Leong Hop, "Chinese Contributions to Sports," *A History of Recreation in Hawaii* (Honolulu: Recreation Commission, City and County of Honolulu, TH, 1936), 104.
4. *Pacific Commercial Advertiser*, 24 September 1906; *Decatur Review*, 8 June 1907; *Washington Post*, 14 March 1908.
5. *Chicago Daily Tribune*, 18 December 1911, p. 14.
6. *Pacific Commercial Advertiser*, 8 January 1912, p. 3.
7. *Honolulu Star-Bulletin*, 22 June 1914, 29 June 1914; *New York Times*, 6 December 1914.
8. *New York Times*, 6 December 1914.
9. *Pacific Commercial Advertiser*, 2 April 1915; *Honolulu Star-Bulletin*, 9 March 1915, 15 March 1915, 19 March 1915, 22 March 1915, 26 March 1915.
10. *Honolulu Star-Bulletin*, 27 March 1915.
11. *Ibid.*, 28 April 1915.
12. *Ibid.*, 8 April 1915, 16 June 1915.
13. *Adams County News*, 19 June 1915.
14. *Honolulu Star-Bulletin*, 28 May 1915.
15. *Ibid.*, 3 June 1915.
16. *Ibid.*
17. *Ibid.*, 5 June 1915, 23 June 1915.
18. *Pacific Commercial Advertiser*, 17 February 1916; *Honolulu Star-Bulletin*, 3 June 1915, 19 June 1915, 14 October 1915.
19. *Sporting News*, 27 May 1915.
20. *Honolulu Star Bulletin*, 22 June 1915, 23 June 1915.
21. *Ibid.*, 26 June 1915, 28 June 1915.
22. *Ibid.*, 6 July 1915.
23. *Ibid.*, 2 July 1915.
24. Jerry Malloy, "The Twenty-Fifth Infantry Takes the Field," *National Pastime*, no. 15 (1995): 61–62; *Pacific Commercial Advertiser*, 15 October 1915, 30 October 1915, 28 November 1915.
25. *Pacific Commercial Advertiser*, 4 March 1912, 6 May 1912, 20 May 1912, 21 June 1912, 19 August 1912.
26. *Ibid.*, 16 September 1912.
27. *Ibid.*, 30 September 1912, 4 October 1912.
28. *Ibid.*, 30 September 1912.
29. *Ibid.*, 18 October 1912.
30. *Honolulu Star-Bulletin*, 20 January 1913, 20 May 1915, 13 September 1915, 23 September 1915; *Pacific Commercial Advertiser*, 17 October 1915, 19 June 1919; *Reno Evening Gazette*, 24 April 1920; *Thrum's Hawaiian Annals for 1921* (Honolulu:

Thomas G. Thrum, 1920), 167; *Nevada State Journal*, 16 July 1922; *Chicago Daily Tribune*, 18 July 1922.
31. Hop, "Chinese Contributions," 104. *Honolulu Star-Bulletin*, 12 May 1936, p. 4; United States Census Manuscripts, City and County of Honolulu, 1930; Arthur Suehiro, *Honolulu Stadium: Where Hawaii Played* (Honolulu: Watermark, 1995), 32–33.
32. Suehiro, *Honolulu Stadium*, 26; *New York Times*, 5 February 1928; *Honolulu Star-Bulletin*, 29 April 1936, 2 May 1936, 7 January 1949, 15 November 1999;
33. *Honolulu Star-Bulletin*, 22 April 1940, p. 10.
34. *Hawaii Herald*, 1 January 1953, 4 January 1951.
35. www.starbulletin.com, 19 February 1998.
36. Suehiro, *Honolulu Stadium*, 33; *Pacific Commercial Advertiser*, 12 March 1906, 8 January 1912.
37. *Hawaiian Star*, 12 April 1912; *Pacific Commercial Advertiser*, 17 June 1912, 22 March 1914.
38. *Pacific Commercial Advertiser*, 20 May 1912, 25 October 1912; *Honolulu Star-Bulletin*, 2 August 1912.
39. *Pacific Commercial Advertiser*, 22 November 1916.
40. *Honolulu Star-Bulletin*, 30 January 1917.
41. *Honolulu Star-Bulletin*, 20 May 1915, 19 December 1916; *Pacific Commercial Advertiser*, 19 November 1916, 25 November 1916, 26 November 1916, 8 June 1919.
42. *Honolulu Star-Bulletin*, 27 August 1915.
43. *Ibid.*, 23 September 1915, 5 October 1915; Nakagawa, *Through a Diamond*, 6.
44. *Pacific Commercial Advertiser*, 9 March 1914, 21 November 1915, 28 November 1915; Suehiro, *Honolulu Stadium*, 7; Nakagawa, *Through a Diamond*, 6; *Elyria Chronicle Telegram*, 12 May 1921; *Daily Palo Alto*, 4 August 1922; George Sakamaki, "Japanese Athletes in Hawaii," *Bulletin of the Pan-Pacific Union*, August 1931, 12.
45. Suehiro, *Honolulu Stadium*, 35; www.starbulletin.com, 19 February 1998; *Pacific Citizen*, 13 September 1974.
46. *San Francisco Chronicle*, 8 February 1923, 9 February 1923, 12 February 1923; *San Jose Mercury*, 16 February 1923.
47. *Pacific Commercial Advertiser*, 21 February 1912, 9 September 1915, 29 November 1915; *Honolulu Star-Bulletin*, 24 July 1915.

48. *Pacific Commercial Advertiser*, 11 July 1911.
49. *Ibid.*, 20 July 1911, 21 July 1911, 23 July 1911.
50. *Ibid.*, 27 May 1912, 14 November 1915.
51. *Honolulu Star-Bulletin*, 13 September 1915, 20 September 1915, 23 September 1915.
52. *Ibid.*, 16 December 1916.
53. *Pacific Commercial Advertiser*, 2 May 1912, 23 November 1912, 8 December 1912; *Honolulu Star-Bulletin*, 27 March 1915.
54. Marie Booty, "Korean Contributions," *A History of Recreation in Hawaii*, 133; "Ancient Philippines," *A History of Recreation in Hawaii*, 105; *Honolulu Star-Bulletin*, 2 May 1936; Ramon R. Carioga, *The Filipinos in Hawaii: A Survey of Their Economic and Social Conditions* (Honolulu: University of Hawaii, 1936), 89.
55. *Honolulu Star-Bulletin*, 17 March 1947, 23 January 1951, 11 May 1951, 16 April 1961, 19 February 1998, 15 November 1999; *Hawaii Herald*, 16 January 1951; Suehiro, *Honolulu Stadium*, 137; Fred Simprich, Jr., "Honolulu: Midocean Capital," *National Geographic*, May 1954, 592.
56. *Honolulu Star-Bulletin*, 1 January 1949; *Chicago Daily Tribune*, 24 January 1949; Suehiro, *Honolulu Stadium*, 57.
57. Jonathan Y. Okamura, "Baseball and Beauty Queens: The Political Context of Ethnic Boundary Making in the Japanese American Community in Hawaii," in Jonathan Y. Okamura, ed., *The Japanese American Contemporary Experience in Hawaii* (Honolulu: University of Hawaii Press, 2002), 122–126.
58. *Ibid.*, 122–128, 132.
59. *Ibid.*, 127–128.

Chapter 3

1. *Sporting News*, 8 May 1965.
2. Gary Otake, "More Than Just a Game," *Nikkei Heritage* (San Francisco: National Japanese American Historical Society, 1997), 4.
3. *Ibid.*, p. 7; William V. Flores and Rina Benmayor, eds., *Latino Cultural Citizenship: Claiming Identity, Space, and Rights* (Boston: Beacon Press, 1997).
4. Tim Malloy, "Strike Three for Ballpark Memorial at Internment Site," www.asianweek, 24 October 2003.

5. Otake, "More Than Just a Game," p. 6; Nagakawa, *Through A Diamond*, 27, 30–32; *Los Angeles Times*, 23 June 1908, 14 April 1909.
6. *Los Angeles Times*, 31 December 1919.
7. Nomura, "Beyond the Playing Field," p. 16
8. *Ibid.*, 17; Nakagawa, *Through a Diamond*, 16–18.
9. Nomura, "Beyond the Playing Field," p. 18;
10. Nakagawa, *Through a Diamond*, 18, 19; *Oakland Tribune*, 4 August 1924; Ship's Manifest SS *Taiyo Maru*, Honolulu, TH, 30 August 1927.
11. *Sacramento Bee*, 20 January 1923, 12 May 1924, 5 March 1927; Nakagawa, *Through a Diamond*, 20; *San Francisco Chronicle*, 5 October 1926.
12. *Sacramento Bee*, 14 April 1923, 2 June 1925.
13. Samuel O. Regalado, "Incarcerated Sport: *Nisei* Women's Softball and Athletics During Japanese Internment." *Journal of Sport History* 27, no. 3 (Fall 2000): 133; *Sacramento Bee*, 2 July 1933; *Los Angeles Times*, 26 May 1935.
14. *San Francisco Chronicle*, 3 February 1923.
15. *Los Angeles Times*, 16 September 1922, 4 February 1923, 3 February 1930, 8 December 1941; *Nichi Bei Times*, 1 January 1973; Otto Friedrich, *City of Nets: A Portrait of Hollywood in the 1940s* (New York: Harper & Row, 1986), 102.
16. *Los Angeles Times*, 10 September 1930, 18 February 1931, 15 March 1937, 21 June 1937, 31 January 1938, 14 November 1938, 15 May 1939.
17. Feldman, "Baseball Behind Barbed Wire," p. 37
18. *San Jose Mercury*, 7 May 1922, 3 February 1923, 19 February 1923, 28 March 1935; *San Francisco Chronicle*, 14 August 1925; *Los Angeles Times*, 21 April 1929; Pearce, *From Asahi to Zebras*.
19. *San Francisco Chronicle*, 11 July 1925, 3 May 1926; *San Jose Mercury*, 15 December 1928, 4 July 1935; *San Francisco Examiner*, 7 June 1937; *Stanford Daily*, 9 April 1931.
20. *San Francisco Examiner*, 1 March 1937.
21. Feldman, "Barbed," 37–39; Regalado, "Incarcerated," 435; Nakagawa, *Through a Diamond*, 83–86; Carol Jung, "Baseball Helped East Assimilation," *San Jose Mercury*, 17 July 1996, p. 1D; Tim Malloy, "Strike Three for Ballpark Memorial at Internment Site," www.asianweek.com, 24 October 2003.
22. *Manzanar Free Press*, 22 July 1944.
23. Bill Hosokawa "From the Frying Pan," *Pacific Citizen*, 5 June 1947, 9 August 1947, 20 September 1947; *San Jose Mercury*, 5 September 1947, 15 August 1947, 17 August 1947, 3 September 1949, 17 March 1951, 19 July 1953, 5 May 1954; *San Francisco Chronicle*, 19 August 1951; *Utah Nippo*, 26 April 1950; *Placerville Mountain Democrat*, 10 May 1951; *Sacramento Bee*, 8 June 1953.
24. Pearce, *From Asahi to Zebras*, 96.
25. *Placerville Mountain Democrat*, 9 August 1962; *Rafu Shimpo*, 9 September 1974.
26. *San Francisco Chronicle*, 3 May 1905, 2 May 1911; *Los Angeles Times*, 18 May 1905, 19 May 1905; Nomura, "Beyond the Playing Field," p. 16; Takaki, *Strangers*.
27. *San Francisco Chronicle*, 2 March 1935, 3 March 1935, 10 March 1935; *Sporting News*, 25 February 1953; *Santa Ana Register*, 1 April 1960.
28. *San Francisco Chronicle*, 18 August 1947; Harold Peterson, *The Man Who Invented Baseball* (New York: Charles Scribner's and Sons, 1963), 162.
29. *New York Times*, 12 May 1900; *Sacramento Bee*, 1 April 1912; *San Francisco Chronicle*, 16 February 1918; *San Jose Mercury*, 23 August 1919, 25 August 1919.
30. *Chicago Daily Tribune*, 28 June 1908.
31. *Los Angeles Times*, 16 September 1922, 19 May 1924, 9 March 1925; George and Elise Yee, "The 1927 Chinese Ball Team," *Gam Saan Journal*, December 1986, pp. 1, 2.
32. Yee, "Chinese Ball Team," pp. 2, 3, 5.
33. *Ibid.*, pp. 4–5.
34. *Ibid.*, p. 5
35. *Ibid.*, pp. 4–5.
36. Connie Young Yu, *Chinatown San Jose, USA* (San Jose, CA: Historical Museum Association, 1991); Eve Armentrout Ma and Jeong Hui Ma, *The Chinese of Oakland: Unsung Builders* (Oakland, CA: Chinese History Research Committee, 1982), 54; *Oakland Tribune*, 8 April 1930; *East/West*, 1 February 1967; *San Francisco Examiner*, 20 September 1932, 6 March 1934.
37. *San Francisco Chronicle*, 8 September 1945.
38. *Ibid.*, 31 July 1950; *Chinese Press*, 4 July 1950; *San Francisco Examiner*, 25 November 1947, 12 March 1950.

39. *San Francisco Chronicle*, 1 April 1946, 19 August 1951; *Chinese Press*, 31 March 1950, 19 May 1950, 30 June 1950; *San Francisco Examiner*, 20 May 1951; *Sacramento Bee*, 25 March 1950.
40. *Sporting Life*, April 13, 1912; *Sacramento Bee*, 5 April 1912; *Honolulu Star-Bulletin*, 10 October 1912; *San Francisco Chronicle*, 1 April 1913; *Los Angeles Times*, 14 March 1914, 15 March 1914.
41. *Chicago Daily Tribune*, 15 May 1922; *San Francisco Chronicle*, 1 March 1927; 15 March 1936; *San Francisco Examiner*, 9 June 1935; *Philippine News*, 13 July 1998.
42. Carlos Bulosan, *America Is in the Heart* (Seattle: University of Washington Press, 1979), 102.
43. *Rafu Shimpo*, 23 August 1972; Clark Walker, "On the Diamond, In the Bleachers," www.asianweek.com, August 29, 1997; Jeff Weinstock, "Park's Place," *Sport*, August 1998; *Los Angeles Times*, September 14, 1997.
44. *East/West*, 20 July 1983; Carolyn Jung, "Assimilation"; Walker, "On the Diamond."
45. Ethen Leiser, "St. Paul Hmong Is First Southeast APA in State Office," *Asian-Week*, February 8, 2002–February 14, 2002.
46. *East/West*, 3 June 1981; AP Online, "Philly Chinese Leaders Rip Ballpark," 7 June 2000.
47. Flores and Benmayor, *Cultural Citizenship*.

Chapter 4

1. *Los Angeles Times*, 14 March 1915, 28 March 1922, 7 March 1925,18 February 1931; *San Jose Mercury*, 9 April 1922, 10 February 1930, 11 February 1930, 18 February 1930; Nomura, "Beyond," p. 17; Elliot G. Mears, *Resident Orientals on the Pacific Coast* (Chicago: University of Chicago Press, 1928), 366; *Gastonia Daily Gazette*, 12 November 1926; Otake, "More Than Just a Game," *Nikkei Heritage* (Spring 1997), 8; *San Francisco Examiner*, 22 February 1931; *San Francisco Chronicle*, 21 April 1935, 17 March 1936, 3 May 1936; Nakagawa, *Through a Diamond*, 92.
2. *Sporting News*, 17 March 1938, p. 4.
3. Nakagawa, *Through a Diamond*, 60.
4. *Pacific Citizen*, 4 June 1942; Gary Y. Okihiro, *Storied Lives: Japanese American Students and World War II* (Seattle: University of Washington Press, 1999), 90, 94–95; Nakagawa, *Through a Diamond*, 92–93.
5. *Los Angeles Times*, 30 May 1946; *San Jose Mercury*, 3 May 1946; 19 September 1946, p. 10; 23 March 1947; *San Jose Mercury*, 17 July 1996; *Pacific Citizen*, 23 August 1947, p. 7; 21 January 1950; *Sacramento Bee*, 24 March 1950, 30 March 1950; *Seattle Post-Intelligencer*, 6 June 1955, 11 June 1955; *New York Times*, 27 August 1959.
6. *Santa Ana Register*, 1 April 1960; *Nichi Bei Times*, 1 January 1973, 30 August 1973.
7. Kerry Yo Nakagawa, "*Nisei* Baseball Project provides diplomacy through sports world," *Fresno Bee*, 8 January 2000; *Pacific Citizen*, 23 August 1947, 20 February 1950, 11 March 1950; *Honolulu Star-Bulletin*, 8 June 1951.
8. *Los Angeles Times*, 1 February 1951, 5 April 1951, 14 April 1951; *Pacific Citizen*, 17 March 1951, 14 April 1951; *Honolulu Star-Bulletin*, 8 June 1951; Red McQueen, "Lopat Stars Win 6 in Hawaii, But Draw Only Slim Crowds," *Sporting News*, 27 October 1954; Bob Cole, Jr., "4 Hawaii Sandlotters Receiving O.B. Trials," *Sporting News*, 30 May 1956.
9. *San Francisco Examiner*, 20 May 1951, 24 Mary 1951; Bruce Farris, "A Lifelong Labor of Love," *Fresno Bee*, 13 March 2000.
10. *Pacific Citizen*, 11 March 1950, 17 March 1951, 8 June 1973; *San Francisco Examiner*, 20 May 1956; *Rafu Shimpo*, 18 March 1972, 29 March 1972, 25 March 1972; Cisco, *Hawai'i Sports*, 27.
11. *Chicago Daily Tribune*, 11 June 1953; *New York Times*, 16 August 1953, 26 August 1953.
12. *Sporting News*, 15 September 1973; *Honolulu Star-Bulletin*, 29 January 1997; www.huskerwebcast.com, 19 September 1999, 14 March 2000; Ethen Leiser, "Komine Shucks Hitters in the Cornhusker State," *Asian Week*, 18 June–24 June 2002.
13. Ron Kroichik, "USF's Title Hopes Are on the Horizon," *San Francisco Chronicle*, 3 April 1998; www.usfdons.com, accessed 12 June 2005.
14. Travis Gauchay, "Quiet, But with Big Bat," *The Signpost*, 7 March 2001; www.bigwest.org, accessed 5 December 2004; *Sports Illustrated*, 9 May 2005.
15. www.gostanford.com, accessed 5 December 2004.
16. Bob Jacobsen, "A Man for All Seasons," www.asu.edu/alumnivision, accessed

30 August 2002; *The Phoenician*, Phoenix High School Yearbook, 1933, www.ancestry.com, accessed 27 May 2006.
17. "Scott's Scrapbook," *Marion Star*, 9 April 1940; Jacobsen, "A Man," *Pacific Citizen*, 15 April 1943, 12 July 1947.
18. *Chicago Daily Tribune*, 26 June 1908; *Los Angeles Times*, 22 March 1908; *Pacific Commercial Advertiser*, 22 November 1912, 12 March 1914; *Chinese Digest*, 29 November 1935, March 1938; *San Jose Mercury*, 1 March 1942.
19. *Los Angeles Times*, 26 February 1942, 28 April 1942, 9 February 1947.
20. Cole, "Sandlotters;" *East/West*, 3 April 1968, 15 June 1983; *Ahead in the Count: 130 Years of Women & Baseball*: 1995 Colorado Silver Bullets Souvenir Program; Michael Learmouth, *Metro Magazine, San Jose Mercury*, 21 August 1997; http://calwomensbaseball.thewavemedia.com/teams.html, accessed 5 September 2005.
21. *Pacific Commercial Advertiser*, 23 December 1911, 12 March 1913; *Daily Palo Alto*, 20 April 1911; Cole, "Sandlotters"; Rube Samuelson, "Hawaiian Ane One Hula-Va Tackler USC Foes Learn," *Sporting News*, 3 December 1952; Joe Bertagna, "A Drive In History," www.fans.harvard.edu, accessed 9 June 2001; John Strege, "The Other Raymond Townsend," *Los Angeles Times*, 12 May 1976, *Asian Week*, 19 July 1996–25 July 1996.
22. *New York Times*, 4 March 1941, 16 April 1941, 21 February 1956, 11 December 1956, 5 May 1960; *Washington Post*, 9 February 1952; *Berkshire Evening Eagle*, 31 July 1952; William T. "Buck" Lai, *Championship Baseball from Little League to Big League* (New York: Prentice Hall, 1954); Keoni Everington, "Remembering Buck Lai," *Asian Week*, 23 November–28 November 2001.
23. *Honolulu Star-Bulletin*, 9 July 1999; www.byucougars, accessed 2 February 2001; www.athletics@swarthmore.edu., accessed 3 July 2005.
24. Sidney L. Gulick, *Mixing the Races in Hawaii: A Study of the Coming Neo-Hawaiian Race* (Honolulu: Hawaiian Board Book Room, 1937), 123.
25. *Pacific Commercial Advertiser*, 24 December 1911, 6 January 1912, 8 January 1912, 18 September 1912, 27 November 1912, 8 December 1912, 6 April 1915, 13 November 1916; *Honolulu Star-Bulletin*, 22 January 1913, 6 May 1913, 20 May 1915.
26. *Pacific Commercial Advertiser*, 12 April 1912, 16 April 1912, 28 April 1912, 11 May 1912, 13 November 1916, 27 December 1916; *Honolulu Star-Bulletin*, 3 May 1915, 4 May 1915, 10 May 1915, 11 May 1915.
27. *Pacific Commercial Advertiser*, 22 April 1912, 25 November 1916, 9 June 1919; *Honolulu Star-Bulletin*, 23 August 1915.
28. *Honolulu Advertiser*, 3 March 1935, 11 March 1935.
29. *Pacific Commercial Advertiser*, 27 March 1916.
30. *Honolulu Star-Bulletin*, 6 September 1915.
31. *San Jose Mercury*, 4 August 1908; *Pacific Commercial Advertiser*, 2 May 1912, 26 June 1912, 19 August 1912, 21 October 1912, 2 November 1912; *Honolulu Star-Bulletin*, 2 June 1951.
32. U.S Census Manuscripts, Hilo, Hawaii, 1930; Cisco, *Hawaii Sports*, 30; *Honolulu Star-Bulletin*, April 16, 1936, 3 September 1940, 6 April 1942, 17 March 1947; *Honolulu Advertiser*, 5 April 1936; Franklin S. Odo, *No Sword to Bury: Japanese Americans in Hawai'i During World War II* (Philadelphia: Temple University Press, 2003), 208; Suehiro, *Honolulu Stadium*, 32.
33. *Helena Independent*, 13 September 1935; *Sporting News*, 28 November 1935; U.S. Census Manuscripts, City and County of Honolulu, 1930.
34. *Honolulu Star-Bulletin*, 12 May 1936; *San Francisco Chronicle*, 25 February 1936, 1 March 1936, 2 March 1936, 14 March 1936.
35. Cisco, *Hawai'i Sports*, 30; *Honolulu Star-Bulletin*, 16 April 1936, 22 April 1940; *Honolulu Advertiser*, 14 July 1947.
36. Suehiro, *Honolulu Stadium*, 33; *Honolulu Star-Bulletin*, 17 March 1947, 12 May 1951; *Sporting News*, 5 July 1961; Kate McKee, "And the Winner Is," www.islandscene.com, 2 April 1999; David Reardon, "Cris Mancao and the Pitch Count Theory," www.islandscene.com, 5 January 2000.
37. *Honolulu Star-Bulletin*, 3 March 1999.
38. U.S. Census Manuscripts, City and County of Honolulu, 1930; *Honolulu Star-Bulletin*, 6 April 1936, 12 May 1936, 8 August 1942, 3 May 1944; 19 February 1998; *Honolulu Advertiser*, 12 March 1944; Beth Bailey and David Farber, *First Strange Place: The Alchemy of Race and Sex in World War II Hawaii* (New York: Free Press, 1992), 166; *San Francisco Chronicle*, 10 March 1946; *Honolulu Star-Bulletin*, 25 June 1946, 7 May

1956, 8 May 1956; *Honolulu Advertiser*, 14 July 1947.
39. *Honolulu Star-Bulletin*, 2 May 1956, 5 May 1956, 9 May 1956.
40. *Pacific Citizen*, 23 August 1947; Milton Bracker, "Hawaiian Lads Homesick at Series," *New York Times*, 27 August 1959; *Los Angeles Times*, 15 January 1964; *San Jose Mercury*, 19 August 1965.
41. *Honolulu Star-Bulletin*, 9 June 1999.
42. *San Francisco Chronicle*, 26 July 1947; *Pacific Citizen*, 16 August 1947, 16 August 1947, 30 August 1947, 7 January 1950; *San Jose Mercury*, 2 August 1947; Rod Ohira, "Stellar Tour," *Honolulu Star-Bulletin*, 28 December 1999.
43. Ohira, "Stellar Tour;" *Los Angeles Times*, 13 June 1948. *Honolulu Star-Bulletin*, 1 July 1948, 4 September 1948.
44. *Sports Illustrated*, 10 October 1955, p. 14; *Official Baseball Annual 1956, Rules, Teams, Photos* (Wichita, KS: National Baseball Congress, 1956), 14–19.
45. *Pacific Commercial Advertiser*, 18 November 1916, 19 November 1916; *Pacific Commercial Advertiser*, 2 December 1916, 3 December 1916, 4 December 1916; Suehiro, *Honolulu Stadium*, 45; Mike Davis, *Dead Cities and Other Tales* (New York: The New Press, 2002), 112; *San Francisco Examiner*, 10 March 1947.
46. Sakamaki, "Japanese Athletes," p. 12; *Honolulu Advertiser*, 3 March 1935; *Pacific Citizen*, 15 February 1950; *Honolulu Star-Bulletin*, 17 March 1947, 5 April 1950, 27 January 1951; Cisco, *Hawai'i Sports*, 14, 15.
47. www.hawaii.edu, accessed 1 January 1997; Cisco, *Hawai'i Sports*, 12, 14–15; Ferd Lewis, " Murakami Put Program on Sturdy Foundation," *Honolulu Advertiser*, 5 November 2000; *Honolulu Star-Bulletin*, 23 April 1999.
48. *Honolulu Advertiser*, 5 January 2000, 8 February 2000; Cisco, *Hawai'i Sports*, 11–12; *Honolulu Star-Bulletin*, 6 January 2001; Elliot Almond, "Rainbows Find the Pot of Gold in Baseball," *Los Angeles Times*, 27 April 1979.
49. www.hawaii.edu, accessed January 1, 1997; Cisco, *Hawai'i Sports*, 14–15.
50. www.uhvulcans.edu, accessed February 2, 2001; Cisco, *Hawai'i Sports*, 21–23; *Honolulu Star-Bulletin*, 15 December 1999.
51. Cisco, *Hawai'i Sports*, 24–25.
52. *Honolulu Star-Bulletin*, 22 April 1940, 17 March 1947; *San Francisco Examiner*, 23 May 1956; *Nevada State Journal*, 4 April 1957; *Pacific Citizen*, 17 March 1951.
53. *Pacific Citizen*, 31 March 1951, 30 August 1974; Gallagher, *Giants Magazine*, July-August 1994, p. 35; *Nichi Bei Times*, 28 August 1973; *San Francisco Giants 1963 Yearbook*, p. 16.
54. Michael Lewis, *Moneyball: The Art of Winning an Unfair Game* (New York: Norton, 2003), 23–24.
55. Cisco, *Hawai'i Sports*, 33; *Honolulu Star-Bulletin*, 16 April 1961; *San Jose Mercury*, 18 January 1965; *Sporting News*, 15 July 1972.
56. www.maui.net., accessed 21 April 1999; *Honolulu Star-Bulletin*, 24 August 1998.
57. *Asian Week*, 8 April 1998, p. 8; "Dodgers' Ng Subject of Racial Remarks," 21 November 2003.
58. "Dodgers' Ng Subject of Racial Remarks."
59. Russell Leong, "Batter Up for Kim Ng," *ibid.*, 14 May 2004.
60. Samson Wong, "Sports and APA Heritage Month, " *ibid.*, 14 May 2004.
61. "Suit Alleges Anti-Asian Bias," *ibid.*, 24 October 2003.

Chapter 5

1. Everington, "Remembering Buck Lai," *Honolulu Advertiser*, 4 April 1964.
2. *Honolulu Advertiser*, 4 April 1964.
3. Everington, "Remembering Buck Lai"; United States Census Manuscripts, City and County of Honolulu, 1900, 1910, 1930; *Honolulu City Directory, 1890*, www.ancestry.com, accessed March 3, 2001.
4. *Pacific Commercial Advertiser*, 13 March 1913.
5. Joel S. Franks, "Uncle Sam's Old Tricks," unpublished book length manuscript.
6. *Elyria Evening Telegram*, 19 August 1912; *Chicago Daily Tribune*, 6 September 1912.
7. *Pacific Commercial Advertiser*, 11 April 1912; *Honolulu Star-Bulletin*, 25 July 1913; *Reno Evening Gazette*, 29 April 1916.
8. *New York Sun,* 25 May 1912; *Pacific Commercial Advertiser*, 6 September 1912.
9. *Los Angeles Times*, 29 March 1912; *San Francisco Call*, 2 April 1912.
10. Cited in *Honolulu Star-Bulletin*, 5 April 1915.

11. *New York Sun*, 23 May 1912; "The Crack of the Baseball Bat Goes Echoeing Around the World," *Current Opinion*, November 1913.
12. *Daily Palo Alto*, 5 April 1913; *Fort Wayne Journal-Gazette*, 15 May 1914; cited in the *Honolulu Star-Bulletin*, 23 September 1915.
13. Cited in *Pacific Commercial Advertiser*, 5 April 1913; cited in the *Honolulu Star-Bulletin*, 17 April 1915.
14. *Indianapolis Star*, 13 September 1914.
15. *Sheboygan Press*, 9 July 1912; *Elyria Evening Telegram*, 19 August 1912; *Honolulu Star-Bulletin*, 10 May 1915.
16. United States Census Manuscripts, Maui, 1900, 1930; *Pacific Commercial Advertiser*, 11 March 1913, 20 March 1913; *Washington Post*, 13 July 1913; *Honolulu Star-Bulletin*, 22 July 1913; *Los Angeles Times*, 15 March 1914.
17. Ship's Manifest SS *Honolulan*, left Honolulu 3 March 1914 and arrived in San Francisco 11 March 1914, www.ancestry.com, accessed 17 September 2004; U.S. Draft Registration Cards, Philadelphia, Pennsylvania, June 5, 1917, www.ancestry.com, accessed 28 September 2004.
18. *Washington Post*, 11 June 1913; *New York Times*, 19 June 1913.
19. *Pacific Commercial Advertiser*, 13 September 1912, 14 September 1912, 7 November 1912, p. 3; *Indianapolis Star*, 13 September 1914.
20. *Honolulu Star-Bulletin*, 23 April 1915; "Our Letter Box," *Baseball Magazine*, July 1915.
21. U.S. Census Manuscripts, City and County of Honolulu, 1930; *New York Times*, 23 May 1912; *Pacific Commercial Advertiser*, 17 April 1913, 11 March 1915.
22. *Pacific Commercial Advertiser*, 24 April 1912, 11 March 1913; *New York Times*, 13 May 1912; *Washington Post*, 14 May 1912.
23. *Honolulu Star-Bulletin*, 5 April 1915, 27 July 1915.
24. *Ibid.*, 19 August 1912, 13 September 1912; *Pacific Commercial Advertiser*, 17 May 1912.
25. *Chicago Tribune*, 24 September 1912; *Oakland Tribune*, 17 January 1915.
26. U.S. Census Manuscripts, City and County of Honolulu, 1930; *Pacific Commercial Advertiser*, 1 June 1912, 11 March 1913; *Honolulu Star-Bulletin*, 10 October 1912.
27. *Pacific Commercial Advertiser*, 20 March 1915; *Honolulu Star-Bulletin*, 8 June 1915, 22 June 1915; *Indianapolis Star*, 2 October 1916; U.S. Census Manuscripts, City and County of Honolulu, 1930.
28. *Honolulu Advertiser*, 4 April 1964.
29. *Washington Post*, 22 December 1911; *Pacific Commercial Advertiser*, 14 February 1912; U.S. Census Manuscripts, City of Chicago and County of Cook [Illinois], 1910.
30. *Pacific Commercial Advertiser*, 16 April 1912, 17 May 1912, 22 May 1912, 1 October 1912.
31. S.H. Hoe, "America Invaded by Oriental Foes," *Baseball Monthly*, March 1914, p. 68.
32. *Honolulu Star-Bulletin*, 27 March 1915.
33. *Ibid.*, 19 May 1915.
34. *Ibid.*
35. *Ibid.*, 19 July 1915.
36. *Gettysburg Star and Sentinel*, 16 August 1914.
37. *Honolulu Star-Bulletin*, 7 August 1912.
38. *Ibid.*
39. *Pacific Commercial Advertiser*, 18 March 1914.
40. *Ibid.*, 21 March 1915; *Honolulu Advertiser*, 4 April 1964; *Honolulu Star-Bulletin*, 20 October 1913; *Elyria Evening Telegram*, 13 May 1913.
41. *Pacific Commercial Advertiser*, 28 November 1912.
42. *San Jose Mercury*, 12 March 1915, 14 March 1915, 15 March 1915.
43. *Ibid.*, 15 March 1915; *Los Angeles Times*, 15 March 1915; *San Francisco Examiner*, 19 March 1915.
44. *Decatur Review*, 29 July 1912; *Honolulu Advertiser*, 4 April 1964.
45. *Chicago Defender*, 27 September 1913, 4 October 1913.
46. *New York Age*, 24 September 1914, 2 September 1915.
47. *Ibid.*, 9 September 1915.
48. *New York Times*, 6 September 1915.
49. *New York Age*, 16 September 1915, 30 September 1915; *Baltimore Afro-American*, 18 September 1915.
50. *Indianapolis Star*, 13 May 1916, 2 October 1916; *Chicago Defender*, 20 May 1916.
51. *Honolulu Star-Bulletin*, 14 October 1912, 15 October 1912; *Pacific Commercial Advertiser*, 19 September 1912, 14 October 1912.
52. *Honolulu Star-Bulletin*, 13 October

1913, 20 October 1913, 25 October 1913.
53. *Pacific Commercial Advertiser*, 2 March 1914, 3 March 1914, 4 March 1914, 5 March 1914.
54. *Ibid.*, 9 March 1914.
55. *Ibid.*, 11 March 1914.
56. *Ibid.*, 16 March 1914.
57. *Pacific Commercial Advertiser*, 14 February 1912; *Honolulu Star-Bulletin*, 23 July 1912.
58. *Pacific Commercial Advertiser*, 15 October 1912.
59. *Ibid.*, 13 October 1913.
60. *Honolulu Star-Bulletin*, 20 October 1913.
61. *Pacific Commercial Advertiser*, 3 March 1913.
62. *Honolulu Star-Bulletin*, 14 October 1912, 8 May 1913, 15 July 1913.
63. *Ibid.*, 10 March 1913.
64. *Ibid.*
65. *Ibid.*, 12 March 1913, 13 March 1913, 17 March 1913.
66. *Pacific Commercial Advertiser*, 17 November 1915, 5 December 1915, 12 December 1915.
67. *Ibid.*, November 1916, 19 November 1916, 26 November 1916.
68. *Nevada State Journal*, 5 December 1914; *Washington Post*, 3 December 1914, 4 December 1914.
69. *Oakland Tribune*, 17 January 1915.
70. *Portland Oregonian*, 19 December 1914.
71. *Sporting News*, 6 January 1915, 7 January 1915.
72. *Pacific Commercial Advertiser*, 7 January 1915.
73. *Ibid.*, 22 March 1917.
74. *San Francisco Examiner*, 21 February 1915; Everington, "Buck Lai."
75. *Honolulu Star-Bulletin*, 13 May 1913, 22 February 1915, 8 October 1915; *Williamsport Grit*, 3 August 1913.
76. *Pacific Commercial Advertiser*, 13 November 1912; *Honolulu Star-Bulletin*, 17 May 1913, 25 July 1913.
77. *Sporting News*, March 15, 1917, March 22, 1917.
78. *Ibid.*, 22 March 1917.
79. *Ibid.*, 5 April 1917.
80. *Honolulu Star-Bulletin*, 22 January 1913; *Indianapolis Star*, 13 September 1914; "Our Letter Box, *Baseball Magazine*, July 1915; U.S. 1917–1918 Draft Registration Cards, Philadelphia, PA., www.ancestry.com, accessed April 27, 2005; *Pacific Commercial Advertiser*, 7 November 1912; *Washington Post*, 10 April 1918, 7 December 1918.
81. *Honolulu Star-Bulletin*, 31 March 1914.

Chapter 6

1. *Pacific Citizen*, 12 July 1947.
2. U.S. Census Manuscripts, City and County of Honolulu, 1930.
3. *Washington Post*, 27 December 1906, 24 March 1907; *Fort Wayne Daily News*, 29 March 1907; *Los Angeles Times*, 17 March 1907; *San Francisco Examiner*, 1 April 1907, 11 April 1907.
4. *San Francisco Examiner*, 11 April 1907; *Los Angeles Times*, 22 June 1907, 26 June 1907; *Reno Evening Gazette*, 10 August 1907.
5. *Sporting Life*, 19 August 1907; *Sporting News*, 12 December 1907.
6. *Washington Post*, 4 September 1907, 8 September 1907, 16 November 1907; *Pacific Commercial Advertiser*, 14 November 1911; U.S. Census Manuscripts, City and County of Honolulu, 1910.
7. *Pacific Commercial Advertiser*, 11 January 1912, 6 March 1912, 5 April 1912.
8. *Ibid.*, 9 April 1912, 21 April 1912, 8 June 1912; *Oakland Tribune*, 27 March 1912; *Los Angeles Times*, 5 July 1912.
9. *Sporting News*, 23 December 1920, 5 October 1922.
10. *Pacific Commercial Advertiser*, 13 November 1912; *Honolulu Star-Bulletin*, 12 December 1916; *Connelsville Daily Courier*, 7 January 1917.
11. *Honolulu Star-Bulletin*, 1 January 1917; *Daily Northwestern*, 1 March 1917.
12. *Sporting News*, 22 March 1917.
13. *Washington Post*, 22 April 1917; *Fort Wayne News*, 17 April 1917; *Fort Wayne Sentinel*, 28 May 1917.
14. *Seattle Post-Intelligencer*, March 26, 1917.
15. *Ibid.*, April 1, 1917, April 3, 1917, April 4, 1917.
16. *Ibid.*, April 15, 1917.
17. *Ibid.*, April 13, 1917, April 24, 1917.
18. *Ibid.*, 21 May 1917; *Sporting News*, 10 May 1917, 31 May 1917.
19. *Sporting News*, 5 July 1917; *Fort Wayne News*, 28 July 1917.
20. *Philadelphia Inquirer*, 28 April 1918; *Chicago Defender*, 4 May 1918; U.S. 1917–1918 Draft Registration Cards, Portland,

Oregon, www, ancestry, com, accessed January 9, 2006; U.S. 1942 Draft Registration Cards, Penns Grove, New Jersey, www.ancestry.com, accessed 28 June 2006; Social Security Death Index. www.ancestry.com, accessed 17 February 2005.

21. *Honolulu Star-Bulletin*, 21 November 1916; *Gettysburg Times*, 27 September 1938.

22. *Gettysburg Times*, 8 May 1917, 12 May 1917, 17 May 1917, 18 May 1917.

23. *Ibid.*, 21 May 1917, 23 May 1917; *New Oxford Item*, 25 May 1917.

24. *Gettysburg Times*, 5 June 1917.

25. *Gettysburg Compiler*, 20 January 1945, p. 4; *Sporting News*, 13 September 1917, 20 December 1917; *Bridgeport Telegram*, 22 May 1918.

26. *Bridgeport Telegram*, 22 May 1918, 28 May 1918.

27. *Ibid.*, 29 May 1918, 1 June 1918, 27 June 1918.

28. *Frederick Post*, 11 December 1918, p. 5; *Bridgeport Telegram*, 6 May 1919; *Sporting News*, 8 January 1920; *Gettysburg Times*, 4 August 1919, p. 4, 19 January 1920, p. 1.

29. U.S. Census Manuscripts, City and County of Honolulu, 1930; *New York Times*, 24 June 1932.

30. U.S. 1917–1918 Draft Registration Cards, Philadelphia, Pennsylvania, www.ancestry.com, accessed February 17, 2005.

31. *Middletown Times*, 21 July 1917.

32. *Washington Post*, 24 March 1918.

33. *Philadelphia Inquirer*, 16 March 1918, 18 March 1918, 25 March 1918, 26 March 1918.

34. *Ibid.*, 31 March 1918, 3 April 1918, 7 April 1918, 8 April 1918; *Sporting News*, 4 April 1918, 11 April 1918.

35. *Sporting News*, 23 May 1918; *Bridgeport Telegram*, 16 May 1918, 17 May 1918, 20 May 1918.

36. *Ibid.*, 22 May 1918, 27 May 1918.

37. *Ibid.*, 28 May 1918, 29 May 1918, 1 June 1918, 3 June 1918.

38. *Ibid.*, 13 June 1918, 20 June 1918, 28 June 1918.

39. *Ibid.*, 13 June 1918.

40. *Ibid.*, 12 July 1918.

41. *Sporting News*, 18 July 1918.

42. *Bridgeport Telegram*, 29 July 1918.

43. *Ibid.*, 14 April 1919, 19 May 1919, 3 July 1919.

44. *Ibid.*, 24 June 1919; *Sporting News*, 29 May 1919, 8 January 1920, 16 December 1920.

45. *Sporting News*, 23 September 1920, 24 February 1921, 5 July 1928; *Bridgeport Telegram*, 21 June 1920, 23 June 1920,14 August 1920, 19 August 1920, 2 May 1921, 1 September 1921.

46. Everington, "Lai"; Ben Gould, "Max Rosner Who Operated Legendary Bushwicks Dies," *Sporting News*, 9 December 1953; United States Census Manuscripts, City of Audubon and County of Camden, New Jersey, 1920.

47. *New York Times*, 13 October 1927.

48. *Florence Morning News*, 19 January 1928; *Helena Independent*, 10 January 1928; *Gettysburg Times*, 14 January 1928; *Los Angeles Times*, 28 February 1928; *New York Times*, 10 January 1928.

49. *Zanesville Signal*, 28 March 1928, p. 13; *New York Times*, 4 March 1928, 14 March 1928, 15 March 1928; Everington, "Lai"; *Circleview Herald*, 13 March 1928; *Appleton Press-Crescent*, 14 March 1928.

50. Red Smith, "Red Reeder's Heisman Trophy Day," *New York Times*, 31 October 1977.

51. *New York Times*, 13 April 1928, 16 April 1928; *Sporting News*, 26 April 1928, 5 July 1928.

52. *New York Times*, 13 October 1928, 24 July 1930, 1 June 1931, 9 July 1931, 24 September 1932, 18 October 1934; *Middletown Times Herald*, 25 July 1933.

53. Everington, "Lai"; *Honolulu Advertiser*, March 3, 1935; *Helena Independent*, 24 May 1936; *Hammond Times*, 21 August 1937.

54. *Honolulu Advertiser*, 5 March 1935, 24 March 1935; *Honolulu Star-Bulletin*, 13 March 1936.

55. *Honolulu Advertiser*, 1 April 1935, 7 April 1935, 20 April 1935.

56. *Chicago Daily Tribune*, 1 June 1935.

57. *Chicago Defender*, 22 June 1935; *Middletown Times-Herald*, 2 July 1935; *Syracuse Herald*, 10 August 1935.

58. *Helena Independent*, 24 May 1936.

59. *Ibid.*, 27 May 1936, p. 8.

60. *Olean Times-Herald*, 15 August 1936; *Chicago Daily Tribune*, 20 May 1936, 31 August 1936, 5 September 1936.

61. *Clearfield Progress*, 26 June 1937; *Mansfield News-Journal*, 1 September 1937.

62. *Chicago Daily Tribune*, 1 June 1937, 23 August 1937, 25 August 1937; *Hammond Times*, 21 August 1937; U.S. Census Manuscripts, City and County of Honolulu, 1930.

63. *Ada Evening News*, 16 May 1937; *Newark Advocate and American Tribune*, 9 June 1937.
64. *Mansfield News Journal*, 10 August 1937, 11 August 1937.
65. *Helena Independent*, 24 May 1937, 26 May 1936; *Elyria Chronicle Telegram*, 4 June 1936.
66. *Reno Evening Gazette*, 12 January 1945; *Sporting News*, 18 January 1945; *Berkshire Evening Telegram*, 9 August 1952; *Berkshire Eagle*, 8 October 1956.
67. EH, "The All-Nation Baseball Club," *Baseball Monthly*, February 1914, pp. 347–348; Bruce, *Kansas City*, 15, 133.
68. U.S. Department of Labor, Passenger List, "All Aliens Arriving from a foreign port or port of Insular possession, Siberia Maru, Sailing From Honolulu, August 12, 1928; *Sacramento Bee*, September 16, 1932, sports, p. 1; *Oakland Tribune*, 27 September 1932, p. B20; Yoichi Nagata, "The First All-Asian Pitching Duel in Organized Baseball: Japan vs. China in the PCL," *Baseball Research Journal*, no. 21, p. 14.
69. *Los Angeles Times*, 16 September 1932.
70. *Oakland Tribune*, 20 September 1932.
71. *Ibid.*, 28 September 1932; Nagata, "Pitching Duel, p. 14.
72. *Oakland Tribune*, 29 September 1932; Nagata, "Pitching Duel;" Social Security Death Index. www.ancestry.com, accessed April 15, 2006.
73. John E. Spalding, *Sacramento Senators and Solons: Baseball in California's Capital, 1886–1976* (Manhattan, KS: Ag Press, 1995), 84; *Los Angeles Times*, 18 February 1931; *Sporting News*, 28 June 1934; *Charleston Gazette*, 8 August 1934.
74. *Sacramento Bee*, 26 June 1935; List or Manifest of Alien Passengers for the United States, Chichibu Maru, Leaving Yokohama, Japan, 14 February 1935.
75. *Chicago Daily Tribune*, 19 November 1935, p. 27; *Sporting News*, 28 November 1935, p. 3; Grantland Rice, "Who is Our Top Athlete," *Sport*, October 1946.
76. *San Francisco Chronicle*, 19 February 1950; 21 February 1950; *San Francisco News*, 11 March 1950; *Sporting News*, 15 March 1950; *San Francisco Examiner*, 26 March 1950; *Honolulu Star-Bulletin*, 3 April 1950.
77. *Sporting News*, 19 June 1950.
78. *Ibid.*, 9 March 1933, 23 March 1933, 1 June 1933; *Washington Post*, January 27, 1933; U.S. Census Manuscripts, City and County of Honolulu, 1930; *Honolulu Advertiser*, March 31, 1935.
79. *Sporting News*, 11 June 1942, 9 July 1942.
80. *Ibid.*, 23 July 1942, 30 July 1942, 20 August 1942.
81. *Ibid.*, 28 August 1946, 19 May 1948.
82. *Ibid.*, 3 August 1949, 20 August 1952; Larry Tajiri, "Yonamine of the Bees," *Scene*, July 1950, p. 42; *San Francisco Chronicle*, 29 July 1949; *Pacific Citizen*, 26 July 1947, 28 January 1950; *Oakland Tribune*, 22 July 1948.
83. Dick Meyer, "11-Inning No Hitter by Tanner First Feat of Kind to be Telecast," *Sporting News*, 24 May 1950.
84. Bob Cole, Jr., "4 Hawaii Sandlotters Receiving O.B. Trials," *Sporting News*, 30 May 1956; Red McQueen, "Lopat Stars Win 6 in Hawaii, But Draw Only Slim Crowds," 27 October 1954.
85. *Ibid.*, 16 March 1956, 4 April 1956; Roscoe McGowan, "Dodgers Unveil Honolulu Pitcher," *New York Times*, 10 March 1956; *Ames Daily Tribune*, 30 March 1956.
86. *Ames Daily Tribune*, 26 April 1956, p. 2; *Sporting News*, 2 May 1956, p. 30, 25 July 1956, 8 August 1956.
87. Cole, "4 Hawaii."
88. *Ibid.*, 10 August 1963.
89. *Ibid.*, 21 June 1961, 16 August 1980, 26 April 1982; Reardon, "Mancao."

Chapter 7

1. *Atlanta Constitution*, 19 March 1908.
2. U.S. Census Manuscripts, City and County of Honolulu, 1900; *Pacific Commercial Advertiser*, 16 February 1912; Spalding, *Sacramento*, 25, 29.
3. *Sacramento Bee*, March 8, 1912; *Pacific Commercial Advertiser*, 4 April 1912, 20 May 1912, 7 June 1912.
4. *Pacific Commercial Advertiser*, 29 April 1913, 26 March 1914; *Honolulu Star-Bulletin*, 26 May 1913; *Los Angeles Times*, 8 August 1913; *San Francisco Chronicle*, 1 July 1915; Ray Castello, "16 Islanders Have Played Major League Ball," www.ohanamagazine.com, May–June, 2002.
5. *Honolulu Star-Bulletin*, 2 January 1914; *Pacific Commercial Advertiser*, 25 November 1913, 29 December 1913, 2 January 1914.
6. *Pacific Commercial Advertiser*, 26 March 1914, 22 April 1914; *Honolulu Star-*

Bulletin, 12 May 1914, 17 May 1914; *Fort Wayne News*, 30 May 1914; Castello, "16."
  7. *Los Angeles Times*, 10 September 1914, 1 October 1914, 13 August 1915; *San Francisco Chronicle*, 1 July 1915; *Sporting News*, 29 March 1917, 18 March 1953.
  8. *Hawaii Herald*, 10 February 1951; U.S. Census Manuscripts, City and County of Honolulu, 1930.
  9. Dan Daniel, "'Prince' Oana Pops Into The Big League Melting Pot: Adding Dash of Hawaii to Cuban and Indian Spice," *Sporting News*, 18 January 1934; *Honolulu Star-Bulletin*, 20 June 1914.
  10. United States Census Manuscripts, Ewa Plantation, Oahu, 1920; Kaulukukui, *Development*, 33; Castello, "16."
  11. Zeke Handler, "Hornsby Told Oana He Batted Like Pitcher," *Sporting News*, 16 July 1942; Kaulukukui, "Development," 22; Ship's Manifest, SS *Wilhelmina*, 26 November 1928. www.ancestry.com, accessed June 4, 2005.
  12. *Helena Independent*, 14 January 1929; *San Francisco Examiner*, 2 May 1929; *Sporting News*, 11 July 1929.
  13. *San Francisco Chronicle*, 8 January 1931; Paul J. Zingg and Mark D. Medeiros, *Runs, Hits, and an Era: The Pacific Coast League, 1903–58*, (Urbana: University of Illinois Press, 1994), 71; *Nevada State Journal*, 4 April 1933; *Los Angeles Times*, 5 April 1933; Cy Kritzer, "Happy Go Roars on Texas Trail," *Sporting News*, 31 July 1946.
  14. Kritzer, "Happy;" *Lima News*, 19 November 1933.
  15. *Sporting News*, 18 January 1934.
  16. *Ibid*.
  17. *Ibid*.
  18. *Ibid*., 3 May 1934; Krizer, "Happy."
  19. *Sporting News*, 11 October 1934; Krizer, "Happy."
  20. *Ibid*., 18 June 1936, 24 September 1936, 4 March 1937, 24 March 1938, 14 April 1938, 28 April 1938, 12 May 1938, 15 February 1940, 2 May 1940, 16 July 1942; *Syracuse Post-Standard*, 14 December 1963.
  21. *Ibid*., 13 June 1940; *Honolulu Star-Bulletin*, 8 August 1942; *Clearfield Progress*, 3 August 1942.
  22. Handler, "Hornsby," *Sporting News*, 4 March 1943.
  23. *Sporting News*, 4 March 1943, 19 August 1943.
  24. *Ibid*., 19 August 1943, 26 August 1943, 15 March 1945.
  25. *Ibid*., 25 May 1944, 7 June 1945, 17 October 1945.
  26. *Ibid*., 30 April 1947; *Marion Star*, 21 May 1946; *San Jose Mercury*, 1 September 1946; *Official Baseball Guide 1947*, (CC Spink and Son: St. Louis, 1948), 260, 270.
  27. *Sporting News*, 19 July 1950, 14 February 1951, 8 August 1951; *Syracuse Post-Standard*, 14 December 1963; www.starbulletin.com, 9 April 1997.
  28. United States Census Manuscripts, City and County of Los Angeles, 1930; Emil Guillermo, "Diversity on the Diamond," *Asian Week*, 3 October 1997.
  29. *Sporting News*, 3 August 1949; Dick Peebles, "Balcena 'Goes for Broke'"; *Sporting News*, 3 June 1953, 5 February 1990; Guillermo, "Diversity," *Nevada State Journal*, 11 May 1949; *Reno Evening Gazette*, 28 June 1949, 23 December 1948; *Sporting News*, 3 November 1948; Charles Hillinger, "Big Leagues' Only Filipino Reminisces About the 50s," *Los Angeles Times*, 10 February 1983.
  30. *New York Times*, 6 April 1951; *Sporting News*, 28 March 1951.
  31. *Sporting News*, 21 May 1951, 4 July 1951, 19 September 1951; Peebles, "Balcena"; *Syracuse Herald-Journal*, 8 July 1951.
  32. *Sporting News*, 27 August 1952, 10 September 1952; Peebles, "Balcena."
  33. *Ibid*., 4 February 1953; Peebles, "Balcena"; *Reno Evening-Gazette*, 16 October 1953.
  34. *Bradford Era*, 13 October 1953; *Los Angeles Times*, 22 March 1954, 16 April 1954, 2 March 1955; *Sporting News*, 14 April 1954, 2 June 1954, 20 October 1954.
  35. *Sporting News*, 8 December 1954, 22 December 1954; *Seattle Post-Intelligencer*, 6 March 1955, 3 April 1955, 5 April 1955.
  36. *Seattle Post-Intelligencer*, 8 April 1955.
  37. *Ibid*., 9 April 1955, 19 April 1955, 20 April 1955.
  38. *Ibid*., 25 April 1955.
  39. *Ibid*., 14 June 1955; *Nevada State Journal*, 15 September 1955; *Los Angeles Times*, 25 January 1956; *Official Baseball Guide 1956*, 182.
  40. *Sporting News*, 16 May 1956, 8 August 1956, 5 September 1956, 21 November 1956; *Los Angeles Times*, 27 August 1956; *Coschocton Tribune*, 14 September 1956.
  41. *Sporting News*, 26 September 1956, 10 October 1956; "Only Filipino."
  42. *Sporting News*, 3 October 1956, 24 October 1956, 9 January 1957; *Zanesville Sig-*

nal, 17 February 1957, 27 February 1957, 3 April 1957.
43. *Sporting News*, 15 May 1957, 5 June 1957, 31 July 1957, 13 November 1957.
44. *Ibid.*, 10 September 1958; *Toronto Mail and Globe*, 6 August 1958; *Lancaster Eagle*, 5 August 1958.
45. *Sporting News*, 22 June 1960, 14 September 1960, 27 June 1961, 5 July 1961, 21 July 1962, 11 August 1962; "Only Filipino"; California Death Index, www.ancestry.com, accessed 6 January 2005. Marcia C. Smith, "Legaspi Motivation Kept in the Family," *Orange County Register*, 24 May 2005.
46. www.starbulletin.com, 29 January 1997; Castello, "16 Islanders."
47. Furman Bisher, "Braves Suffer Dizzy Feeling as Hurlers Ride Teeter-Totter," *Sporting News*, 16 April 1966; Arlene Lum, *Sailing for the Sun: The Chinese in Hawaii, 1789–1989* (Honolulu: Center for Chinese Study, University of Hawaii, 1988), 139; Bill Kwon, "Sports Watch," *Honolulu Star-Bulletin*, 29 July 2000, Castello, "16 Islanders."
48. *Pacific Citizen*, 6 September 1974.
49. Anthony Hayes, "All American Pastime," www.asianweek.com, 25 May 2000.
50. Ethen Lieser, "It's Designed to Break Your Heart," *Asian Week*, 10 August–16 August 2000.
51. "Tiger Among Us," *Asian Week*, 12 February–18 February 1998; Robin Carr, "Happy Days on the Farm," *Giants Magazine*, no. 2 (1987), p. 37.
52. Clark Walker, "On the Diamond, in the Bleachers," www.asianweek.com, 29 August 1997; www.starbulletin.com, 16 January 1998.
53. Guillermo, "Our Benny," *Asian Week*, 6 April–12 April 2000.
54. Hayes, "Pastime."
55. Guillermo, "Our Benny."
56. *Ibid*; www.geocities.com/s_borisov/jb2004/plleaders.html, 31 October 2004.
57. Castello, "16 Islanders"; *www.starbulletin.com*, 6 January 1998.
58. www.asianweek.com, 16 January 2004.
59. members.aol.com/toliasolaita, accessed 15 December 2004.
60. *Ibid.*
61. *Ibid.*
62. Ray Buck, "Solaita Dreams of Bigs — And Church for Father," *Sporting News*, 5 June 1971; Jim Ogle, "Yankees Need Many Things," 4 December 1971.

63. members.aol.com/toliasolaita.
64. *Sporting News*, 26 January 1980; members.aol.com/toliasolaita.
65. members.aol.com/toliasolaita; *Sporting News*, 28 May 1990.
66. *Sporting News*, 18 July 1970; Joseph Durso, "Reds and Orioles Sweep Series," *New York Times*, October 6, 1970; John Feinstein, "Out and In the Tigers Door," *Washington Post*, 12 October 1984.
67. Hayes, "Pastime;" Tom Boswell, "Mets Win in the 11th," *Washington Post*, 2 October 1985; George Vecsey, "Ron Darling in the Fourth," *New York Times*, 20 October 1986.
68. www.cincinnati.com, 18 May 2000.
69. www.asianweek.com, 28 August 2001.
70. www.singaporesoxfan.com/2004/10/dave-roberts-japanese-base-stealing.html, 4 October 2004.
71. *Honolulu Star-Bulletin*, 9 November 1949; www.alohafame.com, accessed August 11, 1999; Nakagawa, *Through a Diamond*, 19, 60–62; *Pacific Citizen*, 11 March 1950; *Hawaii Herald*, 17 February 1951; www.starbulletin.com, 7 August 1996.
72. United States Census Manuscripts, Maui, Hawaii, 1930; Suehiro, *Honolulu Stadium*, 35; *Fresno Bee*, 8 January 2000.
73. *Hawaii Herald*, 9 February 1950; *Honolulu Advertiser*, 31 January 1950; *Pacific Citizen*, 7 January 1950.
74. *Pacific Citizen*, 4 March 1950, 11 March 1950; *Hawaii Herald*, 25 March 1950; Tajiri, "Yonamine of the Bees," *Scene*, July 1950, p. 42; *Utah Nippo*, 5 April 1950.
75. *Los Angeles Times*, 10 April 1950; Tajiri, "Yonamine"; *Pacific Citizen*, 3 March 1951; *Sporting News*, 10 May 1950, 8 April 1953; Sotaro Suzuki, "Talent Hungry Japan Clubs Inks U.S. Players," *Sporting News*, 25 August 1962.
76. *Honolulu Advertiser*, 17 April 1951; *Pacific Citizen*, 31 March 1951.
77. Jerry Izenberg, "Another Side of the Rising Sun," *New Jersey Online*, 12 July 1997; *Honolulu Advertiser*, 4 March 1967; Robert K. Fitts, *Remembering Japanese Baseball: The Oral History of the Game* (Carbondale, IL: Southern Illinois University Press, 2005), 22–23.
78. John Saito, "*Nisei* Inducted into Japan's Hall of Fame," *Nikkei Northwest*, March 1, 1994.
79. *Ibid.*; Frank Ardolino, "Wally Yon-

amine: In Japan's Hall of Fame," *The National Pastime*, no. 19 (1999), p. 11; Louinn Lota, "Misaka Is NBA's Forgotten Minority," *Los Angeles Times*, 7 May 2000; Gordon Sakamoto, "Yonamine Braved Threats Playing in Japan After World War II," Associated Press, Nando Media, 24 August 1998.

80. Sakamoto, "Yonamine Braved"; Izenberg, "Another Side."

81. *Coschocton Tribune*, 24 October 1957; Sadaharu Oh and David Faulkner, *A Zen Way of Baseball* (New York: New York Times Books, 1984), 78.

82. Saito, "*Nisei*."

83. *Sporting News*, 25 February 1953, 1 April 1953; *Los Angeles Times*, 2 March 1953.

84. Robert Trumball, "Tokyo Plays Host to *Nisei* Parlay," *New York Times*, 27 October 1957; "Japanese Baseball in November Like Broadway New Year's Eve," 31 October 1957; Lee Kavetski, "Three Rookies Dot American Total of 14 in Nippon," *Sporting News*, 20 April 1960.

85. *Nevada State Journal*, 22 October 1974; *Appleton Post-Crescent*, March 6, 1975; *Sporting Press*, 6 April 1987; Saito, "*Nisei*."

86. *Honolulu Advertiser*, 23 January 1958; www.hawaii.gov, 10 January 1999; *Tokyo Weekender*, 17 July 1998.

87. Mark Harris, "An Outfielder for Hiroshima," *Sports Illustrated*, 1 August 1958.

88. *Ibid.*, 57, 59; *Nichi Bei Times*, 1 January 1973; Fitts, *Remembering*, 59–66.

89. *Pacific Citizen*, 11 March 1950; Yoichi Nagata and John Holway, "Japanese Baseball," in *Total Baseball.*, John Thorn and Peter Palmer, eds. (New York: Warner Books, 1994), 594; Brandon Masuoka, "'Curly' Hirota, Japanese Baseball Star, Dead at 81," www.honoluluadvertiser.com, 9 September 2003; *Blue Book of College Athletics*, 1967–1968 (Cleveland: Akron Engraving, 1967), 108.

90. *Sporting News*, 1 April 1953; Feldman, *Barbed*, 37–38; *Honolulu Advertiser*, 13 February 1954; *New York Times*, 9 November 1955, 31 October 1957; Red McQueen, "Lopat Stars Win 6 in Hawaii, But Draw Only Slim Crowds," *Sporting News*, 27 October 1954; Fitts, *Remembering*, 51.

91. Sotaro Suzuku, "Talent Hungry."

Afterword

1. Hayes, "Pastime."
2. *Ibid.*

References

Annuals, Programs, Reports

Ahead in the Count: 130 Years of Women & Baseball: 1995 Colorado Silver Bullets Souvenir Program.
Blue Book of College Athletics, 1967–1968. Cleveland: Akron Engraving, 1967.
California Death Index, Bobby Balcena. www.ancestry.com. Accessed 6 January 2005.
Honolulu City Directory, 1890.
Official Baseball Guide 1947. CC Spink and Sons, St. Louis, 1948.
Official Baseball Annual 1956, Rules, Teams, Photos. Wichita, KS: National Baseball Congress, 1956.
Recreation Commission of City and County of Honolulu. *A History of Recreation in Hawaii.* Honolulu, TH: 1936.
San Francisco Giants 1963 Yearbook.
Ship's Manifest, SS *Honolulan*, Honolulu, TH, 11 March 1914. www.ancestry.com., accessed 17 September 2004.
Ship's Manifest, SS *Taiyo Maru*, Honolulu, TH, 30 August 1927. www.ancestry.com. Accessed 17 September 2004.
Ship's Manifest, SS *Wilhelmina*, Honolulu, TH, 26 November 1928. www.ancestry.com. Accessed June 4, 2005
Ship's Manifest, *Chichibu Maru*, Yokohama, Japan, 14 February 1935. www.ancestry.com. Accessed 17 September 2004.
Spalding's Official Base Ball Guide, Thirty-Seventh Year 1913, edited by John B. Foster, American Sports Publishing Company.
Social Security Death Index. Vernon Ayau. www.ancestry.com. Accessed 17 February 2005.
_____. Kenso Nushida. www.ancestry.com. Accessed 15 April 2006.
The Phoenician, Phoenix High School Yearbook, 1933. www.ancestry.com. Accessed 27 May 2006.
Thrum's Hawaiian Annals for 1921. Honolulu: Thomas G. Thrum, 1920.
United States Census Manuscripts. Ewa Plantation, Oahu, 1920
_____. Hilo, Hawaii, 1930.
_____. City and County of Honolulu, 1900.
_____. City and County of Honolulu, 1910.
_____. City and County of Honolulu, 1920.
_____. City and County of Honolulu, 1930.
_____. City and County of Los Angeles, 1930
_____. City of Audubon and County of Camden, New Jersey, 1920.
_____. City of Chicago and County of Cook [Illinois], 1910.
_____. Maui, Hawaii, 1900, 1930.
United States Department of Labor, Passenger List, All Aliens Arriving from a foreign port or port of Insular possession, Siberia Maru, Sailing From Honolulu, August 12, 1928.
U.S. 1917–1918 Draft Registration Cards. Philadelphia, Pennsylvania, www.ancestry.com. Accessed 28 September 2004, 17 February 2005.

_____. Portland, Oregon, www.ancestry.com. Accessed 9 January 2006.

U.S. 1942 Draft Registration Cards, Penns Grove, New Jersey, www.ancestry.com. Accessed 28 June 2006.

Newspapers and Periodicals

Ada Evening News
Adams County News
Ames Daily Tribune
Appleton Post-Crescent
Asian Week
Atlanta Constitution
Baltimore Afro-American
Baseball Monthly
Berkshire Evening Eagle
Berkshire Evening Telegram
Bradford Era
Bridgeport Telegram
Charleston Gazette
Chicago Daily Tribune
Chicago Defender
Chinese Digest
Chinese Press
Circleview Herald
Clearfield Progress
Connelsville Daily Courier
Coshocton Tribune
Current Opinion
Daily Commonwealth
Daily Northwestern
Daily Palo Alto
Decatur Review
East/West
Elyria Chronicle Telegram
Elyria Evening Telegram
Florence Morning Times
Fort Wayne Daily News
Fort Wayne Gazette
Fort Wayne Sentinel
Frederick Post
Fresno Bee
Gastonia Daily News
Gettysburg Compiler
Gettysburg Star and Sentinel
Gettysburg Times
Giants Magazine
Hammond Times
Hawaii Herald
Hawaiian Gazette
Hawaiian Star
Helena Independent
Honolulu Star-Bulletin
Indianapolis Star
Lancaster Eagle
Lima News
Los Angeles Times
Mansfield News Journal
Manzanar Free Press
Marion Star
Metro Magazine
Middletown Times-Herald
Nevada State Journal
New York Age
New York Sun
New York Times
Newark Advocate and American Tribune
Nichi Bei Times
Nikkei Northwest
Oakland Tribune
Olean Times-Herald
Orange County Register
Pacific Citizen
Pacific Commercial Advertiser
Philadelphia Inquirer
Placerville Mountain Democrat
Portland Oregonian
Rafu Shimpo
Reno Evening Gazette
Sacramento Bee
San Francisco Call
San Francisco Chronicle
San Francisco Examiner
San Francisco News
Santa Ana Register
Scene
Seattle Post-Intelligencer
Sheboygan Press
Sport
Sporting Life
Sporting News
Sports Illustrated
Stanford Daily
Syracuse Herald
Syracuse Post-Standard
The Playground
Tokyo Weekender
Toronto Mail and Globe
Utah Nippo
Washington Post
Williamsport Grit
Zanesville Herald
Zanesville Signal

Books and Articles

Anzaldua, Gloria. *Borderlands/La Frontera: The New Mestiza*. San Francisco: Spinsters/Aunt Lute, 1987.

Ardolino, Frank. "Wally Yonamine: In Japan's Hall of Fame." *The National Pastime*, no. 19: 1999.

Bailey, Beth, and David Farber. *First Strange Place: The Alchemy of Race and Sex in World War II Hawaii*. New York: Free Press, 1992.

Beren, Janice A. "Physical Education and Sport in the Philippines," in *Sport in Asia and Africa: A Comparative Handbook*. Edited by Eric A. Wagner. Westport, CT: Greenwood Press, 1989.

Bulosan, Carlo. *America is in the Heart*. Seattle: University of Washington Press, 1979.

Chan, Sucheng. *Asian Americans: An Interpretive History*. New York: Twayne, 1991.

Davis, Mike. *Dead Cities and Other Tales*. New York: The New Press, 2002.

Feldman, Jay. "Baseball Behind Barbed Wire," *The National Pastime: A Review of Baseball History*, no. 12.

Fitts, Robert K. *Remembering Japanese Baseball: The Oral History of the Game*. Carbondale, IL: Southern Illinois University Press, 2005.

Franks, Joel S. *Hawaiian Sports in the Twentieth Century*. Lewiston, NY: Edward Mellen Press, 2002.

———. "Uncle Sam's Old Tricks." Unpublished book-length manuscript.

Friedrich, Otto. *City of Nets: A Portrait of Hollywood in the 1940s*. New York: Harper & Row, 1986.

Gramsci, Antonio. *Selections from the Prison Notebooks*. Edited by Q. Hoare and G. Smith. New York: International Press, 1971.

Gulick, Sidney L. *Mixing the Races in Hawaii: A Study of the Coming Neo-Hawaiian Race*. Honolulu: Hawaiian Board Book Room, 1937.

Hall, Stuart. "Gramsci's Relevance for the Study of Race and Ethnicity." *Journal of Communication Inquiry* 10, Summer 1986.

James, C.L.R. *Beyond a Boundary*. New York: Pantheon Books, 1983.

Kaulukukui, Thomas. "The Development of Competitive Athletics in the Schools of Hawaii." Master's thesis, University of Hawaii, 1941.

Kim, Elaine. "Preface," *Charlie Chan Is Dead: An Anthology of Contemporary Asian American Fiction*. Edited by Jessica Hagedorn. New York: Penguin Books, 1993.

Lai, William T. "Buck." *Championship Baseball from Little League to Big League*. New York: Prentice Hall, 1954.

Levine, Peter. *Ellis Island to Ebbets Field: Sport and the American Jewish Experience*. New York: Oxford University Press, 1992.

Lewis, Michael. *Moneyball: The Art of Winning an Unfair Game*. New York: Norton, 2003.

Lopez, Ian Haney. *White by Law: The Legal Construction of Race*. New York: New York University Press, 1998.

Lowe, Lisa. *Immigrant Acts: On Asian American Cultural Politics*. Durham and London: Duke University Press, 1996.

Lum, Arlene. *Sailing for the Sun: The Chinese in Hawaii, 1789–1989*. Honolulu: Center for Chinese Study, University of Hawaii, 1988.

Ma, Eve Armentrout, and Jeong Hui Ma. *The Chinese of Oakland: Unsung Builders*. Oakland Chinese History Research Committee, 1982.

Malloy, Jerry. "The Twenty-Fifth Infantry Takes the Field." *National Pastime*, no. 15, 1995.

Mears, Elliot G. *Resident Orientals on the Pacific Coast*. Chicago: University of Chicago Press, 1928.

Nagata, Yoichi. "The First All-Asian Pitching Duel in Organized Baseball: Japan vs. China in the PCL." *Baseball Research Journal*, no. 21, 2001.

———, and Jerry Malloy. "Japanese Baseball," in *Total Baseball*. Edited by John Thorn and Peter Palmer. New York: Warner Books, 1994.

Nakagawa, Kerry Yo. *Through a Diamond: 100 Years of Japanese American Baseball*. San Francisco: Rudi, 2001.

Nomura, Gail M. "Beyond the Playing Field: The Significance of Pre–World War II Japanese American Baseball in the Yakima Valley," in *Bearing Dreams, Shaping Visions: Asian Pacific American Perspectives*. Edited by Linda A. Revilla, Gail M. Nomura, Shawn Wong, and Shirley Hune. Pullman, WA: Washington State University Press, 1993.

Odo, Franklin S. *No Sword to Bury: Japanese Americans in Hawai'i During World War II*. Philadelphia: Temple University Press, 2003.

Okamura, Jonathan Y. "Baseball and Beauty Queens: The Political Context of Ethnic Boundary Making in the Japanese American Community in Hawaii," in *The Japa-*

nese American Contemporary Experience in Hawaii. Edited by Jonathan Y. Okamura. Honolulu: University of Hawaii Press, 2002.

Okihiro, Gary Y. *Margins and Mainstreams: Asians in American History and Culture*. Seattle: University of Washington Press, 1994.

———. *Storied Lives: Japanese American Students and World War II*. Seattle: University of Washington Press, 1999.

Omi, Michael, and Howard Winant. *Racial Formation in the United States: From the 1960s to the 1990s*. 2nd ed. London and New York: Routledge, 1994.

Otake, Gary. "More Than Just a Game." *Nikkei Heritage*. San Francisco: National Japanese American Historical Society, 1997.

Pearce, Ralph M. *From Asahi to Zebras: Japanese American Baseball in San Jose, California*. San Jose, CA: Japanese American Museum of San Jose, 2005.

Peterson, Harold. *The Man Who Invented Baseball*. New York: Charles Scribner's and Sons, 1973.

Pope, S.W. *Patriotic Games: Sporting Traditions in the American Imagination, 1876–1926*. New York: Oxford University Press, 1997.

Powers-Buck, Jeffrey. *The American Indian Integration of Baseball*. Lincoln: University of Nebraska Press, 2004.

Reaves, Joseph. *Taking in a Game: A History of Baseball in Asia*. Lincoln: University of Nebraska Press, 2002.

Regalado, Samuel O. "Incarcerated Sport: Nisei Women's Softball and Athletics During Japanese Internment." *Journal of Sport History* 27. (Fall 2000).

———. "Sport and Community in California's Japanese American 'Yamato Colony' 1930–1945." *Journal of Sport History* 19 (Summer 1992).

Rosaldo, Renato. *Culture and Truth: The Remaking of Social Analysis*. Boston: Beacon Press, 1989.

———, and William V. Flores, "Ideology, Conflict, and Evolving Latino Communities: Cultural Citizenship in San Jose, California," in *Latino Cultural Citizenship: Claiming Identity, Space, and Rights*. Edited by William V. Flores and Rina Benmayor. Boston: Beacon Press, 1997.

Sakamaki, George. "Japanese Athletes in Hawaii." *Bulletin of the Pan-Pacific Union*. August 1931.

Seymour, Harold. *Baseball: The People's Game*. New York: Oxford University Press, 1990.

Simprich, Fred, Jr. "Honolulu: Midocean Capital." *National Geographic*, May 1954.

Spalding, Albert G. *America's National Game*. Lincoln and London: University of Nebraska Press, 1992.

Spalding, John E. *Sacramento Senators and Solons: Baseball in California's Capital, 1886–1976*. Manhattan, KS: Ag Press, 1995.

Suehiro, Arthur. *Honolulu Stadium: Where Hawaii Played*. Honolulu: Watermark Publishing, 1995.

Takaki, Ronald. *Strangers from a Different Shore: A History of Asian Americans*. Boston: Little, Brown, 1989.

Tygiel, Jules. *Past Time: Baseball as History*. New York: Oxford University Press, 2000.

White, Richard. *The Middle Ground: Indians, Empires, and Republics in the Great Lakes Region, 1650–1815*. New York: Cambridge University Press, 1991.

Williams, Raymond. *Marxism and Literature*. New York and London: Oxford University Press, 1977.

Wilson, Jeffrey. "Chinese History, Even in Baseball, Stretches Back Far in Time." *International Baseball Rundown*, August 1996.

Yee, George, and Elise Yee. "The 1927 Chinese Ball Team." *Gam Saan Journal*, December 1986.

Young Yu, Connie. *Chinatown San Jose, USA*. San Jose, CA: Historical Museum Association, 1991.

Zieff, Susan G. "From Badminton to the Bolero: Sport and Recreation in San Francisco's Chinatown." *Journal of Sport History* 27 (Spring 2000).

Zingg, Paul J., and Mark D. Medeiros. *Runs, Hits, and an Era: The Pacific Coast League, 1903–58*. Urbana: University of Illinois Press, 1994.

Index

Abele, Wekiki 147
Abo, George 75
Achi, William 84
Agbayani, Benny 12, 96, 174–175
Ah Yat, Paul 96
Akana, Albert 45, 88, 102, 120
Akana, Lang 42, 53, 88, 89, 98, 101, 102, 109, 112, 117, 118, 121, 122–123, 191
Akisada, Bryan 79
Ako, Jerry 156
All-Hawaiian Traveling Team 30–31
American of Japanese Ancestry (AJA) (Hawaii) 46–47, 51, 54–55, 182
Ane, Charlie 84
Apau, William 39
Arakawa, Wallace 145
Asahi Baseball Team: Honolulu 25, 47–48, 49–51, 53–54; San Jose 61; Seattle 58
Asato, Jimmy 96
Ayau, Vernon 45, 95, 101, 102, 108–109, 121, 124, 131–134, 191
Aylett, James 102

Balcena, Bobby 83, 166–172
Blukoi, Frank 149
Bowen, Al *see* Hong, Lee Gum
Bulosan, Carlos 70

Capilla, Doug 175–176
Chinese Americans (Mainland) 56, 65–71
Chinese Athletic Club Baseball Team (Honolulu) 45
Chinese Athletic Union Team Baseball (Honolulu) 38–43, 118
Chinese Baseball League (Honolulu) 45–46

Chinese Dragons Baseball Team (San Francisco) 68–69
Chinese Hawaiians 19–20, 24, 25, 26–29, 36–46, 51–52, 53–54, 103–104, 116–119
Chinese Optimists Baseball Team (San Francisco) 69
Chinese Tigers Baseball Team (Honolulu) 45, 53, 91, 92
Ching, Percy 93, 154
Ching, Richard 53
Choe, Sam Su 147
Chong, W. Tin 41, 42, 43, 118

Damon, Johnny 3, 12, 180–181, 191, 192
Darling, Ron 12, 179–180, 192
De Sa, Joey 176
Desha, Jack 84
Desha, William 30–31, 35–36

Enemoto, Kenichi 148
Estrella, Joey 97

Fetters, Mike 176
Filipino Americans (Mainland) 70
Filipino Hawaiians 52, 53, 54
Fuji Club Baseball Team (San Francisco) 57
Fujie, Clayton 51
Fujioka, George 154
Fujishige, George 155
Fukada, Frank 58
Fukuoroka, Royce 81
Funai, Francis 92

Goo, Francis 145
Gouthro, Laurie 84
Goya, Glen 76

Graves, Danny 12, 180
Gunda, Masa 54

Hammaker, Atlee 12, 71, 178–179
Harada, Cappy 97–98
Hasegawa, Fred 94
Hashimoto, Stan 189
Hawaii 19–20, 22–33, 85–97, 101–126, 172–176
Hawaii Baseball League (HBL) 29–30, 45, 53, 92–93
Hawaiian All-Stars 93–94; Buck Lai's 30, 91, 145–148
Hawaiian Travelers (also known as All Chinese, Chinese University of Hawaii, Chinese Travelers) 2, 5, 39, 51–52, 69–70, 88, 90, 101–126
Hayashi, Eddie 51, 97
Hayashi, Ross 96
Higuchi, Mateo 92
Hinaga, Alice 74
Hinaga, George 75
Hinaga, Russ 61, 74
Hip Lungs Baseball Team (Chicago) 65–66
Hirata, Clyde 51
Hirayama, Fibber 76, 154, 187, 188
Hirota, Jyun 53, 94, 95, 187–188
Hirota, Lefty 46
Hmong Americans 71
Ho, Chinn 98
Ho, George 153
Ho, King Tong 39, 42, 116
Hoe, Henry Pan 83
Hoe, Sing Hung (also known as Sing Hung Ho) 38, 117, 124
Holt, Milt 84
Honda, Henry 62, 75
Hong, Lee Gum (also known as Al Bowen) 67–68, 150, 156
Hoon, Clarence Chun 98
Hop, Sam 45, 88, 102, 103, 104, 112, 117, 118, 119
Horio, Jimmy 151

Ishii, Dean 95
Ishikawa, Travis 189, 192
Itamoto, Jimmy 51
Ito, Nancy 75, 76, 79, 192
Iwata, Harvey 74

Japanese Americans (Mainland) 56–65, 70, 71, 73–83
Japanese Athletic Club Baseball Team (Honolulu) 47, 48
Japanese Hawaiians 24, 25, 29–30, 46–52, 53–55
Joy, Barney 88, 90, 95, 127–131

Kahanamoku, Duke 94, 118
Kahuha, Al 147
Kahuku, Manuel 148
Kajikawa, Bill 82–83
Kameda, Ted 92, 181
Kameda, Tosh 92
Kamishima, Larry 92, 94
Kan Yen Chun *see* Yen, Kan
Kashiwada, Dick 188
Katsunama, Joe 97
Kau, Apau 101, 107, 114, 115–116, 119, 121, 124–125
Kaulukukui, Charles 90
Kaulukukui, Dick 90
Kaulukukui, Ed 90
Kaulukukui, James 90
Kaulukukui, Joe 90
Kaulukukui, Sal 94–95
Kaulukukui, Tommy 90, 95
Kawakami, Vicki 74
Kawano, Yosh 97
Kawata, Harry 74
Kekoa, Luther 103, 112, 116, 117
Kerr, John 90–91, 145, 146, 148, 151
Ki, Hoon 38, 121
Kim, Bill 98
Kim, Wendell 174
Kitamura, David 51, 76
Kitamura, Dick 94, 95
Kitamura, Eddie 92
Kitamura, Harry 63, 94, 95
Kiyokawa, Kay 74–75
Kojima, Kats 94
Kometani, Katsumi 50
Komine, Shane 80, 189
Kong, Ping 38, 45, 88
Konishi, Chad 80
Korean Americans (Mainland) 70–71
Korean Hawaiians 52–53
Kuali, Henry 90
Kubota, Eric 98
Kuhaulua, Fred 176
Kumalae, Clarence 152
Kunihisa, Lawrence 54, 92, 94, 148
Kurisu, Duane 98
Kurosaki, Ryan 79–80, 172

Ladro, Jack 83, 84, 155
Lai, Buck (also known as Lai Tin, Buck Lai Tin, William Lai, Bill Lai) 30, 38, 39, 43, 46, 85, 90, 101, 102, 108, 112, 114, 116, 117, 118, 119, 121–122, 123, 134, 136, 137–149, 156, 162, 191, 192
Lai, Buck, Jr. 85, 147
Lo, Ship 145
Lo, Tan 38
Los Angeles Chinese Baseball Team 66–67
Los Angeles Nippons Baseball Team 60
Luke, Kai 95

Luke, Kim 43
Lum, Mike 12, 172, 176
Lu'uola, Keith 176

Maehara, Ichiro 46
Maesaka, Lefty 47
Mancao, Crispin 54, 91–92, 93, 94, 156
Markham, Fred (also known as Denny) 88, 89, 90, 102, 103, 117, 134
Matias, Bob 175
Matias, John 175
Matsubu, Hank 154
Miyamoto, Andy 186, 189
Miyasato, Jimmy 47
Mori, Victor 54, 95
Morita, Masa 94
Moriyama, Chinito 30, 47, 103, 109, 117, 121, 124
Moriyama, Tsuneo (also known as Tom) 47, 103, 109
Murakami, David 79, 96
Murakami, Les 47, 96
Murakami, Masanouri 98
Muramoto, Jun 94

Nagakawa, Johnny 74
Nakama, Dave 81–82
Nakama, Keo 74, 98
Nakamura, Jiro 154
Nakamura, Takeo 53
Nakamura, Troy 80
Nalua, Al 145, 147
Native Hawaiians 30–31, 35–36
Ng, Kim 98–99, 100, 192
Nishita, Bill 64, 76, 154–155, 188
Nobriega, Ted 152–153
Noda, Steere 37
Nogami, Kiyoshi 74
Nomura, Babe 75
Nushida, Kenso 48–49, 51, 61, 149–150, 156, 162

Oana, Henry 161–166
Ogaki, Tommy 75
Ogi, Chick 61
Okamura, Futoshi 95
Omori, Greg 80
Oniate, Greg 96
Oshiro, Guy 997

Park, Chan Ho 70–71
Parque, Jim Vo 84, 180
Philippines 15–21, 32–34, 40–41
Pung, En Sue 42, 45, 88, 89, 95, 102, 120, 121, 157–158
Pung, Hans 145

Roberts, Dave 181
Robinson, Alvin 117
Robinson, Foster 88, 90, 103, 106–107, 117, 123
Rural Red Sox Baseball Team (Hawaii) 53–54, 94

Sakamoto, Asaye 74
Sakata, Lenn 12, 172–174, 192
Samoa 32, 176–178
San Fernando Aces Baseball Team 60–61
San Francisco Nisei Clippers Baseball Team 63
San Jose Zebras Baseball Team 62–63, 75
Sardinha, Duke 85, 93
Shimada, Frank 63
Shimada, Greg 81
Shimada, Hank 97
Shimizu, George 74
Shirachi, Tar 59, 61
Shundo, Bill 154
Sing Hung Ho see Hoe, Sing Hung
Solaita, Tony 12, 176–178
Strong, Nat 110, 114–115
Suzuki, Kurt 81
Swan, Fred 95

Takahashi, Sammy 60
Takei, Eddie 189
Tanabe, Colin 96
Tanaka, Earl 73–74
Tanaka, Toku 54, 95–96
Tanaka, Yosh 95, 181
Tanner, Buck 154
Tanner, Rudy 154
Tatsuno, Derek 96
Tominaga, Henry 75–76, 92, 95, 96
Townsend, Raymond 84

Uemoto, Bob 76
Uyehara, Mayo 95
Uyehara, Sam 184

Victor, Raymond 45
Vida, Earl 45, 90, 92, 145

Wa Sung Baseball Team (Oakland) 67
Wakabayashi, Henry (Bozo) 12, 181
Wakamatsu, Don 180
Wapato Nippons Baseball Team (Washington) 58
Wasa, George 92
Wasa, Jimmy 50, 53, 92, 94
Watanabe, Curt 96
Watanabe, Tsuneo 94, 95, 96
Wedemeyer, Herman 84, 151–152
Whaley, William 147
Wilcox, Milt 179
Williams, Jerome 176
Williams, John 152, 158–160
Wong, Allie 67–68, 83

Yamada, Richard 145
Yamamoto, Ryan 80
Yamashiro, Andy (also known as Andy Yim) 50, 90, 102, 103, 109, 121, 134–137, 139, 141
Yap, Albert 106, 109, 111–112
Yap, Ed 104, 119
Yap, Robert 110, 112
Yasui, Bill 94
Yee, Luck 38, 41, 42, 45, 102, 108
Yempuku, Ralph 97

Yen, Kan (also known as Kan Yen Chun) 38, 41, 45, 90, 95, 109, 121, 123, 124
Yim, Andy *see* Yamashiro, Andy
Yim, Harry 45
Yonamine, Masa 46, 51
Yonamine, Wally 12, 64, 92, 181–187, 189
Yuen, Franz 96

Zenimura, Harvey 62, 76, 188–189
Zenimura, Howard 62, 75
Zenimura, Kenichi 49, 51, 58–59, 62, 74

www.ingramcontent.com/pod-product-compliance
Ingram Content Group UK Ltd.
Pitfield, Milton Keynes, MK11 3LW, UK
UKHW041954140426
5217IPUK00015B/798